Web Programming with ASP and COM

Matt J. Crouch

ADDISON–WESLEY

An Imprint of Addison Wesley Longman, Inc.

Reading, Massachusetts • Harlow, England • Menlo Park, California
Berkeley, California • Don Mills, Ontario • Sydney
Bonn • Amsterdam • Tokyo • Mexico City

The publisher offers discounts on this book when ordered in quantity for special sales. For more information, please contact:

AWL Direct Sales
Addison Wesley Longman, Inc.
One Jacob Way
Reading, Massachusetts 01867
(781) 944-3700

Visit AW on the Web: www.awl.com/cseng/

Library of Congress Cataloging-in-Publication Data

Crouch, Matt J., 1974–
    Web programming with ASP and COM / Matt J. Crouch.
        p.   cm.
    ISBN 0-201-60460-4
    1. Internet programming.   2. Web servers—Computer programs.   3. COM (Computer architecture)   4. VBScript (Computer program language) I. Title.
    QA76.625 C76 2000
    005.2'762—dc21   99–051975

ISBN 0-201-60460-4
Text printed on recycled paper
1 2 3 4 5 6 7 8 9 10—MA—0302010099
First printing, December 1999

For LisaMarie

Contents

Preface

It was bound to happen sooner or later.

We've come to take for granted the Internet and all it has to offer. We can research, shop, entertain ourselves, and communicate with others worldwide without leaving our PC. Your average Web surfer does not give any second thoughts to the magic behind the scenes of these Web sites that enable us to carry out these activities, but you are a Web application developer who provides these experiences for the Web-surfing masses. For many businesses, a Web site is not just an attractive marketing tool, but a mission-critical piece of their revenue stream. Your job is to ensure the best possible user experience for the Web surfer, and, unfortunately, the time-to-market for these important Web applications shrinks with each passing day.

So, how are you, the software developer, planning to cope with this trend? Fortunately for you, Web application development has taken turns for the better in recent years. Many new tools have become available that make life easier when programming interactive Web applications. A wonderful technology from Microsoft called *Active Server Pages* shines in this capacity. By using simple scripting languages, coupled with its ability to call on the services of reusable code objects, applications come together with ease. Active Server Pages hides the required low-level details of interactive communications with Web servers, and COM components allow us to take advantage of prepackaged application functionality. Together, Active Server Pages and COM deliver on the promise of rapid application development for the Web.

Is This Book for You?

By now, you may have noticed that I have referred to you, the reader, as a software developer. This book is geared for those software developers who need to deliver first-rate Web applications as quickly as possible. I certainly don't expect you to be an expert in Web application development. In fact, I assume that you have little or no knowledge of how Web applications work.

However, I am forced to set a few prerequisites. Since we are working with Web pages, a working knowledge of basic HTML would be very helpful, which means you should be familiar with the common HTML tags as well as forms. You should also be familiar with URLs. And, it's a good idea to be familiar with the Windows operating system fundamentals, such as file operations (moving, copying, etc.) and navigation. We will be constructing COM components that will be built using Microsoft Visual C++. If you have worked with the C++ language for some time and you feel that you have a good understanding of it, then you are ready to tackle the chapters dealing with COM component construction. If not, you should brush up on your C++ skills by supplementing this text with a good C++ manual. The two primary subject areas of this text vary from moderately easy to somewhat difficult. The most difficult areas deal specifically with the COM architecture and its relationship to C++. Many C++ programmers have varying levels of skill, so, throughout the book, I will thoroughly explain concepts that may be unfamiliar to developers who have limited knowledge in programming using C++ in the Windows environment. This is key since the goal of this book is to bring the subject of ASP and COM to a broader audience, not just to those who develop in C++ exclusively for the Windows platform.

In addition, exposure to relational database management system fundamentals would be beneficial in the chapters dealing with the "database-enabling" of your Web application. If you are comfortable working with tables, records, and key constraints and have basic database administration skills, you should be ready for the database sections in the book.

Note: Here are some books that are recommended for bringing you up to speed on the prerequisites to the material in this book:

HTML 3: Electronic Publishing on the World Wide Web by Raggett, Lam, and Alexander, Addison-Wesley, 1996.

The C++ Programming Language, Third Edition by Stroustrup, Addison-Wesley, 1997.

Fundamentals of Database Systems, Third Edition by Elmasri and Navathe, Addison-Wesley, 1999.

Focus and Goal of This Book

Why is the focus of this book on Active Server Pages and COM components? This book grew out of my own frustrations of trying to find a book that emphasized the importance of these technologies coupled together and how to best implement applications using them. I was also trying to locate a book that addressed the issue of writing efficient ASP applications, and I failed at that as well. My struggles to learn how to construct COM components with Visual C++ were worsened by finding only books that focused mostly on theory and that lacked the code examples I needed to start creating my own COM components quickly. This book will fill in the gaps that were left by others.

Above all, my ultimate goal is to provide you with a flying start toward developing world-class Web applications easily and quickly. Active Server Pages and COM provide the best framework for this. Web application development, which was once possible only by using UNIX-based systems and CGI programs (more on CGI later), is now within the reach of friendly Windows-based servers. With easy-to-understand scripting languages and reusable code modules, developing Web applications becomes as easy as developing other types of programs.

Software and Hardware Tools Used in This Book

To develop ASP applications, you will need a 486 or Pentium-class PC. You will need a minimum of 16MB of RAM, although I advise you to upgrade to at least 32MB. You will find that all the development tools required will use quite a bit of memory. If in doubt, it will not hurt to add more RAM or hard-drive space to your computer!

Ideally, your computer should have Windows NT Server 4.0 installed. NT Server 4.0 is required to install the latest version of Internet Information Server, version 4.0 (IIS version 5.0 is in beta). This configuration will allow you to take advantage of all the material we are going to cover in this book.

I realize that having NT Server 4.0 installed on your computer may not be an option for you. Upgrading your PC with a new operating system, just to follow along with the exercises, may not seem worth it (although this author certainly hopes you think it's worth the trouble!). Windows NT Server 4.0 also carries a heavy price tag, which puts it out of the reach of many home-based PC users or hobbyist programmers. Also, if you have an older PC, its hardware may not be compatible with or powerful enough to run Windows NT.

You will need Microsoft's Web server software, Internet Information Server (IIS). This requires Windows NT Server 4.0. However, if NT Server 4.0 is not possible for you to obtain, Microsoft has a solution for users with low-end hardware. Personal Web Server (PWS) 4.0 can run on Windows 9x and Windows NT Workstation. It provides all the features of Internet Information Server, but it is intended for low-volume Web sites and for development. PWS also cannot use many of the integrated security features of IIS, which makes it unsuitable when site security is an issue. Interactive debugging of Active Server Pages is also not possible with PWS. All that considered, it is to your advantage that you use Windows NT Server for your development. You may download IIS/PWS, which is part of the Windows NT 4.0 Option Pack (for both Windows 9x and NT), from Microsoft's NT Server Web site at: `http://www.microsoft.com/ntserver/nts/downloads/recommended/nt4optpk/default.asp`

This book also focuses on COM object development. The component development chapters of this book require Microsoft Visual C++ 5.0 or greater. In this book, examples will be shown using Visual C++ 6.0. If possible, it would be to your advantage to get v6.0 since it incorporates many time-saving features that make development easier. You may run Visual C++ on either Windows NT or Windows 9x. Depending on the installation, Visual C++ can use several hundred megabytes of disk space, so be selective when installing this software to ensure that you have room for all the other component pieces of the Active Server Platform.

Optional Software

There are some optional software packages that you may find useful to have around while you develop ASP applications. Microsoft Visual Studio includes Visual InterDev 6.0, which features a code editor specifically designed for editing Active Server Pages. Using sophisticated IntelliSense technology, the Visual Studio editor aids the programmer in coding by providing syntax highlighting and automatic statement completion. It is highly recommended, not just for ASP development, but also when building COM components in Visual C++. You can also use any full-featured text editor if you so desire. Let your conscience be your guide.

We will be interacting with relational database management systems (RDBMSs) throughout the book. While a complete RDBMS package is not required, it will be helpful since the utilities provided in the RDBMS package will give you quick control over the administrative functions of the database. The examples in this book will use Microsoft Access databases. IIS and PWS will install all of the necessary database software required to talk to Microsoft Access databases. Installing the complete Microsoft Access package will enable you to quickly query data, administer the database, enter new data, run reports, and more. In later chapters, we will discuss how to migrate this data over to Microsoft SQL Server 7.0. Obviously, if you will be doing any of the exercises in that chapter, you will be required to install SQL Server.

If you want to use some of the COM components that you create in other development environments, you can install those as well. As mentioned, COM components can be reused in many development environments. Visual Basic, Microsoft Office, and others are possible hosts for your COM components.

Special Text Notations

Key code lines are referenced in the text with a ❶. Code lines that wrap are indicated with a ↵.

Other Resources

For your convenience, the enclosed CD-ROM contains all of the code used for our complete Web application, the Megabyte's Pizzeria. It also includes the other code samples scattered throughout the text. You will find installation instructions in Appendix A.

Feedback

I am always trying to improve the quality of this book. So, please send me your comments, suggestions, rants, raves, and so on. I can be reached at `matt_crouch@hotmail.com`. I look forward to hearing from you!

Acknowledgments

To say that writing a book is a tremendous effort is an understatement. It would be unfair to say that putting this text together was a solo act. So, credit to the souls who helped me is in order.

My editors at Addison Wesley Longman, Mary O'Brien and Elizabeth Spainhour, deserve my most heartfelt thanks for the project "go-ahead," their helpful input, and their faith and trust in me to see this project to completion. I would also like to thank Tyrrell Albaugh, Mariann Kourafas, Chanda Leary, Ben Ames, and Robin Bruce for all their production and marketing efforts.

My coworkers and associates at Centillion Digital Systems provided me with much needed assistance throughout this endeavor. Mark Hayton patiently answered all my stupid questions about ASP and COM and warned me about the coming pain and discomfort that would result from writing a book. Throughout my career at Centillion, he has kept my wild ideas about software development in check and provided valuable knowledge and guidance. It was all worth it, Mark, in spite of what you said! Thanks also to Dave Trepanier and Jon Cardwell, who provided encouragement and support throughout the project, to Steve Hedderick for giving me my "start," and to Jennifer Green for being "nit-picky" about items in the text and providing very helpful criticism. Thanks to all the rest of the Centillion staff who threw kind words of encouragement and support my way. Thanks also to Kathy Glidden and Jean Peck for applying the final coat of shine to the text.

Thank you, my very good friend Clinton Wong, who provided the initial inspiration and continuing support for this project through reviews and light-hearted words of encouragement over e-mails. To my reviewers Bud Crittenden and Gordon Diamant: thanks a bundle!

Thanks to Manohar Kamath, who provided very good review of the ASP and ADO sections of the text.

To R.J. Snyder, who went well beyond the call of duty of reviewing the critical sections of the text—thanks, R.J., for making this project a success.

Thanks also to my parents, Pam and John, for their support and for teaching me to be responsible and independent. Gratitude and thanks also go to my uncle, Gregory Comella, who knows how to lift up spirits even when they are at their lowest. Thanks to the rest of my family (both present and future), the Crouches, the Canino family, the Comellas, and the Lewises. Much love to you all.

But, most of all, my fiancée, Lisa Canino, deserves my most sincere and heartfelt thanks. Were it not for her guidance and encouragement, this book would not have been possible.

Matt J. Crouch
Indianapolis, IN
August 1999

The Active Server Platform

Introduction

Welcome to *Web Programming with ASP and COM*! Chapter 1 will introduce you to the *Active Server Platform,* the collection of technologies that make programming with ASP and COM possible. This chapter is designed to give you a taste of topics to come in the text and to show you the many benefits of programming with ASP and COM.

The phrase "The Web means business" has become such a cliché that it's hard to imagine a time when the World Wide Web was just about serving up static documents. Indeed, it has developed into an interactive medium of global proportions and has presented a wealth of opportunity for business to become more profitable. However, many obstacles stood in the way of achieving the high level of interactivity that Web sites commonly feature today. Highly skilled programmers were needed to crank out arcane code to access a corporation's data and intellectual assets and present that material in a Web format. To make matters worse, effective tools for Web development were in short supply. As a result, Web development projects ranked as some of the most expensive software projects for companies. Early Web applications were mainly restricted to the UNIX operating system, which confined their development and maintenance to a small group of privileged individuals. The road along the way to highly interactive Web sites was certainly treacherous, but it paved the way for wonderful technologies like Active Server Pages (ASP) and its marriage to the Component Object Model (COM).

The Web Client/Server Model

Before we begin to discuss ASP and COM, let's discuss how all the components of a Web-based network environment fit together.

Web Clients and Web Servers

At the highest level, communication in a Web-based environment takes place between two entities:

1. A Web *client,* which is the software that requests files, data, and services.
2. A Web *server,* which fulfills the client's requests for content.

In most cases, the Web client is the ubiquitous Web browser, such as Microsoft Internet Explorer or Netscape Navigator. The Web server software could be software such as Microsoft Internet Information Server (IIS). We will investigate IIS in further detail later in this chapter.

Protocols for Web Client/Server Communication

TCP/IP Protocol

The Web browser and the Web server send information back and forth using the *Transmission Control Protocol/Internet Protocol* (TCP/IP). This is the same network protocol used by many other Internet services, such as e-mail and the File Transfer Protocol (FTP). It's a common language that all computers connected to the Internet (and some local area networks) speak. A digital software conduit, or socket, connects computers using the TCP/IP protocol.

A *socket* is a line of "plumbing" that is established by either the client or the server software that is used to move packets of data back and forth between them. It is through this "channel" that requests and responses are sent inside packets of data. A *packet* is a fragment of data that includes information about its origination, its destination, and so forth. The TCP/IP protocol handles the encapsulation of user data into these packets for transmission. Packets transmitted along sockets arrive at their destination in exactly the order in which they were transmitted. Web applications communicate over sockets using a higher-level protocol—the HyperText Transfer Protocol.

HyperText Transfer Protocol

The *HyperText Transfer Protocol* (HTTP) is a simple command–response system used for communication on the Web. It functions just as described: A command is issued, a response is received, and the data exchange is completed. HTTP contains roughly ten commands in its instruction set. Typically, the commands sent by the client are requests for files, such as HTML documents and images. The HTTP protocol is *stateless*, which means that when a client request is completed, the Web server normally closes the socket connection with the browser. Later in this chapter, we will discuss why this is an obstacle toward developing a Web application.

The first version of HTTP (v0.9) was extremely limited, so much so that it implemented only one client command—the GET method. This command accepted one parameter (the file pathname) and requested that document from the Web server. In these early days, content was static text only. No multimedia, interactivity, or persistency was supported until the next revision of the HTTP protocol was adopted.

So, HTTP 0.9 went the way of the dinosaurs, and HTTP 1.0 emerged in its place. This upgraded version provided commands not only to retrieve documents but also for the client to send additional information to the server. (HTTP 1.1, the latest incarnation, added more features, such as the ability to host more than one Web host on the same physical server.) Some of this information could be parameters to an executable program residing on the Web server. Given this information, the external executable program can send data back to the client based on processing it did on the information sent. This method of encoding data to be sent from Web client to Web server is called the *Common Gateway Interface* (CGI). Applications and scripts that read the CGI encoding scheme are called *CGI scripts* or *CGI applications* (or simply *CGIs*).

Server-Side Processing with CGI Programs

CGI works by processing the data sent by the Web browser (typically data that originates from an HTML form) on the Web server. The data contained in the form fields is encoded using the *x-url-encoding* system by the browser before transmission. The data is sent by one of two methods:

1. Encoding the data in the body of an HTTP POST command (a "post").
2. Passing the data as arguments to a script file in the URL (a "get" request).

(GET and POST requests are covered in more detail in the coming chapters.)

The Web server receives this data and passes it to a CGI application for processing. The CGI application processing can include any programming logic and code necessary to produce the desired output. The CGI then sends the results to the Web browser as HTML or other data that the browser can

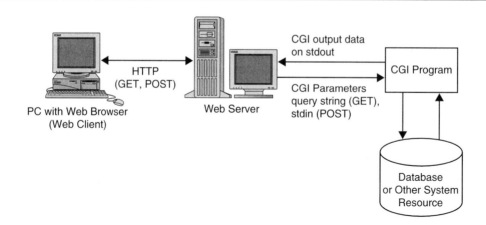

Figure 1-1. Diagram of Web client/server environment with CGI.

render. Figure 1-1 shows how a Web browser and a Web server communicate with HTTP and CGI.

Disadvantages of the Common Gateway Interface

CGI provides the "plumbing" functionality for Web client/server communication, but interpreting the CGI encoding can be difficult. Although this architecture may seem simple and elegant on the surface, it is very much at a disadvantage when compared to programming with ASP. Let's do some brief comparisons of ASP and CGI to illustrate.

■ *Writing CGI programs is the least cost-effective method of Web development.* Since CGI is simply an encoding scheme for passing data back and forth between Web client and Web server, CGI programs typically need extra code to interpret the encoding. This is only a preliminary step; after decoding the CGI data, we must then do some processing on it. ASP solves both of these problems by (1) making it extremely easy to parse CGI data using built-in code objects designed for CGI decoding and (2) providing a framework for using many different interpreted languages, like VBScript and JScript, to process the data. Using ASP clearly eliminates many monotonous programming steps associated with CGI development, thus freeing the programmer to concentrate more on the main application logic of the program.

■ *CGI programs run separately from the Web server process in a separate application.* When the Web browser makes a request for a CGI program, the CGI executes in another system process independently from the Web server. On the Windows platform, CGI applications are typically implemented as executables (EXEs). The largest problem with this is the CPU resources involved in launching this application. In most cases, valuable CPU time and memory are stolen from the Web server when resources are at a premium. This occurs because one EXE process is created for each request of the CGI program—a very costly operation in Windows NT. When coupled with a high number of users requesting files from the Web server, the server can quickly be exhausted of its resources. ASP is designed to use minimal system resources by executing in the process space of the Web server, thereby sharing its system resources.

Advantages of the Active Server Platform

The Active Server Platform addressed the technical limitations of CGI programming and took a completely new approach to Web client/server interaction. Both ASP and CGI accomplish the same goal of dynamically generating HTML content, but that's where the similarities end. Let's explore the architecture of the Active Server Platform and see how each piece of this architecture contributes to making a Web application.

Software Pieces of the Active Server Platform

Here are the component pieces of the Active Server Platform that we will discuss in greater depth in succeeding sections:

■ *Internet Information Server,* which is the core server software that delivers Web content to the user's browser.

■ *Active Server Pages,* which are HTML pages with interpreted script code to dynamically generate content and to act as a "glue" for the presentation layer and the application services.

■ *Transaction Server,* which is coordinating software that controls the resources and execution of COM servers and the management of database transactions.

Internet Information Server (IIS)

Internet Information Server (IIS) is Microsoft's software for serving up content to Web clients. In addition to supporting delivery of Web content via HTTP, IIS also supports the File Transfer Protocol (FTP) as well. The functionality of IIS is extendable through the *Internet Server Application Programmer's Interface* (ISAPI). ISAPI programs come in two flavors: ISAPI extensions and ISAPI filters.

ISAPI Extensions

ISAPI *extensions* bear a striking resemblance to CGI traditional programs. Both programs are invoked in much the same manner. They can receive URL-encoded form data from an HTTP "post" request as well as from an HTTP "get" request. However, unlike CGI programs, which are executables (EXEs), ISAPI extensions exist as Windows *dynamic link libraries* (DLLs). DLLs are compiled code modules whose functions are called by another program during runtime. DLLs share the memory of the program that is calling the DLL. In this case, the program calling the ISAPI DLL extension is IIS. Therefore, ISAPI extensions don't incur the overhead associated with EXEs when they allocate memory. ISAPI extensions are also *multithreaded,* which enables them to run many times concurrently without impacting the precious resources of the server. ISAPI extensions can be used when a problem calls for a CGI-like program, but when performance must remain paramount.

ISAPI Filters

ISAPI *filters* differ from CGIs or ISAPI extensions. Like ISAPI extensions, they exist as DLLs, are multithreaded, and run in the memory space of IIS. However, these programs are not invoked by a request from a Web browser. An ISAPI filter's job is to intercept requests from a Web browser and send back some kind of alternative response to the Web browser. In effect, it modifies the default behavior of the Web server and how it returns data—hence, the name *filter.* To illustrate how this works, let's look at what happens during a normal request–response transaction between Web server and Web browser.
    For a Web server with no ISAPI filter,

1. The user requests a URL, and the browser sends the appropriate HTTP command to the Web server.
2. The Web server receives the command and requests the file in the URL. This could be either a static HTML file or a server-side script or program.

3. The content of the file (or output of the script program) is sent back to the client, and the connection is closed.

For a Web server with an ISAPI filter,

1. The user requests a URL, and the browser sends the appropriate HTTP command to the Web server.

2. The Web server receives the request and passes that request data as parameters to the ISAPI filter code. This step is transparent to the user. The user has no knowledge of the ISAPI filter at work on the server.

3. The ISAPI filter performs some server-side processing and then sends back customized data to the Web browser, bypassing the normal action taken by the Web server.

ISAPI filters have many applications. Here are some examples:

■ Customized logging of user activity on the server.

■ An advanced security system that examines the origin of the HTTP request and determines whether the user is allowed to enter.

■ On-the-fly decryption of files on the Web server based on a password.

■ Modification of the output stream of the Web server. An example is Microsoft's Cookie Munger. It works by attaching an ID to HTML anchor tags (<A>) in the HTML file before the file is delivered.

In essence, ISAPI filters do exactly as their name implies; they filter incoming requests from Web clients. In the next section, we will cover the most important ISAPI filter of all—the technology of Active Server Pages.

Active Server Pages (ASP)

In the preceding section, we described the two different types of ISAPI applications, the filter and the extension. *Active Server Pages* (ASP) is a special type of ISAPI filter. It acts as an interpreter for script code embedded inside HTML files. When an ASP file is requested, its contents are parsed for any script code. This script code is executed, and the results are inserted in the location where the script code was placed in the file. The results are then sent to the user's Web browser. The script code that executes on the server is stripped out, effectively hiding it from the user. This is the mechanism in which ASP produces dynamic Web content.

ASP is an extremely versatile development environment. Not only does it free the programmer from the complexities of CGI, but it also gives the programmer the ability to develop ASP code in a variety of languages. The programmer specifies what language to use when executing a script and is free to mix any number of languages within the Web application. ASP provides tools for interactive debugging as well, much like most integrated development environments do.

As just stated, ASP is language independent. ASP is built around a Microsoft standard called *ActiveX Scripting.* The specification for this standard is freely available. As a result, several third-party companies have made their scripting languages compliant with the ActiveX Scripting standard. Microsoft ships two languages in the default installation of ASP: JScript and VBScript.

JScript

In an effort for Microsoft's Internet Explorer to be more compatible with the many emerging interactive Web sites, Microsoft released its own flavor of Netscape's client-side scripting language, JavaScript, and dubbed it *JScript.* Not only can JScript execute on the user's Web browser, but it also can be used for server-side ASP development. The syntax of the language is similar to C. JavaScript has a large following, and it has become a de facto standard for scripting on the Web.

VBScript

The Visual Basic Scripting Edition language, or *VBScript,* is a subset of Microsoft's popular development environment, Visual Basic. It provides most of the features of the original language, and its syntax is very easy to understand. Many ASP developers come from a Visual Basic background, so their learning curve is very small. Whether you are a seasoned programmer or a beginning programmer looking for a first language to learn, VBScript is an excellent choice. This book focuses on VBScript for ASP development.

The Component Object Model (COM) and COM Servers

The *Component Object Model* (COM) is a software specification that allows for the creation of object-oriented, compiled software components. It's also the standard way that software objects communicate with one another in the

Microsoft software universe, and it's the underlying technology behind 32-bit Windows (9x and NT) operating systems. Many services of the Windows operating system such as ActiveX, OLE, OLE-DB, and ADO are built to conform to COM standards. These pieces come together to create complete applications.

Some Advantages of COM

Using COM programming methodologies to build components has many advantages. Let's discuss some of them briefly.

Business Logic Encapsulation

Many times throughout the text, you will see the term *business object*. A business object is a COM object in the usual sense, but business objects encapsulate critical business rules and logic. To illustrate this, let's examine the programmatic steps that a hypothetical order-entry system performs to fulfill a customer order.

For this order-entry system,

1. A customer fills out ship-to information, billing information, and order detail. Upon completion, the user sends the data to the server.

2. The server receives the data. The system compares the order detail with in-stock items. If the items requested are in stock, it logs the order to a database showing that the order was received and is pending processing. If the items requested are out of stock, it informs the customer that the order can't be fully fulfilled.

3. The system then calculates total cost and shipping charges and sends the order to the company's distribution warehouse via e-mail. The customer's credit card information is sent for processing. If credit is approved, it informs the customer that the order is now being processed.

4. The e-mail is received at the warehouse, and the order is picked. Once the order-picking system is fulfilled, the order-picking system sends an e-mail message to the customer that the order has been shipped.

Although the complexity involved in making a complete order-entry system is not apparent in the preceding four steps, they nonetheless serve as a good example of how the steps (some or individual parts) of this order-processing system can be "wrapped up" into an order-entry business object. We could use a scripting language by itself to implement the order-entry system, but this has disadvantages. The first problem is the lack of information hiding.

One of the main objectives of object-oriented programming is to hide the implementation details of a code module. The scripted implementation of the ordering system won't allow us to do this. However, if we create a COM component that performs the functionality of the ordering system, we gain the advantage of having the code completely hidden inside a compiled binary. The COM component is object-oriented, plus it will execute much faster since it is no longer interpreted code. Once the business object development is complete and tested, it can be used over and over again in other software projects without the need to adapt the script code to fit the application that uses the ordering system's logic.

Faster Code Execution for Web Applications

ASP provides a simple way to add application functionality to a Web site. Since ASP code is interpreted, it needs no compilation before running. This makes developing easier since modification and corrections to the code can be made quickly. However, interpreted code will never be as fast as compiled code, and this is a weak point of the scripted nature of ASP. In high-traffic sites that use a lot of ASP code, this can spell disaster for the Web server.

We can make the Web application more scalable by moving script code and putting it inside COM objects. Remember that COM objects are compiled code. This makes the logic that was previously in script code run much faster once it is inside a compiled COM component.

Reusable Compiled Components

It's true that object-oriented programming relieved programmers from having to write code from scratch for each project they worked on. C++ classes have proved very popular and successful in this capacity. They allow the programmer to define a data object along with a well-defined set of operations to perform on the object. Many programmers share the source code to objects they build in hopes that other programmers will find them useful. This approach has some drawbacks. For example, a C++ object that implements a desired functionality that is required in a Visual Basic application won't be of any use to the Visual Basic developer. The Visual Basic programmer would need to translate the C++ code into Visual Basic, which is a costly and error-prone process (not to mention all the time required to test the new code). Another problem involves the nature in which objects like C++ classes are distributed. They are distributed as source code. This creates a twofold problem:

1. The potential exists that company trade secrets will be exposed since the implementation details of the object are available for everyone to see.

2. The programmer using the object might have difficulty compiling the code on his/her platform due to implementation-dependent code that could exist in the object.

So, how does COM address these issues? We mentioned earlier that COM components are compiled code objects. The objects require no special tweaking to get them to work in the development environment you are working in since compile-time code complications are eliminated, and they are very well *encapsulated,* hiding all the implementation details of the object from the programmer. You just "drop" them into your application code, and you are ready to roll.

More Advantages of COM

A Standard for Interobject Communication

COM components, regardless of where the components are located, can communicate with one another thanks to standards that COM provides. This makes *distributed applications* possible. For example, COM objects can call on the services of other COM objects on the local computer or request the services of COM objects located on a networked computer. Communication between components is facilitated by a variety of network protocols, such as TCP, UDP, IPX/SPX, and HTTP. Various security models can be used to transport the data between COM objects, including NT security, SSL, and others.

Language Independence

The COM binary standard explicitly defines how the methods of COM objects are exposed to a programmer. Any language that can support the conventions set forth in the standard can create and use COM objects. The entire Microsoft Visual Studio suite of tools can create and use COM objects, and many other tools vendors are quickly jumping on the COM bandwagon.

Capability to Call COM Components from ASP

This point is extremely important, and it is not a coincidence that it's the focus of this book. Throughout the text, you will see how COM, coupled with ASP, can make complicated server-side functionality a snap to implement. Just as COM and ActiveX make it easy for Windows application developers to piece together a complete application, ASP and COM give that same flexibility to the Web application developer.

ASP ships with a set of COM objects that perform Web-related tasks. These are referred to as *intrinsic objects.* These objects can perform duties such as retrieving HTML form data, sending content back to the browser, and keeping track of session and application state. These objects are always globally available throughout your ASP application.

In addition to the intrinsic objects, many companies provide ready-to-use COM objects that perform a number of common programming tasks. Toward the end of the book, you will find links to ASP Web sites that feature COM objects available for download and use in your projects.

Microsoft Transaction Server (MTS)

Microsoft Transaction Server (MTS) performs several functions that aid in the operation of an ASP application. As its name implies, MTS manages transactions. A *transaction* is a series of operations or steps that are carried out as a group. The reliability and integrity of a system depend on the successful execution of these transactions. In order for a transaction to be successful, all of its steps must be successful. If a failure occurs, MTS can "undo" all of the previous successful steps, leaving any modified data untouched. This makes MTS a good choice for keeping database integrity intact.

In addition to keeping database integrity in check, MTS makes the execution of COM components more efficient. MTS controls the creation and destruction of COM object instances used in ASP applications in such a way that objects created in one ASP application can be used in another when the first application is not using the component. This maximizes precious server resources and prevents one application from using resources when it doesn't need to.

It should be noted that MTS is not required for ASP applications. ASP applications are free to use COM objects that are not under the control of MTS. However, when high amounts of usage become the norm on your ASP-enabled site, you will find MTS to be a most valuable ally. Figure 1-2 provides an overview of the Active Server Platform.

Alternatives to the Active Server Platform

Although the Active Server Platform has some powerful features, other products have some features that are designed to make Web application development easier. Let's briefly discuss some of these products to provide some background.

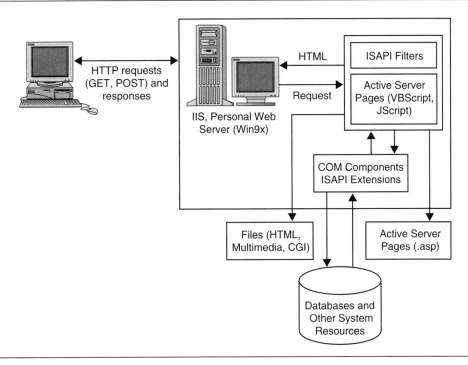

Figure 1-2. Overview of the Active Server Platform.

Allaire Cold Fusion

Cold Fusion's ability to generate dynamic content lies in the way that it extends HTML. With these extensions, Cold Fusion has the ability to perform such tasks as accessing databases and sending e-mail by placing special language tags inside standard HTML files. This makes Cold Fusion easy for novices to understand. Cold Fusion contains its own programming language, similar in style to the scripting languages offered with ASP.

Netscape Enterprise Server API

Netscape bundles a server-side JavaScript engine with its Enterprise Server product. You have the ability to write JavaScript that executes on the server in much the same way that ASP runs script code on the server. Before server-side JavaScript can run, it must be processed through a manual compilation into bytecodes (in much the same way as Java applets). The server-side script provides access to many services on the Web server, such as ODBC data sources.

Common Gateway Interface (CGI)

CGI is still very much in widespread use on the Internet as a means of delivering interactive content to the Web. CGI is the underlying encoding scheme that external programs use to process data sent by the Web browser to the Web server. Most Web servers in operation on the Internet run some version of the UNIX operating system. Most of these UNIX computers run CERN, Apache, or NCSA httpd as their Web server software. With these packages, CGI is the most popular way of providing interactive content. The CGI craze was further fueled with the introduction of the Practical Extraction and Reporting Language (PERL). PERL is an interpreted programming language, available on many platforms, that simplifies many text-processing tasks. PERL contains code libraries that make CGI programming easier, which played a big part in its success.

ASP-Supported Platforms

ASP is rapidly gaining widespread acceptance in the Web development community, so it is only natural that it supports a number of different software platforms. Most of the platforms are Microsoft Windows-based, and these versions will be used in this book.

Windows NT 4.0

At the base of the Active Server Platform is the Web server, Internet Information Server (IIS). At the time of this writing, the most current shipping version of IIS is v4.0 (IIS v5.0 is in beta). This version runs on Windows NT Server 4.0.

Windows 95/98

IIS comes in another flavor, dubbed *Personal Web Server* (PWS). You can think of this application as IIS "Lite." PWS is designed to run on Windows NT 4.0 Workstation and Windows 95/98. It is not designed to handle high levels of concurrent use like IIS. However, PWS supports most of the features of its larger sibling and is a good choice for development of ASP applications because of its lesser memory and operating system requirements. ASP applications developed using PWS can be deployed on IIS servers as well. MTS also exists in two versions: one for Windows NT and one for Windows 9x.

Other Platforms

The Active Server Platform consists of many software packages, some for which Microsoft has made the specifications freely available. This has opened up the opportunity for other vendors to provide ASP/COM capabilities in their products. Chili!Soft (`http://www.chilisoft.com`) offers an ASP-compatible system that runs on Netscape Web servers on Windows NT as well as various flavors of UNIX. The Chili!Soft version of ASP is functionally equivalent to the Microsoft version. Microsoft's Personal Web Server for MacOS also supports a limited version of ASP.

In addition, the ActiveX Scripting languages from Microsoft (VBScript and JScript) are freely licensable as binaries for use in your applications. The source code for the scripting languages and engine are also available through a special license from Microsoft (see `http://msdn.microsoft.com/scripting` for details).

What's Ahead

You'll soon be introduced to Megabyte's Pizzeria, our fictional online restaurant. The Megabyte's Pizzeria is a partial implementation of an e-commerce application. The term *e-commerce* is used to describe an interactive Web site that allows users to order products online and that handles the financial transactions.

Here is a functional overview of the application. With each section of the program, key Active Server and COM concepts will be explored.

■ Customers begin using the application by visiting the main Megabyte's Pizzeria Web site. They are presented with a menu of options. Among these options is a choice to enter the customer ordering system. The opening page will display the current date and time and check to see whether the restaurant is open for business. Based on the store hours, the system will display an appropriate message and either enable or disable menu options based on the hours of operation.
Objective: You will learn the basics of the VBScript language, including its semantics and how it is embedded into an HTML page.

You will also become familiar with some commonly used VBScript functions and statements and with how to work with variables. The process in which ASP files are parsed will also be explored.

■ After customers visit the Welcome Page, they will enter the ordering system with a username and password. If they don't have an account, an area in which they can set one up is provided. When the account information is collected, the server will save the account information in a cookie. If the user successfully logs into the system, the cookie information is retrieved, and a personalized welcome message is displayed.

Objective: You will learn about the `Request` and `Response` ASP objects in this section and how they can be used to process HTML form data and send data back to the browser. Various methods of implementing security within ASP applications will be explored. Other methods of the `Request` and `Response` objects will be explored, including methods that send raw binary data back to the browser and manage cookies.

■ Once logged into the system, customers can begin browsing food selections. Several items will be available, and customers will be able to browse the selections. They will also be able to enter their orders online and have them logged in the database.

Objective: In this section, you will learn how to access databases within ASP using ActiveX Data Objects (ADO). The ADO object model will be introduced, and you will see how each of ADO's objects are involved in retrieving and updating databases.

The complexity of the Megabyte's Pizzeria application will grow with each successive chapter. Upon completion of the book, you will have a fully functional ASP application ready for deployment. Good luck and welcome to the Active Server Platform!

■ Further Reading

■ *Microsoft COM Web Site*—`http://www.microsoft.com/com`. This site provides an executive overview of COM, what it offers, and the potential market for COM-based applications.

■ *Internet Information Server*—`http://www.microsoft.com/ntserver/web/default.asp`. This site offers resources related to IIS and other NT-based server software, like Transaction Server.

■ *CGI*—`http://hoohoo.ncsa.uiuc.edu/cgi`. This site at the University of Illinois explains CGI very well.

The VBScript Programming Language

Introduction

We are now ready to begin programming our application! Chapter 2 will explore the Visual Basic Scripting Edition language (VBScript) and show its power and ease of use. In this chapter, we will leverage the VBScript skills we acquire and build the Welcome Page of Megabyte's Pizzeria. We will also be setting the stage for using VBScript in more advanced ways later on in the book.

You will learn some essential fundamentals in this chapter. By constructing the Welcome Page, you will have gained substantial experience with the following:

- Controlling the display of HTML with VBScript.
- Using variables, constants, and operators.
- Creating procedures to modularize code.
- Working with variable types.
- Executing conditional processing, looping, and flow control.

So, let's begin!

The Megabyte's Pizzeria Welcome Page

When users first log into the Megabyte's Web site, they will encounter the Welcome Page. Unlike some Web sites that display only a static HTML page, we want to make our page display some dynamic content. The Welcome Page will do two things: (1) It will display the local time of day, and (2) based on the time of day, it will determine whether or not the restaurant is open and able to fulfill orders. We do this by creating an Active Server Page, commonly referred to as an .asp file.

The .asp File

Let's discuss for a moment how an .asp file differs from an HTML file. The most obvious difference is the file extension. IIS uses that piece of information to determine how the file is processed. In effect, the .asp file extension signals IIS that the file contains scripting code to execute. The second difference is the contents of the file. Both can contain HTML, but an .asp file contains special escape characters that distinguish script code from HTML. To illustrate, let's look at the very simple .asp file shown in Listing 2-1.

Listing 2-1. A Simple .asp File (example2-1.asp)

```
<!-     Example 1 ASP File
                              Web Programming with ASP and COM
->
<BODY>

<!- This is just HTML ->
<H1>Sample ASP File</H1>
This text is HTML and is static in nature.<BR>
We will perform a simple arithmetic operation with VBScript.<BR>
The VBScript code will calculate the expression 9 + 7 and display the ⏎
result.<BR><BR>

<!-     The "less-than/percent and percent/greater-than characters ⏎
            are opening and closing tags for scripting code.
->
❶ 9 + 7 = <% = 9 + 7 %>
</BODY>
```

At first glance, this file should look very familiar to you. It contains mostly HTML code. The interesting element that makes this an .asp file is what happens at ❶.

```
9 + 7 = <% = 9 + 7 %>
```

Here, the system displays the 9 + 7 string as static HTML text. Then, IIS encounters the opening <% tag and knows that it should begin processing the following text as executable script. The equal sign (=) is VBScript shorthand that sends the value of the expression to the right of the equal sign to the browser. In this case, VBScript evaluates the expression 9 + 7. When IIS encounters the closing %> tag, it knows that the script code has ended and that normal HTML output should resume.

Testing Your .asp File (Running from the Web Root Directory)

To see this .asp file in action, you need to place the file in the Web server's content directory space. This directory space begins in a directory called the *Web root*. The Web root directory is a directory that you designated during the install of IIS/PWS. (For information on installing IIS/PWS, see Appendix A.) Every file and directory under the Web root directory is potentially accessible by your Web site visitors, given that proper security settings have been established. If you are uncertain as to the location of your Web root directory, you can find its location by launching the IIS/PWS configuration program and looking at the properties for the Web server. Figure 2-1 shows the Personal Web Server with the Home directory (Web root) highlighted.

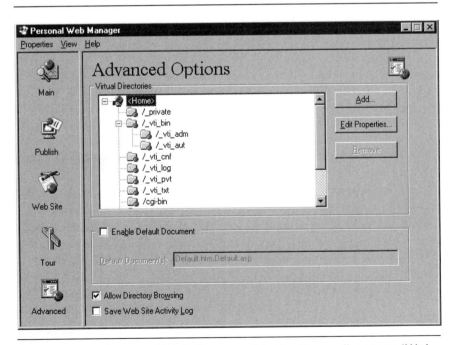

Figure 2-1.   Personal Web Server with the Home directory (Web root) highlighted.

Let's test out this example `.asp` file. Copy the `example 2.1.asp` file into your Web root directory. Make sure that your Web root directory has "Scripts" permission set (see Figure 2-2). You can "run" it by requesting the URL for your browser (`http://your-server/example2-1.asp`).

You should see the following output:

```
Sample ASP File

This text is HTML and is static in nature.
We will perform a simple arithmetic operation with VBScript.
The VBScript code will calculate the expression 9 + 7 and display the ⅃
result.
9 + 7 = 16
```

You will notice that only the results of the VBScript execution are displayed in the browser. Even an inspection of the HTML source of the results will show no signs of VBScript. After the code executes on the server, IIS "strips" all of this from the output before display. This is especially desirable since we don't want the user to view our VBScript source code.

This example is not very exciting (although it is far superior to the ubiquitous "Hello World," which we have seen ad nauseam infinitum), but it does do something other than introducing itself. The details of the VBScript language have been purposely avoided at this point in order to familiarize you with the way `.asp` files are structured. From here on, we will begin to program the Megabyte's Pizzeria application using more advanced VBScript functions.

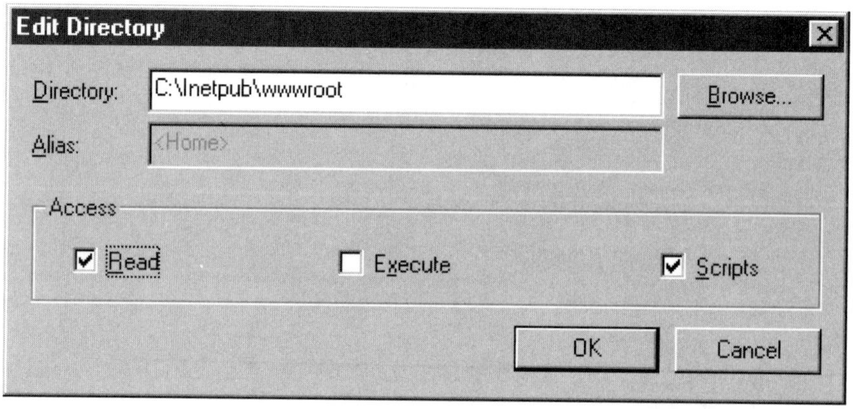

Figure 2-2.   Home directory (Web root) with "Scripts" set.

VBScript Data Types

Microsoft has kept things simple with VBScript variables. Variables come in one flavor—the variant. A *variant* is a special variable type that can store different types of string and numeric data. Variants are similar to the union constructs in C/C++. Each of the different kinds of data that the variant can work with are called *subtypes*. Table 2-1 lists the subtypes of a variant with a description of each.

VBScript provides conversion functions to coerce one subtype to another. VBScript is not considered to be a strongly typed language since the versatility of the variant allows us the flexibility to convert freely between types. In many cases, different variable types can be converted implicitly. That is, no function call is required to convert the variable's value to a different type.

Table 2-1. VBScript Data Types

Subtype	Description
Boolean	A true or false value
Byte	An 8-bit value, more specifically a number from 0 to 255
Integer	A number ranging from –32,767 to 32,767
Currency	A number ranging from –922,337,203,685,477.5808 to 922,337,203,685,477.5807
Long	A number ranging from –2,147,483,648 to 2,147,483,647
Single	A floating-point number from (–3.402823E38 to –1.401298E–45) to (1.401298E–45 to 3.402823E38)
Double	A floating-point number from (1.79769313486232E308 to –4.94065645841247E–324) to (4.94065645841247E–324 to 1.79769313486232E308)
Date	A date ranging from January 1, 100 to December 31, 9999
String	A sequence of characters up to 2 billion in length
Object	An object, such as an instance of a COM object
Error	An error number

Variables in VBScript

VBScript uses *variables* to hold data. Unlike compiled languages, variables in VBScript do not need explicit declaration in order to be used. By simply assigning a value to a variable, we implicitly declare it. Variables can be declared at any point in the code. In a sense, this can make coding very fast since the programmer doesn't need to be concerned with the extra work of defining variables. However, the joy here is short-lived. When the programmer begins to debug code after receiving unexpected results, he/she will find that a misspelling of a variable name could be to blame. The programmer will then have to check every place where the variable was used and make the corrections—a painstaking process, indeed. Fortunately, VBScript can enforce a rule in which variables must be explicitly declared. Runtime errors are produced when a variable name is encountered that is not previously defined.

Variables in VBScript also have scope. If a variable is declared outside of a procedure block, it is referred to as a *script-level* variable. Script-level variables are accessible in any part of the .asp file (global to the file). When the script inside the .asp file finishes execution, the variables are freed. Variables can also be declared as *local* to a procedure. Local variables cannot be used outside of the procedure in which they are declared. When the procedure exists, the memory that the variable uses is freed.

VBScript can hold data in scalar or array variables. Arrays can have as many as sixty dimensions. Arrays can also be *dynamic*. A dynamic array can be resized after it is declared. The elements of the array can be of any data type that VBScript supports.

All VBScript code used in our application will enforce the "must declare" rule for variable usage. To enforce the rule, place the following code at the beginning of your .asp file:

```
<% Option Explicit %>
```

To declare a variable, the Dim statement is used. Variable names are unique to 255 characters. They can be made up of any alphanumeric characters but cannot contain a period (.). Variable names must also be unique in their scope. Multiple variables can be declared by separating each one with a comma. In the following example, we will declare three variables:

```
Dim sStrOne, sStrTwo, sStrThree     ' declare three variables
```

You can also declare variables individually. This example is functionally equivalent to the preceding code:

```
Dim sStrOne          ' declare variables individually
Dim sStrTwo
Dim sStrThree
```

Note the use of the single quote in our code. This quote indicates that a code comment (text that is ignored by the interpreter) follows. Any text to the right of the quote on the same line is considered to be a comment. As you know, it is always good programming practice to comment your code as much as possible, so don't neglect it with your VBScript projects. When your code is ready for production deployment, it's best to remove comments because, unlike compiled languages that strip out comments before compiling, the VBScript interpreter must process them like any other statement.

Another good programming practice is to give your variables meaningful names. Microsoft recommends that you name your variables following a set of established conventions.

1. Prefix your variable name with its intended scope:

   l for local

   g for global (script-level)

   p for procedure parameter

2. Show what type the variable is by using the following prefixes:

   bln for Boolean

   byt for byte

   dtm for date/time

   dbl for double

   err for error

   int for integer

   lng for long

   obj for object

   sng for single

   str for string

3. Give the variable a meaningful name that briefly describes how the variable is used in the application.

To illustrate, let's declare a variable using the preceding conventions. We want to create a local integer variable that is used for a counter. We could say something like this:

```
Dim lintMyCounter        ' a local integer variable
```

Notice how we alternated between case when naming the variable. This styling improves the readability of our code.

Constants in VBScript

VBScript uses *constants* to assign meaningful, easily recognizable names to pieces of data. Unlike variables, the value of a constant cannot be changed once it is defined. VBScript provides a number of predefined constants to make programming easier. You may also define your own constants throughout your VBScript code.

The syntax for defining a constant is as follows:

```
Const myConstantName = value
```

The equal sign (=) is the assignment operator in VBScript. Use it when assigning values to variables or constants. Constants can be strings or numbers. Strings must be enclosed in double quotation marks. You can also specify date/time values by enclosing a properly formatted date/time within pound signs (#). When using constants, it's a good idea to use ALL CAPS to help distinguish them from variables.

Controlling Program Flow

All programming languages need to be able to conditionally execute code based on previous results. VBScript provides two methods for accomplishing this: the If . . . Then . . . Else statement and the Select Case statement.

If . . . Then . . . Else

The general syntax of If . . . Then . . . Else is as follows:

```
If expression Then
        [statements1]
[ElseIf expression2
        [statements2]
        . . . more ElseIf statements]
[Else
        [statements3]]
End If
```

where *expression* is any expression (numeric or string) that evaluates to true or false. If *expression* is true, then the statements in the *statements1* block are executed. The `Else` clause is optional. If supplied, the statements in the *statements3* block are executed if *expression* is false.

The `ElseIf` statement performs another expression check if the previous expression was false. If that expression is true, then the following statement block is executed. If not, then more `ElseIf` statements that follow are each evaluated in turn.

Select Case

If you must check the value of an expression against several values and execute code based on each of those choices, then a `Select Case` statement will be most appropriate for this type of comparison. The `Select Case` statement was designed to eliminate the overly complex code that would result from using `ElseIf` statements to conditionally branch on the value of an expression. The syntax of a `Select Case` statement is as follows:

```
Select Case test-expression
      Case expression1
         .
       . [statements1]
         .
      Case expression2
         .
       . [statements2]
         .
      Case expression n
         .
       . [statements n]
         .
      Case Else
         .
       . [statements]
         .
End Select
```

VBScript first evaluates *test-expression*. If *test-expression* equals the value of *expression1*, then the statements in the *statements1* block are executed. After that, program flow resumes with the statement following the `End Select`. If *test-expression* is false, then *test-expression* is compared against *expression2*, *expression n*, and so on. If *test-expression* does not match any of the expressions in any of the `Case` clauses, the statements after the `Case Else` statements are executed. Although optional, including the `Case Else` clause in your `Select Case` is a good idea because you want your script to catch unexpected values in *test-expression*.

　　Note: Some languages, like C/C++, allow constant expressions only in `Case` clauses. VBScript, however, can accept any valid VBScript expression for a `Case` clause.

Comparing Values of Expressions

When you want to compare the value of one expression with another, use VBScript's comparison operators. The comparison operators in VBScript should look familiar to you. You have come across them many times in your programming career. They are outlined in Table 2-2.

　　Note in the examples of Table 2-2 that we used the VBScript operators to compare both numeric data and strings. Remember that VBScript knows of

Table 2-2.　Sample Expressions Using VBScript Comparison Operators

Comparison Operator	Meaning	Example*
<>	Not equal to	`76 <> 2` `"MezzaLuna" <> "Ambrosia"`
>=	Greater than or equal to	`23 >= 3.14` `"Italy" >= "America"`
<=	Less than or equal to	`24 <= 56` `"daVinci" <= "Sinatra"`
=	Equal to	`5 = 5` `"COM" = "COM"`
>	Greater than	`12 > 6` `"pizza" > "calzone"`
<	Less than	`3 < 5` `"spaghetti" < "ziti"`

*All expressions evaluate to true.

only one type of variable—the variant. So, our comparison operators are overloaded. If you recall operator overloading from C++, you know that you can use a single operator in expressions using many different data types.

What happens if we try to compare, say, a string to a number expression? In this case, the numeric expression will always be less than the string. Sometimes, one of the expressions or variables will be Empty, which is a special value in VBScript used to indicate that the variable is zero if it is numeric or contains a zero-length string if it is a string variable.

Logical Operators

You can use logical operators in your expressions to perform Boolean logic. VBScript offers a full range of logical operators, as outlined in Table 2-3.

Functions and Subroutines

Like any good programming language, VBScript allows us to modularize our code for better readability and reuse. These "code modules" also come in

Table 2-3. Truth Table for Various VBScript Logical Operators

Logical Operator	Meaning		
And	true And false	=	false
	false And true	=	false
	false And false	=	false
	true And true	=	true
Or	true Or false	=	true
	false Or true	=	true
	false Or false	=	false
	true Or true	=	true
Not (unary)	Not true	=	false
	Not false	=	true
Xor (exclusive or)	true Xor false	=	true
	false Xor true	=	true
	false Xor false	=	false
	true Xor true	=	false

handy when a series of statements needs to be executed multiple times. VBScript procedures come in two flavors—*functions* and *subroutines*—both of which accomplish the same goal of grouping statements into callable code blocks. Functions can return a value to the caller based on the results of the execution of the function's code. Subroutines do not return a value after they are executed. Subroutines are useful when you need to do some procedural task but the results of the task are of no importance, such as displaying a static block of text. Both functions and subroutines can take parameters as input. Let's look at the general syntax of a function and a subroutine:

```
Function function-name [( param1, param2, …, param n )]
.
. [statements]
.
End Function


Sub subroutine-name [( param1, param2, …, param n )]
.
. [statements]
.
End Sub
```

Creating Loops

Loops are quite common for any programming language. VBScript provides several different kinds of loops, as shown in Table 2-4.

Table 2-4.   Loop Types in VBScript

Loop Type	Description
While . . . Wend	Execute statements as long as *test-expression* is true.
Do . . . Loop	Execute statements inside loop as long as *test-expression* is true. (Do . . . Loop comes in two varieties.)
For . . . Next	Execute statement inside loop a specified number of times.
For Each . . . Next	Use this special type of For . . . Next loop to traverse arrays and collections.

While . . . Wend

Here's an example of a `While . . . Wend` loop:

```
' Wait until quitting time
❶ While ( Time >= #08:00:00# And Time <= #17:00:00# )
        DoSomeWork( "Matt" )
❷       If ComputerCrashed Then
                ' Cannot do any work, too bad..
                Exit While
End If
Wend
' Time to go home!
GoHome( "Matt" )
```

The *test-expression* for this `While . . . Wend` loop❶ is the comparison of the current time against the times of a typical workday (for a nonprogrammer!). If the system time (returned by the `Time` function) is in the range of 8:00 A.M. and 5:00 P.M., the expression is true. This means that the code inside the `While . . . Wend` block gets executed.

Inside our loop, notice that an `If . . . Then`❷ statement has checked the value returned by the function `ComputerCrashed`. If true, the `Exit While` statement will cause an immediate exit from the loop. Code execution then resumes with the statement following the `Wend`.

Do . . . Loop

`Do . . . Loop` comes in two flavors. It can execute statements either until the *test-expression* is true (`Do Until`) or as long as the *test-expression* is true (`Do While`).

Here, we use `While`:

```
Do While EnergyLevel > 50
        WriteInBook
        If BookComplete Then
                Exit Do
        End If
Loop
```

If you prefer, you can use the following syntax instead. It works the same as the previous loop example, except that this loop is "bottom driven." This means that the code in the loop is executed first, and then the continuation expression is evaluated. Here is the syntax:

```
Do
        WriteInBook
        If BookComplete Then
                Exit Do
        End If
Loop While EnergyLevel > 50
```

And here, we use Until:

```
Do
        WriteInBook
Loop Until BookIsComplete Or EnergyLevel <=50
```

For . . . Next

The For . . . Next loop is used to execute a group of statements a specified number of times. A For . . . Next loop has a counter variable that increments or decrements with each pass through the loop. The statements inside the loop are executed until the destination value for the counter is reached.

To illustrate, let's look at a For . . . Next loop inside the small .asp script shown in Listing 2-2. The output of this script is as follows:

Listing 2-2. A For . . . Next Loop (example2-2.asp)

```
<HTML><BODY>
<% str = "Spaghetti" %>
<% = str %> is spelled:
<% For x = 1 to Len( str ) ' Start at the beginning of the ⤶
    string to
' the end (determined by the Len()
' function.
%>
<%     ' The Mid() function gets one character
       ' at position x in the string
%>
        <% = Mid( str, x, 1 ) %>
        <% If x <> Len( str ) Then
               ' If this is the last
               ' letter then do not
```

```
                        ' display a dash.
%>

              -

<%      End If
        Next                          ' Loop back to get the next letter
%>
</BODY></HTML>
```

Spaghetti is spelled: S - p - a - g - h - e - t - t - i

For Each . . . Next

The For Each . . . Next loop is used to iterate through items in an array or a collection. The For Each . . . Next loop in Listing 2-3 is used to do a summation on the elements of an integer array. The VBScript Array() function is used to assign values to an array. Then, that value is divided by the number of elements in the array, and the division is rounded off using the VBScript Round() function.

Listing 2-3. A For Each . . . Next Loop (example2-3.asp)

```
<%
Function Average( intNumberArray )

        Dim intElement
        Dim intSum
        Dim intCount

        intSum = 0
        intCount = 0
        For Each intElement In intNumberArray
%>
                <% = intElement %><BR>
<%
                intSum = intSum + intElement
                intCount = intCount + 1
        Next
        Average = intSum / intCount
%>
<HR>
<%
End Function
%>
```

```
<%
Dim intMyArray
intMyArray = Array( 5, 3, 56, 12, 87, 34 )
%>
<% = Round( Average( intMyArray, 6 ) ) %> is the average
```

Building the Megabyte's Welcome Page

We have covered the basics of VBScript to this point. Let's begin building the Megabyte's Welcome Page. Armed with the knowledge presented thus far, we should be able to start adding some "intelligence" to the page.

Let's begin with the code for welcome.asp, as shown in Listing 2-4.

Listing 2-4. The Complete welcome.asp File

❶
```
    <%
Option Explicit              ' Force VBScript to check for explicit
                             ' declaration of our variables.
```

❷
```
    Const SUNDAY_OPEN =     #11:30:00#
    Const SUNDAY_CLOSE =    #22:00:00#
    Const MONDAY_OPEN =     #10:30:00#
    Const MONDAY_CLOSE =    #23:59:59#
    Const TUESDAY_OPEN =    #10:30:00#
    Const TUESDAY_CLOSE =   #23:59:59#
    Const WEDNESDAY_OPEN =  #10:00:00#
    Const WEDNESDAY_CLOSE = #23:59:59#
    Const THURSDAY_OPEN =   #11:00:00#
    Const THURSDAY_CLOSE =  #23:59:59#
    Const FRIDAY_OPEN =         #10:15:00#
    Const FRIDAY_CLOSE =    #23:00:00#
    Const SATURDAY_OPEN =   #10:00:00#
    Const SATURDAY_CLOSE =  #23:59:59#
    Const OPEN_MSG =            "We are open for business!"
    Const CLOSED_MSG =          "Sorry, we are closed. Come back ↵
later!"
    Const MORNING_MSG =     "Good morning!"
    Const AFTERNOON_MSG =   "Good afternoon!"
    Const EVENING_MSG =     "Good evening!"
```

❸
```
    Dim gdteCurrentDateTime ' The current date/time will be ↵
stored here
```

```
        Dim gtmeCurrentTime      ' the current time will be stored here


        ' Get the current date and time and store it in gdteCurrentTime
        gdteCurrentDateTime = Now
        gtmeCurrentTime = Time


❹      Public Function GetTimeBasedGreeting()
          ' Is it morning, afternoon, or night?
❺      If gtmeCurrentTime >= #00:00:00# and gtmeCurrentTime ↵
   < #12:00:00# Then
              GetTimeBasedGreeting = MORNING_MSG
        End If
❻      If gtmeCurrentTime >= #12:00:00# and gtmeCurrentTime ↵
   < #18:00:00# Then
              GetTimeBasedGreeting = AFTERNOON_MSG
        End If
❻      If gtmeCurrentTime >= #18:00:00# and gtmeCurrentTime ↵
   < #23:59:59# Then
              GetTimeBasedGreeting = EVENING_MSG
        End If
      End Function


      Public Function RestaurantOpen()
        ' Check the hours of operation according to the day of the week
        Select Case DatePart( "w", gdteCurrentDateTime )
              Case vbSunday
                    If gtmeCurrentTime > SUNDAY_OPEN And ↵
   gtmeCurrentTime < SUNDAY_CLOSE Then
                          RestaurantOpen = true
                    Else
                          RestaurantOpen = false
                    End If
              Case vbMonday
                    If gtmeCurrentTime > MONDAY_OPEN And ↵
   gtmeCurrentTime < MONDAY_CLOSE Then
                          RestaurantOpen = true
                    Else
                          RestaurantOpen = false
                    End If
              Case vbTuesday
                    If gtmeCurrentTime > TUESDAY_OPEN And ↵
   gtmeCurrentTime < TUESDAY_CLOSE Then
                          RestaurantOpen = true
                    Else
```

```
                              RestaurantOpen = false
                        End If
               Case vbWednesday
                        If gtmeCurrentTime > WEDNESDAY_OPEN And ⌐
gtmeCurrentTime < WEDNESDAY_CLOSE Then
                              RestaurantOpen = true
                        Else
                              RestaurantOpen = false
                        End If
               Case vbThursday
                        If gtmeCurrentTime > THURSDAY_OPEN And ⌐
gtmeCurrentTime < THURSDAY_CLOSE Then
                              RestaurantOpen = true
                        Else
                              RestaurantOpen = false
                        End If
               Case vbFriday
                        If gtmeCurrentTime > FRIDAY_OPEN And ⌐
gtmeCurrentTime < FRIDAY_CLOSE Then
                              RestaurantOpen = true
                        Else
                              RestaurantOpen = false
                        End If
               Case vbSaturday
                        If gtmeCurrentTime > SATURDAY_OPEN And ⌐
gtmeCurrentTime < SATURDAY_CLOSE Then
                              RestaurantOpen = true
                        Else
                              RestaurantOpen = false
                        End If
               Case Else
          End Select
     End Function
     %>


     <HTML>
     <HEAD>
     <META HTTP-EQUIV="Content-Type" CONTENT="text/html; ⌐
charset=windows-1252">
     <META NAME="Generator" CONTENT="Microsoft Word 97">
     <TITLE>welcome</TITLE>
     </HEAD>
     <BODY TEXT="#000000" LINK="#0000ff" VLINK="#800080" ⌐
BGCOLOR="#ffffff">
```

```
<P><IMG SRC="Image1.gif" WIDTH=132 HEIGHT=97>
<FONT FACE="Arial" SIZE=6>Megabyte's Pizzeria<IMG SRC="Image2.gif" ⏎
WIDTH=117 HEIGHT=73>
</P></FONT>
<I><P ALIGN="CENTER">"Italy's Finest, from your desktop to your door!"
</P/I>

<B><FONT FACE="Arial" SIZE=2>
<P>
<% = GetTimeBasedGreeting() %> - It is now <% = ⏎
gdteCurrentDateTime %> </P>
<P>
<% If RestaurantOpen() Then %>
 <% = OPEN_MSG %>
<% Else %>
 <% = CLOSE_MSG %>
<% End If %>
```

.

.

.

(Remaining static HTML code removed for clarity and length.)

The file begins with a beginning script bracket❶ (<%) and ends with a closing script bracket (%>). This code contains our logic to determine the messages we need to display.

Toward the top of the file, we declared all of our global variables and our constants for use in the `.asp` file using the `Const` statement.❷ The two variables that we declare will hold the current system date and time.❸ The variable `gdteCurrentDateTime` holds the value returned from the VBScript function `Now()`, which returns the current system date and time. The value is of the subtype date, which allows for any date-related function to be applied to it. Similarly, the `Time()` function returns the current system time. The variables `gdteCurrentDateTime` and `gtmeCurrentTime` were declared outside any procedure, which makes their scope global (within the file).

In this `.asp` file, we demonstrate the use of declaring functions. The `GetTimeBasedGreeting()` function❹ will return a string value that is the message that we display for our time-of-day greeting. This function does not take any parameters; instead, it uses the value of `gtmeCurrentTime`, which is a global variable.

Taking a look inside the `GetTimeBasedGreeting()` function, we see VBScript comparison operators at work. As mentioned, these operators can make comparisons of many types of data, including dates and times. In order for us to compare a date/time variable against a constant date/time expression, the constant expression must be enclosed in pound signs (#). In our example, we use three If . . . Then statements to compare the current time against a range of values. The first If . . . Then statement shows the current time being checked to see whether it falls in the range of A.M. hours (12:00 midnight to 11:59:59 A.M.).❺ If the current time falls within this range, the expression is true, and the value of the GetTimeBasedGreeting() function becomes that of the morning greeting. The following If . . . Then statements test the current time to see whether it falls within afternoon hours and evening hours, respectively.❻ In each case, the value of the function is set appropriately.

Chapter Review

Let's take a moment to review the key concepts we've learned in this chapter.

- An Active Server Page has a file extension of .asp, which instructs IIS/PWS that there is executable script inside the file and that it should be preprocessed before delivering the HTML to the client browser.
- VBScript is an interpreted programming language used for creating dynamic Web content. It's a "weakly typed" language that relies on the multipurpose variant data type to hold different kinds of data.
- VBScript variables have scope; they can be either local or global. They do not need to be explicitly declared, although it's a good idea to do so.
- Constants can be used in substitution for data values for convenience.
- VBScript has two mechanisms for flow control: If . . . Then . . . Else and Select Case.
- VBScript supports a full range of comparison operators that work on many different data types, and a full range of Boolean operators are also supported.
- VBScript provides many different kinds of program loops, like Do While, While . . . Wend, and so on. These program loops can be used to iterate through arrays or through a range of values.
- VBScript code can be partitioned into blocks of procedures. These are functions and subroutines.

What's Next

Congratulations on reaching this point! You've taken the first steps in creating a Web application. In Chapter 3 you will introduced to the Active Server Pages object model. You will learn how the internal ASP object model can be used to perform many different Web application tasks. You'll also get a glimpse of what COM components are and how they are used in ASP. We'll explore how to process user input from an HTML form. And, of course, the Megabyte's application will continue to evolve into a more complex system with more features. So, stay tuned!

■ Further Reading

- ■ *Scripting (VBScript and JScript)*—`http://msdn.microsoft.com/scripting`. This is the Microsoft Developer Network's site on ActiveX Scripting. You'll find tons of information about VBScript, JScript, and other scripting-related resources, including a very good online help system that describes all the available scripting functions. Microsoft offers the latest version of the scripting languages, plus documentation of all the available commands in VBScript.

Fundamentals of Active Server Pages

Introduction

We have covered some substantial ground so far. We learned about VBScript, the powerful programming language used to drive dynamic content in Web pages. By having a full-featured programming language at your disposal, you quickly discovered the possibilities available to help your Web site move out of its static HTML universe and into the exciting dimensions of dynamic content.

A scripting language is just one piece of the Web application puzzle that we will put together in the coming chapters. Chapter 3 will introduce you to the Active Server Pages application framework and the intrinsic ASP objects. The ASP objects and the application framework allow us access to many utility functions useful to Web application developers.

The term *Web application* is used very frequently, most often in an incorrect context. Many people are quick to call a Web site a "Web application" even if it contains mostly static content with just a few application-like features. In order to make a Web application, we need to effectively mimic the architecture of traditional applications such as client/server applications.

In Chapter 1, we mentioned that the HTTP protocol is stateless. No record (other than an entry in the Web server log files) is kept of the data exchange between the Web browser and the server when a file is requested and sent. In other words, no information sent by the user's Web browser is stored by the Web server's memory space. In a desktop application environment, the memory used by the application is persistent until the user exits the application. This memory can hold whatever data is necessary to keep track of items such as the user's location in the program, user settings, and internal data caches. A possible workaround to the data persistence problem with Web servers would be to send the data to the server via a CGI script and then have that CGI script pass that same data along to another script using hidden

HTML input variables. This chain would continue throughout the application. If many variables are reused in many areas of the application, the code could become considerably complex and difficult to maintain.

Web Applications

So, what makes a Web site behave more like a traditional application? To make a Web application (in the IIS/PWS/ASP environment), we must meet certain criteria.

- *A Web application is contained inside a virtual directory under the IIS Web root content directory.* All files and directories under the virtual directory are considered part of the application. The files could include `.asp` as well as HTML files. A Web server may contain many virtual directories—hence, many Web applications.

- *The Web application can store variables that are accessible by all users of the application.* These variables have application global scope. Typical uses of these *application variables* include tracking concurrent usage of the Web application and keeping settings for the application. An application starts when a user requests any `.asp` file within the virtual directory for the first time and ends when the Web server is shut down.

- *Web applications can track the session of the user.* A session starts when a user requests an `.asp` file inside a virtual directory for the first time and ends when a specified amount of time passes without any further requests. We can store information in session-scope variables much like application variables that relate to the user's session. These *session variables* are associated with the user's session ID, which is assigned when the session is created. For example, we can store items that the user has selected for an online purchase in session variables. We can then retrieve this information at a later time in the application.

By combining these features, we can make persistent, state-enabled applications in a Web environment.

The Active Server Pages Object Model

ASP comes with a set of six intrinsic COM components that facilitate Web application development. The word *intrinsic* here means that the components don't need to be explicitly created by your scripts and that they are always available for use in your scripts.

The ASP intrinsic objects are the magic behind a Web application. Each one plays a critical role in many different server-side related tasks. The ASP intrinsic objects encapsulate functionality that a Web application programmer using other development environments would have to code "by hand." Web applications, regardless of the platform or tools that they were built with, have a common set of tasks to perform. They need to retrieve information that the user sent in an HTML form and dynamically send a response back to the user's browser based on the information they received from an HTML form, retrieve specifics about the request, manage cookies, and perform other tasks. The ASP intrinsic components provide all of this functionality and more, wrapped up in an easy-to-understand object model.

Let's pause here briefly to examine COM components and how they are used from VBScript. We will cover them in extensive detail in coming chapters, but providing a little background now will get you comfortable using them.

Each COM component object is composed of *properties* and *methods*. You can set and get the value of properties (although some may be read-only). Methods are the procedural commands to perform on the component and often use the values of its properties in the call to the procedure. The notation to reference a component is outlined in the following examples:

- To set a property of an object,

  ```
  Object.Property = value
  ```
- To get the value of a property,

  ```
  variable = Object.Property
  ```
- To call a method of an object,

  ```
  ReturnValue = Object.Method ( param1, param2, …, param n )
  ```

In later chapters, we'll investigate using COM components in more detail. The preceding discussion should be enough to achieve a basic understanding of their use inside ASP.

Application Object

The `Application` object is used to store application-persistent data available for all users to access. The `Application` object stores all of its application variables in a collection. A *collection* is simply a series of name–value pairs. Each name in a collection serves as a unique key into the collection. Each application variable constitutes one item in the `Application` object's collection.

To store an application variable with VBScript, use the following syntax:

```
<%
Application( "variable_name" ) = value
%>
```

The value that is assigned to the application variable can be of any type, including string, numeric, and object variables. To retrieve the value of an application variable, just reverse the notation:

```
<%
variable = Application( "variable_name" )
%>
```

The application variables are very useful for storing information that you need to be constant for the lifetime of the application. You may access an application variable from any script inside your application. Therefore, they are global in scope. These variables exist in the Web server's memory space until the Web server is shut down. If data needs to be more persistent, it's best that it be stored in a file or database (more on this in Chapter 5).

When to Use Application Variables

When should you use application variables? Think of any time that you wish to save a piece of data and share it between Web pages. Maybe you want to keep track of how many times a page has been hit (loaded). Another possible use of application variables could be a repository for application settings. For example, maybe you want to set the background color of your Web pages to a predefined color value. The color value could be stored in the HTML RGB representation (#C0C0C0) as a string. So, we could say the following in our ASP code to change the background color of the page:

```
<% Application( "appBGColor" ) = "#C0C0C0" %>
<BODY BGCOLOR="<% = Application( "appBGColor" ) %>"
```

If we want to reference the `appBGColor` variable value again in another page, we simply access the variable's value in another page. Recall that we are free to repeat this throughout the application since application variables are persistent until the Web server process is terminated.

The Contents Collection

The default collection of the `Application` object is the `Contents` collection. All application variables are stored here when declared, as in the preceding example. (You can also declare objects using the HTML `<OBJECT>` tag, but these objects are not included in the `Contents` collection. More on this in the next section.) When creating and referencing application variables, it is not necessary to use the full `Application.Contents( "…" )` notation. VBScript automatically searches its collections for the variable that you specify using the notation given earlier. Using the unambiguous `Application.Contents` notation, however, removes the extra work in searching through the `Application` object's other collections.

It important to note that when we say "declare an application variable," we do not mean declaring a variable using the `Dim` syntax. When we declare an application variable, we are simply adding it to the object collection.

Here's how to take a peek at all of the defined application variables and their values. We can use a `For Each` loop (since we are iterating a collection) to do this:

```
<% For Each vApplicationVar In Application.Contents %>
    <% = vApplicationVar %> - <% = Application( vApplicationVar ) %><BR>
<% Next %>
```

The variable `vApplicationVar` contains the name of the variable, and we retrieve the value of `vApplicationVar` by referencing it in the collection by that name.

The StaticObjects Collection

If you wish to reference application variables created statically (using the `<OBJECT>` tag—more on the `<OBJECT>` tag later), use the `StaticObjects` collection in the same manner as the `Contents` collection.

You may also determine the number of application variables by using the default `Count` property of a collection. To illustrate, the following code will display the number of script-created application variables:

```
Number of application variables is: <% = Application.Contents.Count %>
```

Volatility of Application Variables

In a multiuser environment, we may find it necessary to "protect" the contents of application variables from being changed by other users of the application. Remember that application variables not only are global in scope but also can be shared among all users (authenticated or otherwise) of the Web application. If one user is executing a script inside an `.asp` file that contains a reference to an application variable, and another user requests that same script and modifies that application variable's value, the first user might experience undesirable results later on in his/her script. For example, consider this script that implements a page visit counter:

```
<HTML>
<BODY>
<H1>Welcome to my Home Page!</H1>
  .
  .
  .
  <%
❶    Application( "concurrentUsers" ) = Application( " ⏎
  concurrentUsers " ) + 1
  %>
❷ The application currently has <% = Application( " ⏎
  concurrentUsers " ) %> visitors.
</BODY>
</HTML>
```

In this simple `.asp` file, the Web server increments the value of the application variable **pageCounter** by 1❶ and displays the result.❷ This script will work just fine if there is just one concurrent user of the application. It's safe to say that there will not be one concurrent user of your Web application. Let's look into some of the issues we run into when working with application variables.

Potential Hazards of Using Application Variables

Recall that the Active Server environment is multithreaded. Quite conceivably, while one user is executing the script that retrieves the **concurrentUsers** application variable, another user running the same script in a different thread can increment the **concurrentUsers** value. If two users retrieve the variable at the same time, they are updated at the same time. This makes the final count only one more than the initial count and not two more, which would be the correct value. The result is in an invalid count.

Protecting Application Variables

The `Application` object helps keep the values of application variables orderly by supplying two methods to control when application variables can be modified. The `Lock` method will protect all application variables from being modified until `Unlock` is called.

Let's look at our sample script again and make the appropriate changes:

```
<HTML>
<BODY>
<H1>Welcome to my Home Page!</H1>
.

.

.

<%
❶     Application.Lock
      Application( "concurrentUsers" ) = Application( " ↵
concurrentUsers " ) + 1
%>
The application currently has <% = Application( " ↵
concurrentUsers " ) %> visitors.
❷ <% Application.Unlock %>
</BODY>
</HTML>
```

Notice that when we called the `Lock` method, ❶ we did not specify any particular variable to lock. In fact, when we call the `Lock` method, we are locking *all* application variables. This brings us to an interesting point: Always remember to call the `Application.Unlock` ❷ method after you are finished modifying application variables in your script. If you don't, then other processes executing the script will not be able to modify the variable. Another important point: Any modifications you make to application variables should be completed as quickly as possible so as not to interrupt application variable modifications from being made by other scripts.

Session Object

The Web server creates a *session* in ASP when a user requests a Web page from the server. Recall that Web client/server communication is stateless. So, in order for us to keep track of persistent data, like user preferences, we must have a way for the Web server to remember this data even after a file request has been made. For sessions to be persistent in your Web application, you'll need to have a `global.asa` file (more on `global.asa` later in this chapter) created for your Web application with the `Session_OnStart()` subroutine defined. By using the `Session` object, you can declare variables that have "session scope." That is, they are available for use in any `.asp` file within the application. We also need to be able to determine when the user has "left," or stopped using the application. This is accomplished by examining how much time has elapsed since the user last requested a page inside the virtual directory. The session is considered ended if that timeout period has elapsed. Unlike application variables, which hold their value for the duration of the Web server process lifetime, session variables are destroyed after the timeout period.

The Contents and StaticObjects Collections

Session variables are stored in the `Session` object's default collection, just like that of the `Application` object. The syntax for setting a session variable is as follows:

```
<%
Session( "variable_name" ) = value
%>
```

If `variable_name` exists in the collection, the value of `variable_name` is replaced with the new value. If `variable_name` does not exist, it is created and assigned the value *value*. To retrieve a session variable's value, just reverse the notation:

```
<%
variable = Session ( "variable_name" )
%>
```

Session variables cannot be accessed by anybody except the user who created them. In that regard, they are useful for storing data relating to a particular user, like the user's personal preferences for the application. Session variables are also useful when you need to reuse a piece of data inside several `.asp` files. Without the use of session variables, you would have to pass that piece of data between `.asp` pages by using URL query strings, as in an HTTP GET request, or using hidden form variables, as in an HTTP POST request.

The Contents and StaticObjects collections of the Session object can also be used to explicitly reference session variables, just as we did with the Application object. Session variables that are created using the <OBJECT> tag are grouped into the StaticObjects collection, and those created without (by assigning a value to a variable in the session default collection) are placed into the Contents collection.

The code fragment shown in Listing 3-1 illustrates how to retrieve all of the session variables in the Contents collection and display their names and values.

Listing 3-1. Iterating a Collection (example3-1.asp)

```
<%
      ' Declare our iterator variable
      Dim vVar

      ' Assign some session variables for us to retrieve
      Session( "myvar" ) = 3
      Session( "anothervar" ) = "pizza"
      Session( "anothervar3" ) = "spaghetti"

      ' Retrieve each one and display the name and value
      For Each vVar In Session.Contents
%>
      <% = vVar & ": " & Session( vVar ) & "<BR>" %>
<%
      Next
%>
```

Anatomy of a Session

When the Web server starts a session, the session is assigned a unique identification number. This number is called the *session ID*. You can determine the session ID of the current session by getting the value of the SessionID property. Even though the session ID is (for most practical purposes) unique, it is best to avoid associating SessionID with a particular user session. The potential exists that the SessionID property could return a duplicate value if the Web server is shut down and another session is started after the Web server has restarted. So, if you have an application that needs to uniquely identify something with a session, it's best to use some other value that you generate yourself.

Controlling Sessions

We said before that since the Web communication environment is stateless, we have a somewhat difficult time determining when the user has disengaged from the application. In order to overcome this limitation, we set a time limit on how long a session can "exist." That parameter is called the *session timeout*. It is expressed in minutes. Sessions default to a timeout of 20 minutes. That is, if the user does not request a page inside the application within this 20-minute period, the session automatically expires, and all session variables are lost. To set the timeout period, just set the `Timeout` property of the `Session` object to an integer equal to the number of minutes. The best time to override the session default timeout period is when you think a particular script's execution will likely exceed the default time limit. Here's how to change it:

```
Session.Timeout = 50
```

Note: The session timeout can also be set for the entire session when placed in the `Session_OnStart` event of the `global.asa` file (see the next section for information on the `global.asa` file).

Suppose you wanted to end a session immediately. For example, your application might include an option for the user to "log off" of your application. Since we are logging off of the application, we want to ensure that we properly "clean up" after ourselves. This means freeing any system resources used to store our session variables. We can accomplish this by calling the `Abandon` method of the `Session` object, like this:

```
Session.Abandon
```

Let's look at another example. In the `.asp` code fragment of Listing 3-2, we illustrate how the methods and properties of the `Session` object are used to set the timeout of the session, display the values of some session variables, assign a few session variables, and explicitly abandon the session.

Listing 3-2. Setting the Timeout (example3-2.asp)

```
<HTML>
<BODY>
Welcome user! Your session identification number is: <% = Session.↵
SessionID %><BR>
<%

' Set the session to expire after 60 minutes of no activity
Session.Timeout = 60
```

```
' Set some session variables
Session( "favorite_food" ) = "lasagna"
Session( "hobby" ) = "playing guitar"
%>
I know that your favorite food is <B><% = Session( "favorite_food" ) ⏎
%></B>,<BR>
and you like <B><% = Session( "hobby" ) %></B>. How thrilling!<BR><BR>


<%
' We will now abandon the session. The Web server will no longer keep ⏎
the session variables.
Session.Abandon
%>
The session has been abandoned, but I still know that your hobby is ⏎
<B><% = Session( "hobby" ) %></B>, but only until the end of this page.
</BODY>
</HTML>
```

It's important to note that a call to `Session.Abandon` does not destroy the session at that moment. It is, in fact, queued for deletion by the Web server. References to the values of session variables can still be made up to the termination of the script. On the next page request, the variables will no longer exist, and, if the new request is to another ASP page, a new session is created.

The global.asa File

Now that we have covered how an ASP application is defined and how a session is created and terminated, it's time to introduce the heart of an ASP application—the `global.asa` file.

Tracking Application and Session Events

What is the `global.asa` file? The `global.asa` file is a single file that resides in the root directory of a Web application. An application can have only one `global.asa` file. It contains script code that executes when a session begins and ends and when the application starts and stops. The `Application` and `Session` objects both contain two event handler procedures: one called `OnStart` and one called `OnEnd`. These event handlers are merely `Sub` functions whose code is executed in the event of an application start or termination or session start or termination.

Structure of the global.asa File

Let's look at how the global.asa file is structured. The following is a minimal global.asa file (it is minimal because we do not have any code to execute for the OnStart and OnEnd events of the Application and Session objects):

```
<SCRIPT LANGUAGE=VBScript RUNAT=Server>

Sub Application_OnStart
End Sub

Sub Application_OnEnd
End Sub

Sub Session_OnStart
End Sub

Sub Session_OnEnd
End Sub


</SCRIPT>
```

The global.asa file is extremely versatile. In general, you can put whatever code you wish inside the Sub procedures for each event. Typically, the global.asa file is used to perform various types of initializations, such as declaring objects and variables that have application and session scope. Another use for the global.asa file is to track concurrent usage of an application. For example, you might want to monitor the number of users currently using your application. By keeping a counter variable (in an application variable), incrementing it whenever a session begins (in the Session_OnStart event), and subtracting from it when a session ends (in the Session_OnEnd event), you can effectively keep track of concurrent usage of the application. It should also be mentioned that a global.asa file is not required in order for a Web application to run. Most Web application developers will appreciate its versatility since it allows them to trap the all-important session and application events.

Using Application and Session Events

The Megabyte's Pizzeria application makes use of a global.asa file. We can begin building it based on the minimal global.asa file listed earlier. We will

use it to store some global variables and to count concurrent users of the
application.

The Megabyte's `global.asa` file needs to be able to assign some values to
a few variables that will be used over and over again throughout our application. The `Application_OnStart` event provides a good facility for us to do this
because the code in the `OnStart` event handler of the `Application` object will
be executed before the Web server processes any content:

```
Sub Application_OnStart
        ' The application begins when the first user requests a file in
        ' the application, so we know the count is 1 at this time.
❶      Application( "ConcurrentUsers" ) = 1

        ' Boolean value indicating whether or not to display our
        ' custom page header
❶      Application( "DisplayPageHeader" ) = true
End Sub
```

The code in the `Application_OnStart` procedure created two application
variables: one called `ConcurrentUsers` and one called `DisplayPageHeader`. ❶
These variables will be used to tally the number of concurrent users of the
application and to control the display of our HTML page header, respectively.
Remember that the lifetime of these variables ends when the Web server is
shut down.

Let's implement the code to increment the count of the concurrent users.
When a new user enters the application space (requests a file in the virtual
directory), a session begins. That's the point when we want to increment the
value of `ConcurrentUsers`. So, as part of the `Session_OnStart` event, we
need to increment the counter:

```
Sub Session_OnStart

        ' Lock the application variables to prevent others modifying them
        Application.Lock

        ' Increment the value
        Application ( "ConcurrentUsers" ) = _
                Application ( "ConcurrentUsers" ) + 1

        ' Unlock the application variables, enabling other access to them
        Application.Unlock
End Sub
```

We want to perform a similar procedure for the `Session_OnEnd` event. When a user's session times out, we need to decrement the value of the `ConcurrentUsers` variable. The steps are almost identical:

```
Sub Session_OnEnd

    ' Lock the application variables to prevent others modifying them
    Application.Lock

    ' Decrement the value
    Application ( "ConcurrentUsers" ) = _
        Application ( "ConcurrentUsers" ) - 1

    ' Unlock the application variables, enabling other access to them
    Application.Unlock
End Sub
```

When you write code for your `global.asa` file, take note that any code that you include outside the `<SCRIPT></SCRIPT>` tags will be ignored. You must also declare each variable in the `global.asa` file to have application or session scope (using the `Application` or `Session` collection); otherwise, your other ASP scripts won't be able to access them. If you make changes to the `global.asa` file while an application is running, the changes will take effect after all current requests to the application have finished processing. During the reprocessing of the `global.asa` file, requests made of the application are returned with an error message. After processing, all sessions are killed, and the application is reset. The next request to the application will execute the code in `Application_OnStart`.

Note: In addition to placing scripts inside the event subroutines, you may also create instances of COM components (see the section about the ASP `Server` object for more information).

Request Object

Web applications would cease to be useful if they could not process information sent to them by the user. When a Web browser makes a request of the Web server, there is a wealth of information that is sent with the request. We learned in Chapter 1 about the header information that accompanies an

HTTP request. Included in these headers is "meta-data" like the IP address of the computer making the request, the query string, cookie information, the type of data being sent in the request, and so on. With traditional CGI programming, a programmer typically had to read in all this data and manually parse out the needed information. The ASP `Request` object provides a convenient, high-level, object-style interface to all the information sent in an HTTP request.

CGI Encoding and Form Variables

The `Request` object is also responsible for retrieving information sent in an HTML form. HTML form data can be sent using two methods: an HTTP `GET` or an HTTP `POST`. The CGI encoding scheme takes each field on the form and represents it as a name–value pair, with the name being the name of the HTML form element and the value being the data that is associated with that form element.

The CGI encoding scheme represents some characters as escape sequences. To illustrate, let's look at how HTML form data is encoded.

Consider an HTML form with three text fields named COLOR, STYLE, and SIZE. Suppose the user entered "green," "sweater/V Neck," and "XL," respectively, for each variable. The string of data that is sent in the HTTP request would be encoded in this manner:

```
COLOR=green&SIZE=XL&STYLE=sweater%2FV+Neck
```

A name–value pair in an HTTP request takes the format `name=value`. The ampersand (&) character delimits the name–value pairs. Notice that forward-slash and space characters in the value for STYLE have been "escaped out." The percent sign is used to prefix a hexadecimal number that represents the ASCII value of the character being encoded (a slash is ASCII 2F in hexadecimal). This is necessary because some characters, like a space character, are represented as other ASCII characters. In this case, a space is represented as a plus sign (+).

The type of request method that you use in your form depends on your application. If the values you are sending in your request are small in size and you don't have a lot of them, a GET request will be adequate. If you are sending large amounts of data, such as blocks of text contained in <TEXTAREA> tags or whole files (as in an HTTP upload), a POST is more appropriate since most Web servers put a limit on the length of a GET query string. You may also opt to use a combination of both methods if the need arises. A POST is also useful if you do not want your users to see the names of your form variables as they are passed in the URL.

ASP conveniently takes care of decoding the request data without any intervention on your part. Whether you use the GET or POST method for sending your HTML form data to the Web server, ASP stores the data of each type of request in two different collections of the Request object. Those collections are the QueryString collection (used for storing data sent in an HTTP GET) and the Form collection (for HTTP POST requests).

As we mentioned, the form data that is sent is stored in collections (like those of the Application and Session objects). We can assess them by referencing the HTML form element name in the collection. Consider the simple HTML form of Listing 3-3.

Listing 3-3. A Simple HTML Form (example3-3.htm)

```
<HTML>
<BODY>
<FORM METHOD=GET ACTION="example3-3.asp">
Enter your e-mail address (if you dare) : <INPUT TYPE=text
NAME=emailAddr SIZE=40>
<INPUT TYPE=submit VALUE="Send">
</BODY>
</HTML>
```

We can retrieve the value in our e-mail address text field, emailAddr, with example3-3.asp. The .asp script file could contain something like the code shown in Listing 3-4.

Listing 3-4. The ASP Script File (example3-3.asp)

```
<%
    Option Explicit
    Dim sEmailAddress       ' Variable to hold the e-mail address

    ' Get the value of the HTML text field "emailAddr" and store it
    ' in the VBScript variable sEmailAddress. Since the form used
    ' the GET method, our form fields will be contained in the
    ' QueryString collection.
    sEMailAddress = Request.QueryString ( "emailAddr" )
%>
```

You entered <% = sEmailAddress %> as your e-mail address. Prepare to
be <B>spammed!</B> Just kidding..

Now consider the next example. We retrieve information from the HTML
form of Listing 3-5—it uses the POST method—and we process it with the
script in `example3-4.asp`, shown in Listing 3-6. Since we specified
METHOD=POST in our HTML form, the values entered in the form are stored in
the Form collection instead of the QueryString collection.

Listing 3-5. Another HTML Form (example3-4.htm)

```
<HTML>
<BODY>
<FORM METHOD=POST ACTION="example3-4.asp">
If you don't have anything nice to say, don't say anything at all:
<TEXTAREA NAME=comments ROWS=10 COLS=30></TEXTAREA>
<INPUT TYPE=submit VALUE="Send">
</BODY>
</HTML>
```

Listing 3-6. Another ASP Script File (example3-4.asp)

```
<%
Option Explicit
Dim sComments

sComments = Request.Form ( "comments" )

%>

We appreciate all you have to say:<BR>
<PRE>
<% = sComments %>
</PRE>
```

Cookies

Another collection that is part of the Request object that you will often be
working with is the Cookies collection. *Cookies* are small fragments of data
that are sent by the Web server and stored on the user's hard drive.

When a request is made for a file on the Web server, the Web server will occasionally send HTTP headers along with the response that contains instructions for the user's Web browser to write a cookie to the user's disk. Cookies are assigned an expiration date and are no longer valid after that date.

The next time a user requests the page for which the cookie has been set, the browser will send the cookie to the Web server along with the request. The cookies sent along in the request are kept in a collection called `Cookies`. The anatomy of a cookie consists of the name of the cookie and its associated value. Some cookies can have multiple values associated with them. These cookies are said to contain *keys*.

To use cookies, you reference them just like any other collection. For example, if you want to retrieve the value of a cookie named `foodchoice`, you could use the following code:

```
I see that you keep asking for <% = Request.Cookies ( "foodchoice" ) ↵
%> ↵whenever you visit here.
```

If the cookie contained multiple values (keys), then you could reference each of the keys of the cookie in this fashion:

```
You have selected: <BR><BR>
<% For Each sKey in Request.Cookies ( "foodselections" ) %>
    <% = Request.Cookies ( "foodselections" ) ( sKey ) %><BR>
<% Next %>
```

Sometimes, you may not know in advance that a cookie contains keys. For this purpose, a function called `HasKeys` can be used to test a cookie for the existence of keys. The `HasKeys` function will return true if the cookie contains keys and false if it does not. Here's an example:

```
<% If Request.Cookies ( "mycookie" ).HasKeys Then %>
    This cookie does not contain any keys.
<% End If %>
```

Cookies are a very useful tool to the Web application developer. With cookies, you can perform tasks such as the following:

- Storing the user's preferences for your Web site and retrieving them on their next visit.
- Storing the user's profile (name, address, phone number, and other personal data) to be used in ordering transactions.
- Storing any small amount of data for later retrieval with little overhead.

It is important to note that while cookies can be very helpful, their convenience comes with a price. First, cookies have raised concern about user privacy in the online community. Many individuals believe that their personal information (name, address, social security number, and credit card number) stored in cookies can be freely retrieved from their browser. Some sites used cookies to store this information for use on return visits. So, if a Web site requests that a cookie be sent from your browser, it seems reasonable to question the security of something like this. Is it possible for an "unauthorized" site to request your private cookie information? (In general, the answer is no, and we'll discuss why in the section on the `Response` object later in this chapter. This section will cover, in detail, the semantics of setting cookies.)

Another problem with cookies is that they do not migrate with the user from workstation to workstation. This can be annoying for the user who regularly visits a particular site that uses cookies to store frequently requested information. Picture this scenario: The user submits some form data on a page, and the server sets cookies with the entered information. Upon returning to the site at a later time, the user doesn't have to repeat the data entry process since it is stored in cookies. What happens if the user accesses the same site from a different computer? As you can probably imagine, the site will request the information once again from the user because it didn't find the cookies.

In summary, cookies are not suitable for persistent storage over extended periods of time. If you require permanent storage of data that the user supplies, it's best to store it in a database. Chapter 4 will cover this topic, so stay tuned.

Server Variables

The HTTP environment variables sent along with an HTTP request are stored in the `ServerVariables` collection. These values are read-only and give information about the HTTP data exchange. Table 3-1 contains a partial list of the most important environment variables supported by IIS/PWS.

We are now ready to return to the Megabyte's application. Let's look at the next part of the program. This section will gather some information about the visitor and echo it back to the browser.

The Megabyte's Pizzeria Order Registration Page

The objective of the Order Registration Page is to collect the essential information we need from the user in order to create an account in the ordering system. We need to collect the user's name, street address, e-mail address, and

Table 3-1.   HTTP Environment Variables

General Server Variables	
Variable	**Description**
ALL_HTTP	Contains a string of all of the HTTP environment variables.
ALL_RAW	Same as ALL_HTTP, but some variable names not prefixed with HTTP.
QUERY_STRING	Contains the query string; this is all the characters following the "?" in a URL.
REMOTE_ADDR	The IP address of the Web client.
REMOTE_HOST	The hostname of the Web client.
REMOTE_USER	The username of the person making the request.
REQUEST_METHOD	The type of request received—specifically, a GET, POST, or HEAD.
SCRIPT_NAME	Virtual path of the executing script.
SERVER_NAME	The server's hostname, DNS alias, or IP address.
SERVER_PORT	Port number the HTTP request was received on.
SERVER_PORT_SECURE	A string of "1" indicates that request came in on a secure port. "0" is not secure.
SERVER_PROTOCOL	The protocol and version used for the Web client/server exchange (example: "HTTP/1.1").
SERVER_SOFTWARE	The Web server software name (example: Microsoft-IIS/4.0).
CONTENT_LENGTH	The length in bytes of the client request.
CONTENT_TYPE	The type of data sent in the request. This is a MIME data type.
GATEWAY_INTERFACE	The version of the CGI standard that is running on the Web server.

(continued)

Table 3-1. (continued)

LOCAL_ADDR	Returns the server address on which the request came in.
URL	The current URL.
PATH_INFO	Path information given by the client.
PATH_TRANSLATED	Translated version of PATH_INFO.

Variables Used in Password Authentication	
Variable	**Description**
AUTH_PASSWORD	The value entered in the client's authentication dialog. This variable is available only if Basic authentication is used.
AUTH_TYPE	The authentication method that the server uses to validate users when they attempt to access a protected script.
LOGON_USER	The Windows NT account that the user is logged into.
AUTH_USER	Raw authenticated username.

Variables Used with Client Certificates	
Variable	**Description**
CERT_COOKIE	Unique ID for client certificate. Returned as a string. Can be used as a signature for the whole client certificate.
CERT_FLAGS	Bit 0 is set to 1 if the client certificate is present. Bit 1 is set to 1 if the Certifying Authority of the client certificate is invalid (not in the list of recognized CAs on the server).
CERT_ISSUER	Issuer field of the client certificate (O=MS, OU=IAS, CN=username, C=USA).
CERT_KEYSIZE	Number of bits in Secure Sockets Layer connection key size (example: 128).

(continued)

Table 3-1. (continued)

CERT_SECRETKEYSIZE	Number of bits in server certificate private key (example: 1024).
CERT_SERIALNUMBER	Serial number field of the client certificate.
CERT_SERVER_ISSUER	Issuer field of the server certificate.
CERT_SERVER_SUBJECT	Subject field of the server certificate.
CERT_SUBJECT	Subject field of the client certificate.
Variables Used in Secure HTTP Communications	
Variable	**Description**
HTTPS	Returns ON if the request came in through secure channel (SSL), or it returns OFF if the request is for a nonsecure channel.
HTTPS_KEYSIZE	Number of bits in Secure Sockets Layer connection key size (example: 128).
HTTPS_SECRETKEYSIZE	Number of bits in server certificate private key (example: 1024).
HTTPS_SERVER_ISSUER	Issuer field of the server certificate.
HTTPS_SERVER_SUBJECT	Subject field of the server certificate.

his/her chosen username and password. For the purposes of our application, we assume that the street address that the user gives is correct and inside Megabyte's delivery area. (We could intelligently detect whether the given street address is inside the restaurant's delivery area, but such an algorithm is beyond the scope of this book and is left as an exercise for the reader.)

The Registration Page is an HTML file. It contains an HTML form, designated by the <FORM> tag. The HTML source that contains the form section is given in Listing 3-7.

Listing 3-7. HTML Source for Megabyte's Registration Page

```
❶ <FORM ACTION="newuser.asp"METHOD=GET></FONT>
  <TABLE CELLSPACING=0 BORDER=0 CELLPADDING=7 WIDTH=570>
  <TR><TD WIDTH="50%" VALIGN="TOP">
  <P><B><FONT FACE="Arial">Name:</B></FONT></TD>
```

```
<TD WIDTH="50%" VALIGN="TOP">
<B><FONT FACE="Arial"><P>

<INPUT TYPE="TEXT" NAME="fullname">

</B></FONT></TD>
</TR>
<TR><TD WIDTH="50%" VALIGN="TOP">
<B><FONT FACE="Arial"><P>Street Address:</B></FONT></TD>
<TD WIDTH="50%" VALIGN="TOP">
<B><FONT FACE="Arial"><P>

<INPUT TYPE="TEXT" NAME="streetaddr">

</B></FONT></TD>
</TR>
<TR><TD WIDTH="50%" VALIGN="TOP">
<B><FONT FACE="Arial"><P>E-Mail Address:</B></FONT></TD>
<TD WIDTH="50%" VALIGN="TOP">
<B><FONT FACE="Arial"><P>

<INPUT TYPE="TEXT" NAME="email">

</B></FONT></TD>
</TR>
<TR><TD WIDTH="50%" VALIGN="TOP">
<B><FONT FACE="Arial"><P>Tell us about your favorite ↵
foods:</B></FONT></TD>
<TD WIDTH="50%" VALIGN="TOP">
<P> </TD>
</TR>
<TR><TD WIDTH="50%" VALIGN="MIDDLE">
<B><FONT FACE="Arial"><P>

<INPUT TYPE="CHECKBOX" NAME="favorite_spag">

</B></FONT><FONT FACE="Arial" SIZE=2>Spaghetti

<INPUT TYPE="CHECKBOX" NAME="favorite_pizza">
Pizza
<INPUT TYPE="CHECKBOX" NAME="favorite_tira">
Tiramisu</P>
<P>
<INPUT TYPE="CHECKBOX" NAME="favorite_salad">
```

```
Salad
<INPUT TYPE="CHECKBOX" NAME="favorite_lasagna">
Lasagna
<INPUT TYPE="CHECKBOX" NAME="favorite_burgers">
Hamburgers?</FONT></TD>

<TD WIDTH="50%" VALIGN="TOP">
<P> </TD>
</TR>
<TR><TD WIDTH="50%" VALIGN="TOP">
<B><FONT FACE="Arial"><P>Have you ordered from Megabyte's ⏎
before?</B></FONT></TD>
<TD WIDTH="50%" VALIGN="TOP">
<B><FONT FACE="Arial"><P>

<INPUT TYPE="RADIO" CHECKED NAME="orderedbefore" VALUE="Yes">

</B></FONT><FONT FACE="Arial" SIZE=2>Yes

<INPUT TYPE="RADIO" NAME="orderedbefore" VALUE="No">No

</FONT></TD>
</TR>
<TR><TD WIDTH="50%" VALIGN="TOP">
<B><FONT FACE="Arial"><P>How did you hear about us?</B></FONT></TD>
<TD WIDTH="50%" VALIGN="TOP">
<B><FONT FACE="Arial"><P>

<SELECT NAME="referral">
<OPTION VALUE="Web Page Banner Ad">Web Page Banner Ad
<OPTION VALUE="Magazine">Magazine
<OPTION VALUE="Radio/Television">Radio/Television
<OPTION VALUE="Other">Other
</SELECT>

</B></FONT></TD>
</TR>
<TR><TD WIDTH="50%" VALIGN="TOP">
<B><FONT FACE="Arial"><P>Choose a username:</B></FONT></TD>
<TD WIDTH="50%" VALIGN="TOP">
<B><FONT FACE="Arial"><P>

<INPUT TYPE="TEXT" MAXLENGTH="8" NAME="username">

</B></FONT></TD>
```

```
</TR>
<TR><TD WIDTH="50%" VALIGN="TOP">
<B><FONT FACE="Arial"><P>Choose a password:</B></FONT></TD>
<TD WIDTH="50%" VALIGN="TOP">
<B><FONT FACE="Arial"><P>

<INPUT TYPE="PASSWORD" NAME="password">

</B></FONT></TD>
</TR>
<TR><TD WIDTH="50%" VALIGN="TOP">
<B><FONT FACE="Arial"><P>Cofnirm your password:</B></FONT></TD>
<TD WIDTH="50%" VALIGN="TOP">
<P>

<INPUT TYPE="PASSWORD" NAME="confirmpwd">

</TD>
</TR>
<TR><TD WIDTH="50%" VALIGN="TOP">
<B><FONT FACE="Arial"><P>

<INPUT TYPE="SUBMIT" VALUE="Send Account Request" ↵
NAME="newusersubmit">

<INPUT TYPE="RESET" VALUE="Reset Form">

</B></FONT></TD>
<TD WIDTH="50%" VALIGN="TOP">
<P> </TD>
</TR>
</TABLE>

<P><HR></P>
<P ALIGN="CENTER"><A HREF="menu.htm"><FONT FACE="Arial">Browse ↵
menu"</FONT></A><FONT
FACE="Arial" SIZE=1> | </FONT><A HREF="order.htm"><FONT ↵
FACE="Arial">Order
Online</FONT></A><FONT FACE="Arial" SIZE=1> | </FONT><A ↵
HREF="status.htm"><FONT
FACE="Arial">Check Order Status</FONT></A></P>
<P ALIGN="CENTER"><A HREF="mailto:support@mbpizza.com"><FONT ↵
FACE="Arial">Contact
```

```
Us</FONT></A><FONT FACE="Arial" SIZE=1> | </FONT><A ↵
HREF="welcome.asp"><FONT
FACE="Arial">Home</FORM></FONT></A></P>
```

In Listing 3-7, the form-related items have been highlighted in boldface. Notice in the opening <FORM> tag, we assign the form to use the GET method when sending the information to the Web server.❶ This means that the form data (coded as name–value pairs) will be passed in the query string. The ACTION attribute of the <FORM> tag gives the URL of a script to execute upon submission of the form. The file called newuser.asp will process the new user information.

Our example uses four different types of input elements: text fields, checkboxes, a drop-down list, and radio buttons. In the case of text fields, the system passes the text typed inside them in a straightforward manner. The "name" in a given name–value pair corresponds to the NAME attribute of an INPUT element, and the "value" corresponds to the text entered in that INPUT element. The drop-down list works in a similar fashion. The name of the <SELECT> element corresponds to the name in the name–value pair. The assigned value is the <OPTION VALUE> associated with the selection. But what information is sent for the checkboxes on the form? What data is sent for a radio button that is selected? Since there is no text entered for these items, what data is passed for these items?

To see how this works, let's look at the query string that is sent by the form after it is filled out with some values:

```
newuser.asp?fullname=Matt+J.+Crouch&streetaddr=123+Main+Street&email=↵
mymail@host.net&favorite ↵
spag=on&favoritetira=on&favorite ↵
lasagna=on&orderedbefore=No&referral=Radio%2FTelevision&use ↵
rname=mcrouch&password=secret&confirmpwd=secret&newusersubmit=Send+↵
Account+Request
```

In this example, notice that the text fields in the form are each assigned to the text that was typed into them. The user also checked the boxes for "Spaghetti," "Tiramisu," and "Lasagna." Each of these items receives a value of "on" to indicate that they were checked. Those checkboxes that were not selected are not sent in the form request.

The registration form also contains two radio buttons, used to facilitate asking for a yes/no response from the user. Both of the radio buttons have the same NAME attribute assigned to them—the name used is "orderedbefore."

One radio button is given a VALUE attribute equal to "Yes." The other radio button's value is assigned to "No."

You should use radio buttons for an input element when you have a specific set of options that you want the user to select from. Each of the options should be mutually exclusive. In other words, you may select only one of the options. This is unlike checkboxes, where the options are independent of one another (i.e., the user may select one or more options).

When the user clicks on one radio button, all other radio buttons with the same NAME attribute are unselected. When the form is submitted, the value of the highlighted radio button is sent in the HTTP request. So, if the user responded "No," in answer to whether or not the visitor ordered from Megabyte's before, the request is sent by the name–value pair `orderedbefore=no`.

The newuser.asp Script

We are now going to take the information submitted by the HTML form and set up an account for this user to use when ordering food. This code will set a cookie on the user's browser that contains the username and e-mail address that the user entered in the form.

Note: Setting cookies in this fashion is an elementary example. We'll talk about cookies in more detail in the section on the Response object later in this chapter.

Later, we will add code to the Welcome Page to greet the user by his/her name. In Chapter 4, we'll expand upon this code by writing the account information to a database. This database will then be used to validate users when they log into the ordering system.

The workhorse of the `newuser.asp` script is a VBScript function called `CreateAccount()`. This function takes the user account information in its parameters and creates a cookie with that information. It also returns a success or failure code upon exiting. Here is the code:

```
Public Function CreateAccount ( username, fullname, email )

' Local variables
Dim liCookie ' cookie iterator

' Set a cookie that holds the user information. This cookie will ⏎
contain keys.
' The "base" of this cookie will be "accountinfo", and the keys will ⏎
contain
```

```
' the fullname and e-mail address.
Response.Cookies ( "accountinfo" ) ( "username" ) = fullname
Response.Cookies ( "accountinfo" ) ( "fullname" ) = fullname
Response.Cookies ( "accountinfo" ) ( "email" ) = email

' Set the cookies to expire a year from now.
For Each liCookie in Response.Cookies
    Response.Cookies ( liCookie ) .Expires = DateAdd ( "yyyy", 1, Now )
Next

' Successful account creation. Return to caller
CreateAccount = 0
End Function
```

The cookie we are setting contains keys. This method makes it convenient for us to file information away on a user and keep it together. The base of the cookie is called `accountinfo`. We will store the user's chosen username, his/her full name, and the e-mail address in the keys of these cookies.

Whenever we are modifying HTTP headers (such as is the case with setting cookies) in an `.asp` script, we must be certain that this is done before any content is sent to the browser because an attempt to modify an HTTP header after content has been sent will raise a runtime error. As the `CreateAccount()` function evolves, you'll notice that we do such a check (refer to the complete `newuser.asp` file). The Web server will first execute the script and, based on the result returned from `CreateAccount`, will start to send content to the browser. Based on the comparisons of the `If . . . Then` statements, different messages are delivered. This method may seem cumbersome at first, but shortly we'll demonstrate a technique with the `Response` object that will allow us to suppress HTTP output until a command is executed. This technique is called *buffering*.

It should be noted that setting the `Expires` property for your cookies is essential. Setting the expiration date on cookies causes the browser to "flush" the cookies from memory to disk. If the expiration of cookies is not set, it is possible that the user's browser will discard the cookies when closed.

Client Certificates

Some Web servers, especially those used for e-commerce, send their data back and forth using encrypted data. This data exchange is carried out using the Secure Sockets Layer (SSL) protocol. When data is sent using this protocol, the server must provide proof of the identity of the company running the server. The proof of authenticity is issued to a company through a third-party organization. The authenticating piece, or *certificate*, is sent in the HTTP responses from the server.

The `ClientCertificate` data, as it is known, is stored in a collection of the `Request` object. The certificate includes data about the issuer of the certificate, the serial number of the certificate, the expiration date, and other parameters. Table 3-2 lists the complete set.

The `Issuer` and `Subject` fields both contain subkeys with additional information. The name of any subkey is a combination of the key name and letter codes. Table 3-3 lists these letter codes, defines the meaning of each code, and indicates what collection it is used by.

Certificate Code Sample

Suppose that we wanted to verify that the date of a particular certificate being sent by the user is still valid. If we connect to a site that is not using Secure Sockets Layer (SSL), then the certificate fields will be empty. If not, we can investigate the contents of the `ValidFrom` and `ValidTo` keys from the `ClientCertificate` to determine whether the certificate is expired.

This sample will provide meaningful results (will actually return data in the `ValidFrom` and `ValidTo` fields) only if IIS 4.0 is set up to accept client

Table 3-2. ClientCertificate Collection

Collection Value	Description
Certificate	Binary. Binary representation of the entire certificate.
Issuer	String. Represents the issuer's name. Contains subkeys that hold the issuer information.
SerialNumber	String. The certificate's serial number.
Subject	String. Represents the issuer's name. Contains subkeys that hold the issuer information.
ValidFrom	Date. The date from which the certificate is valid.
ValidUntil	Date. The date when the certificate expires.

Table 3-3.   Issuer and Subject Subkeys

Code	Description	Used by
C	Country of origin	Issuer
CN	Common name	Subject
GN	Given name	Issuer
I	Initials	Issuer
L	Locality	Issuer
O	Organization name	Issuer
OU	Organization unit name (department)	Issuer
S	State or province	Issuer
T	Person or organization title	Issuer

certificates and communication is over SSL. (For information on this setup, see Appendix A.) Here is the certificate code sample:

```
<%
' Check for valid certificate dates
If Request.ClientCertificate ( "ValidFrom" ) <= Now And
        Request.ClientCertificate ( "ValidTo" ) > Now Then
            ' Certificate still valid, print out its info
                Response.Write "Valid certificate"
                    Response.Write _
     Request.ClientCertificate ( "Issuer" ) ( "IssuerC" ) & "<BR>" & _
     Request.ClientCertificate ( "Issuer" ) ( "IssuerCN" ) & "<BR>" & _
     Request.ClientCertificate ( "Issuer" ) ( "IssuerGN" ) & "<BR>" & _
     Request.ClientCertificate ( "Issuer" ) ( "IssuerI" ) & "<BR>" & _
     Request.ClientCertificate ( "Issuer" ) ( "IssuerL" ) & "<BR>" & _
     Request.ClientCertificate ( "Issuer" ) ( "IssuerO" ) & "<BR>" & _
   Request.ClientCertificate ( "Issuer" ) ( "IssuerOU" ) & "<BR>" & _
    Request.ClientCertificate ( "Issuer" ) ( "IssuerS" ) & "<BR>" & _
      Request.ClientCertificate ( "Issuer" ) ( "IssuerT" ) & "<BR>"
```

```
Else
     Response.Write "Certificate has expired or no certificate sent"
End If
%>
```

This sample code first investigates for valid dates. If a valid certificate is sent, then the certificate's information (about the issuer) is written to the browser by retrieving the subkeys of the `Issuer` collection.

Response Object

The job of the `Response` object is to send data back to the user's browser and control the output of the HTTP stream in a programmatic way. Sometimes, you may need to dynamically insert content into the HTTP stream. You may wish to set cookies as part of your script. You also may need to send customer HTTP headers as part of the output of a script, or you may need to log additional information about the client request. If your programming task involves sending output back to the client, the `Response` object is the vehicle for that task.

Sending Page Output

You can write data to the HTTP output in two different forms—either text or binary. Text output is used for sending an HTML-based response. Binary output is for those applications where an `.asp` script needs to send back data in the form of, say, a JPEG image.

Buffering the Output Stream

ASP has the ability to buffer the output to the HTTP stream. When the output is buffered, no data is sent to the stream until all script processing has completed for the page. You may also send what has currently accumulated in the output buffer by issuing the `Flush` or `End` method. If you wish to enable buffering for your `.asp` script, you must specify it by setting the `Buffer` property to true. This property setting must be made before any output is sent to the browser. If possible, it's a good idea to make it the first statement in your file. By default, all output is not buffered in IIS/PWS. As your script runs, any calls made to the `Write` methods will send output immediately. In addition to controlling buffering programmatically with `Response.Buffer`, you can modify buffering behavior via a setting in the Windows Registry (see the IIS documentation for more information on how to change this setting).

The `Flush` and `End` methods both cause an immediate dump of the buffer contents to the stream. The `End` method also stops script execution. Be careful not to call any of these methods when buffering is not turned on because a runtime error will result.

You may also erase the current contents of the buffer by calling the `Clear` method. This will wipe out any data in the response body only; other HTTP response headers will still persist.

Note: With regard to using buffered output, be advised that HTTP 1.1 contains a special header that is issued by some Web browsers called the `"Keep-Alive"` header. It instructs the Web server to hold open the network connection for subsequent requests, rather than establishing a new connection for each page request, which can save valuable processing time on a busy server.

With all this said, let's look at some examples of using `Write` and `Binary-Write`. The first example uses buffered output. Try the script in Listing 3-8 and pay close attention to the output. Notice that the only lines displayed are ❶, ❷, and ❸. The `Clear` method prevents the further text from appearing, and the `End` method❹ will flush all the output and then stop any processing of the script.

Listing 3-8. Using Buffered Output (example3-5.asp)

```
<%
' Turn on buffering
Response.Buffer = True


' Write out some text to the browser
❶ Response.Write "<H1>Buffering Example</H1>"
❷ Response.Write "This is a test of buffering"


' Flush the output
Response.Flush
' Write some more text and clear it from the buffer
Response.Write "<BR>This text should not show up"
Response.Clear
' Display this text and end script processing
❸ Response.Write "<BR>But this text will show up"
❹ Response.End
```

```
Response.Write "<BR>This text shouldn't appear, Response.End stops ↵
the script"
%>
```

Tip: Before we introduced the `Response.Write` method, we had been sending the results of ASP execution using the shorthand notation <% = *expression* %>. Using this method comes with a performance penalty. The script parser/interpreter switches between HTML and script processing with each script bracket it encounters and causes overhead. A better way to handle output is to use buffered output with `Response.Write` statements. In this way, the script engine just needs to send the output once, rather than multiple times throughout the script.

The `Response.Write` method can display strings, numbers, and dates. It performs the necessary conversions internally. In the event that you need to write the character sequence <% or %> to the browser, you can escape out the less-than symbol or greater-than symbol using the back-slash character(\).

To use the `Binary.Write` method, you need to set the HTTP `Content-Type` Header to a MIME type appropriate to the data that you are writing to the stream. Keep in mind that this must be set toward the beginning of the script before any content is sent to the stream. You must also tell the browser how much data you intend to send to it. This is done by setting the `Content-Length` header to the number of bytes to be sent. The values for `ContentType` and `ContentLength` are properties of the `Response` object. Take a look at the following example to see how working with binary data is done:

```
<%
' Set our MIME type to the data type in binMyBinaryString
Response.ContentType = "application/my-binary-object-type"

' The length of binMyBinaryString is 30 bytes
Response.ContentLength = 30

' Write the string to the HTTP stream
Response.BinaryWrite binMyBinaryString
%>
```

Working with HTTP Headers

The `Response` object, for convenience, maps several common HTTP header values to its object properties. Look at each one in Table 3-4 to see how they are used.

Table 3-4. Response Object Properties

Property	HTTP Header	Description
CacheControl	Cache-control	Set to either public or private. If public, proxy servers will cache the output generated by ASP. Default is private.
Charset	(Part of the Content-Type header)	Use to specify a character set to use when sending text output. In order for Charset to work, a valid character set name must be specified.
ContentType	Content-Type	Set the content type for the response. Can be any valid MIME type. If none is specified, text/html is used.
Expires	Expires	A number specifying the number of minutes until the page expires (the browser will retrieve it from the server again).
ExpiresAbsolute	Expires	Instead of a period of minutes until the content expires, you can supply a specific date/time on which the page will expire.
PICS	PICS-label	The PICS header, which is a string that defines the "rating" of the content.

We've worked with several HTTP headers so far. The HTTP protocol contains many more headers that are used in the Web client/server exchange. When we discussed the Request object's SeverVariables collection, we saw all of the predefined variables available for us to query. For some advanced applications, we may wish to add our own header variables to the list of existing headers. We can do this by using the AddHeader method.

The header that we add can be any arbitrary name–value pair. It's a good idea not to use any underscore characters (_) in the header name to ensure that there is no header name ambiguity. Also, note that any underscores in the header name are translated into dashes. As with any HTTP header modifications, you need to be sure that, if your script uses unbuffered output, calls to AddHeader are placed before any output is written to the stream.

Consider the example in Listing 3-9. Upon investigation of the actual response sent by the Web server, we see our customer header added with the rest of the HTTP response headers:

Listing 3-9. Using the AddHeader Method (example3-6.asp)

```
<%
Response.Buffer = true
Response.AddHeader "MegabytesStatus", "all is well"
Response.Write "<H1>Hello</H1>You might not have noticed, but I sent a
customer header"
%>
```

```
HTTP/1.1 200 OK
Server: Microsoft-IIS/4.0
Date: Thu, 21 Jan 1999 03:42:41 GMT
Connection: keep-alive
MegabytesStatus: all is well
Connection: Keep-Alive
Content-Length: 70
Content-Type: text/html
Set-Cookie: ASPSESSIONIDFFFCVRWD=CINHHIEDLNPFPOLAHEPCHHOB; path=/
Cache-control: private

<H1>Hello</H1>You might not have noticed, but I sent a customer header
```

Custom HTTP headers have a number of applications. You can use them to send back the status of script execution, or, if you have a special application where you are sending other types of data over HTTP, you can send status messages about the transmission using custom headers.

Cookies

We've had an opportunity to work with cookies in our discussions with the Request object. The Response object also has a Cookies collection. This collection is used to set the values of cookies. It's almost identical to the Cookies collection in the Request object, except that you can add items to this collection. The items you add to the Cookies collection correspond to cookies that will be set as part of the server response.

The Megabyte's account creation script shows us an example of setting cookies. Bear in mind that you must set the `Expires` or `ExpiresAbsolute` property to a future date in order for the cookie to be applied to the user's disk.

The `Response.Cookies` collection functions much like the `Request.Cookies` collection (with keyed cookies, the `HasKeys` attribute, etc.) with some additions, which we'll touch on here. When cookies are set, you may opt to specify the circumstances in which they are to be sent back to the server.

Table 3-5 shows each of the cookie attributes you can assign to cookies, which controls how and when cookies are to be sent. `Domain` is used to state that the cookie being set can be retrieved only from the domain specified. This instructs the user's browser to send the cookie only when the request originates from the domain. By default, `Domain` is set to the current domain that the ASP page is running in. `Path` allows us to gain finer control over when the cookie should be sent by the browser. The cookie will be returned only if the request comes from a specific path on the domain. A cookie specified as `Secure` is sent only when the SSL protocol is used (`https://`). You can find out more about SSL in Chapter 9.

Table 3-5. Cookie Attributes

Attribute	Type and Description
Expires	Date. Date for the cookie to expire.
Domain	String. The domain the cookie belongs to.
Path	String. The "home path" of the cookie. Return the cookie for requests to this path only.
Secure	Boolean. Designate the cookie as secure.

Consider the example in Listing 3-10. Running this `.asp` file will generate the following response from the server:

Listing 3-10. Setting Cookies (example3-7.asp)

```
<%
Response.Buffer = true
Response.Cookies ("onesmartcookie") = "Chocolate Chip"
Response.Cookies ("onesmartcookie") .Expires = "June 13, 1999"
Response.Cookies ("onesmartcookie") .Domain = "megabytes.com"
Response.Cookies ("onesmartcookie") .Path = "/megabytes"
```

```
Response.Cookies ("onesmartcookie ") .Secure = FALSE
Response.Write "cookie set"
%>
```

```
HTTP/1.1 200 OK
Server: Microsoft-IIS/4.0
Date: Thu, 21 Jan 1999 05:31:19 GMT
Connection: Keep-Alive
Content-Length: 10
Content-Type: text/html
Set-Cookie: onesmartcookie=74Chocolate+Chip; expires=Sun, 13-Jun-1999 ⏎
05:00:00 GMT;
domain=m
egabytes.com; path=/megabytes
Set-Cookie: ASPSESSIONIDFFFCVRWD=GINHHIEDHIOHMAJDODPAJJAA; path=/
Cache-control: private
cookie set
```

Browser Redirection

A browser *redirection* is simply another HTTP header with its value set to a URL. When the Web browser encounters this header, it moves to the specified URL automatically without any user intervention. This is useful if you want to maintain an outdated link and send the user off to where the updated page is located for that link. It can also be used as part of an `.asp` script that redirects the user to a result page after the script executes.

To use redirection, use `Response.Redirect` in the following manner:

```
Response.Redirect( sURL )
```

where `sURL` is a URL, either relative or full.

Just a reminder: You may not use a redirect if you already have sent some data to the HTTP output stream. For example, consider the script in Listing 3-11. When this ASP page is requested, you'll see something like this for the output:

Listing 3-11. Browser Redirection Error (example3-8.asp)

```
<%
Response.Write "Pizzas on sale: Only $5.00 for a large, one-topping!"
Response.Redirect( "pizzasale.asp" )
%>
```

```
Pizzas on sale: Only $5.00 for a large, one-topping!
Response object error 'ASP 0156 : 80004005'
Header Error
/redirectfail.asp, line 4
The HTTP headers are already written to the client browser. Any HTTP ⏎
header modifications must be made before writing page content.
```

This error happens because the redirect instruction is an HTTP header that is placed in the HTTP response, and anything sent via a `Response.Write` is placed in the content area of the response (after the headers).

Now consider an example that actually works. Check out Listing 3-12. The page you get redirected to is shown in Listing 3-13.

Listing 3-12. Correct Browser Redirection (example3-8-1.asp)

```
<%
Response.Redirect("example3-8-2.htm")
%>
```

Listing 3-13. Browser Redirection Output (example3-8-2.htm)

```
<HTML>
<TITLE>Redirect Demo</TITLE>
<BODY>
<H1>Welcome!</H1>
You have been redirected from example3-8-1.asp

</BODY>
</HTML>
```

Customizing the IIS/PWS Logging Feature

Like many Web servers, IIS/PWS has the capability to log requests to a log file. We can customize the information that is sent to the log file by using the `Response.AppendToLog` method.

Each entry in the IIS/PWS log file is on its own line. The information it logs is the IP address of the host making the request, the date and time, the file requested, and so on. Each piece of information is separated by a comma. We can append our own text to the end of this line by calling the

Response.AppendToLog method (the text you append may have up to 80 characters). Here's an example:

```
<%
    Response.Write "<H1>Web Server Log Test</H1>Will append a string to ⏎
the log"
    Response.AppendToLog "My custom text"
%>
```

And, here's what a log file entry looks like after the Web server served up the preceding script:

```
127.0.0.1 - - [21/Jan/1999:22:57:26 -0500] "GET /logappend.asp?My ⏎
custom text HTTP/1.1" ⏎
200 230
```

Server Object

The Server object contains some miscellaneous utility functions and properties on the Web server. With the Server object, you can perform HTML/URL encoding, resolve physical pathnames on the server, and create instances of COM components (more detail on COM components in later chapters).

HTML Encoding

Sometimes, it is necessary when producing HTML output that special (typically non-ASCII) characters be represented using a special notation. For example, if you wish to display characters that have special meaning to HTML (like the < and > signs used to enclose tags), the characters need some other representation if they are not to be confused with HTML to be processed. There is also an issue with characters used in international languages that extend past the normal ASCII character set (like the character ö). Not all systems will correctly recognize these characters.

Let's say we want to display the following string on our page: *Ruché di Castagnole Monferrato*. We cannot accurately display the string "as-is" in a Response.Write call because of the "*é*" character. We need to do some preprocessing with the Server.HTMLEncode method, as shown in Listing 3-14.

Listing 3.14. HTML Encoding (example3-9.asp)

```
<% Response.Write Server.HTMLEncode( "Ruché di Castagnole Monferrato" )
%>
```

Upon examination of the HTML source result (select View→Source from your browser) of the statement in example 3-9.asp, we see

```
Ruch&#233; di Castagnole Monferrato
```

The &#233 escape sequence represents our special character.

URL Encoding

The Server.URLEncode method prepares strings for use in URLs. Recall our prior discussions with encoding HTML form data. The Server.URLEncode method will perform this type of encoding. A useful application for Server.URLEncode is for manually constructing query strings for a URL. Consider the example in Listing 3-15.

Listing 3-15. URL Encoding (example3-10-1.asp)

```
<%      ' Server.URLEncode example
        Dim sMyStrParam, sURL

        ' Set up our string value to encode
        sMyStrParam = "My very own string-parameter"

        ' Construct the URL with the encoded value string
        sURL = "example3-10-2.asp?param1=" ↵
& Server.URLEncode( sMyStrParam )

        ' Go to the URL
        Response.Redirect( sURL )
%>
```

When the new URL is requested, you will see the full URL in the address bar of your browser:

```
http://localhost/mynewpage.asp?param1=My+very+own+string%2Dparameter
```

The `example3-10-2.asp` file also echoes the `QUERY_STRING`, which also shows our `param1` variable with its encoded value.

Setting the Script Timeout Parameter

When IIS/PWS processes `.asp` files, it gives the script a time limit in which to complete its processing. The reason for such a limit is to protect the client browser from being tied up should script execution go awry due to programming problems. By default, this timeout period is set to 90 seconds. You can change or get the timeout period by referencing the `ScriptTimeout` property, as in

```
<%
    Server.ScriptTimeout = 200
    Response.Write "The script timeout is now " & ↵
            Server.ScriptTimeout & " seconds."
%>
```

Instantiating COM Objects

To create an instance of a COM object, you will use the `Server.CreateObject` method. So far, all of the COM objects we have been working with (`Response`, `Request`, etc.) have been instantiated for us by the ASP environment. To use other objects (some of which will be your own), a call to this method is required. Its syntax is simple, and an example is provided here:

```
<%
    Set objMyObj = Server.CreateObject↵
("Megabytes.SomeObjectOfMine")
%>
```

This code creates an instance of the hypothetical `Megabytes.SomeObjectOfMine` component. COM object names have the form *ProgID.ClassID*. In later chapters, we'll discuss the architecture of COM components and how they are used in more detail. This example should provide some background for those later discussions.

Using the <OBJECT> Tag to Create COM Components

Another way to create instances of COM objects in ASP is to use the HTML <OBJECT> tag. In ASP, the HTML <OBJECT> tag is a special tag that is processed by ASP (rather than by the client browser) and that signals the creation of a COM object. It is accompanied by a RUNAT=server parameter that goes inside the tag. This tells the Web server that the object (COM component) is to be created on the server. Here's an example piece of code showing the creation of a component on the server:

```
<OBJECT RUNAT=server PROGID=WidgetsRUs.MainWidget id=Widget1> </OBJECT>
```

Objects created using the <OBJECT> tag are normally used for creating objects that have application or session scope. To do that, you'll need to put those declarations in the global.asa file. Here, we show a component being created with application scope inside a global.asa file:

```
<OBJECT RUNAT=server Scope=Application PROGID=WidgetsRUs.MainWidget ⏎
id=Widget1> </OBJECT>
<SCRIPT LANGUAGE=VBScript RUNAT=Server>

Sub Application_OnStart
End Sub

Sub Application_OnEnd
End Sub

Sub Session_OnStart
End Sub

Sub Session_OnEnd
End Sub

</SCRIPT>
```

If we want to reference an object in this manner, we need only specify the name of the object. For example, if Widget1 was instantiated with application scope, and we want to reference the object, we simply write

```
<% Widget1.Turn 30 %>
```

The alternate way we could create an object with application/session scope would be to use the method we already know: Server.CreateObject(). Here's how:

```
Set Application( "Widget1" ) = Server.CreateObject(
"WidgetsRUs.MainWidget" )
```

Then, to reference the object, we say something like this:

```
<% Application( "Widget1" ).Turn 30 %>
```

COM components created with the `<OBJECT>` tag are also more efficient since the actual object instance is not created until the component is first referenced.

ObjectContext Object

The `ObjectContext` object is a special object in ASP. It is used in conjunction with Microsoft Transaction Server. Its job is to manage COM objects under a transactional context. The `ObjectContext` object allows us to control transactions in which some COM objects participate. This object is mentioned here for the sake of completeness, but we will revisit it in great detail when we reach the chapter on Microsoft Transaction Server.

Chapter Review

Congratulations on reaching this point in our Active Server journey! In this chapter, we learned about the Active Server Pages application framework, which consists of the following objects:

- `Server`—Manages properties of the server and provides miscellaneous utility functions.
- `Request`—Houses all the data received from a browser's request of a file on the Web server.
- `Response`—Is in charge of sending output back to the user's browser.
- `Application`—Manages the ASP application and stores application-persistent data.
- `Session`—Keeps track of the user's session and stores session-persistent data.
- `ObjectContext`—Is used for executing components under a transactional context.

The Megabyte's Pizzeria application is starting to take shape. We've added the ability to "create" an ordering account for a user and store the user's data in cookies on the user's browser. We've also demonstrated how to retrieve that data for display in the browser.

What's Next

We will expand the user account system to include relational database access. The next chapter covers using the ActiveX Data Objects (ADO), which is the programming interface used to talk to relational databases.

■ Further Reading

- ■ *IIS Documentation*—These docs cover the ASP intrinsic object in detail. It is an optional installation component with the Windows NT Option Pack.

Working with Databases and ActiveX Data Objects

Introduction

An interactive Web site without a back-end database is almost unheard of. In fact, the primary motivation of many Internet and Intranet Web sites is to expose corporate data to a wider audience, such as customers or other departments in the organization. Microsoft has provided the *ActiveX Data Objects* (ADO) for this purpose.

We're going to learn many valuable ASP database access skills in Chapter 4. We'll learn a little about the history of Microsoft's evolution of data access technology. We'll also learn to integrate ADO into our ASP pages to query and update databases on the server. We'll cover database transaction processing and also touch on some new features in the latest version of ADO.

The History of Microsoft Data Access Technology

Open Database Connectivity (ODBC)

ADO has a long history, and its architecture is built from several different data access technologies. At its lowest abstraction level is the technology known as *Open Database Connectivity* (ODBC). ODBC is a single C-language application programming interface (API) that is used to access relational databases on a wide variety of distributed systems. It freed programmers from having to know the specifics about a particular database management system in order to interact with the database. For a database vendor to be ODBC-compliant, the database vendor must provide ODBC driver software that translates the ODBC API calls into the native database query language of the database.

ODBC had two main drawbacks. The first drawback is that ODBC is designed to be used only with C/C++. The API functions had only a call-level interface compatible with this language. If you programmed in another language, you probably used the native API of the database system. The other drawback to ODBC is that programming with it is cumbersome at best. ODBC requires many calls to the ODBC API just to perform the simplest of operations. Many of the low-level details of database access with ODBC are left to the programmer. Development times for programming with ODBC are considerably longer. For these reasons, ODBC is rarely used anymore for programming with databases.

Data Access Objects (DAO) and Remote Data Objects (RDO)

The result was two more technologies—*Data Access Objects* (DAO) and *Remote Data Objects* (RDO). DAO and RDO provide object-oriented interfaces to databases on local and remote servers, respectively. Many low-level details of data access are hidden "under the hood" and away from the programmer. These two technologies were introduced with early versions of Visual Basic and Microsoft Access.

COM-Based OLE-DB

With the introduction of COM and its language-independent architecture, a new version of data access technology was required to take advantage of COM's architecture. This new technology is known as OLE-DB (OLE stands for *Object Linking and Embedding,* which is the forerunner technology of COM). OLE-DB communicates with a *data provider,* which is software that provides access to the physical data. The OLE-DB package that Microsoft distributes comes with a data provider for ODBC drivers. This enables the programmer to write OLE-DB code, which communicates with ODBC data sources, using the COM methodology. In addition to providing access to ODBC data sources, OLE-DB providers are available for specific database management systems. This provides the fastest access to the data. OLE-DB can even talk to data providers for nonrelational database data as well, such as flat files or a store of e-mail messages. Whatever the data source, the programmer's interface remains the same.

ActiveX Data Objects (ADO)

ADO, the latest and greatest data access method, provides the easiest programming interface to data sources, while still being efficient. The object model of OLE-DB is complicated, so ADO serves as another code "wrapper" around OLE-DB to make programming easier. ADO unified the functionality of DAO and RDO and reduced the number of objects in the programming interface as well.

Programming with ADO

Currently, ADO is the recommended way to access all types of data sources. Microsoft dubs all the aforementioned technologies as "Universal Data Access," and this is their strategy for the future of data access to any kind of data, relational or not.

Connection Object

Whenever we need to access a database, we must establish a connection to the database. The purpose of the Connection object is to manage those connections. The Connection object represents a physical connection to the data store and lets you manipulate the parameters of the connection with its properties and methods. The most common Connection object methods and a short description of the function they perform are provided in Table 4-1.

The Open Method

To open a connection to a data source, we need to ensure that our environment is properly set up to do that. The following steps are involved:

1. Obtain all the correct database usernames and passwords (if the database requires a login validation).
2. Get any necessary hostnames or network connection options appropriate for the database server. You may need to consult the documentation for the DBMS for this information.
3. Set up an ODBC data source using the ODBC Control Panel.

Table 4-1.   ADO Connection Object Methods

Method	Description	Parameters
Open	Open a connection to the data source.	ConnectionString (string), UserID (string), Password (string)
Close	Terminate the connection to the data source.	
Execute	Run a SQL statement or stored procedure.	CommandText (string), RecordsAffected (long), Options (long)
BeginTrans CommitTrans RollbackTrans	Start a database transaction. Apply chances made inside a transaction. Undo changes made by a database transaction.	
OpenSchema	Get various database schema information.	QueryType (long), Criteria (array), SchemaID (GUID)

The Megabyte's application will be retrieving and updating data from a relational database. Our database will be used to store several types of information. It will store information on customers, the food menu, order detail data, materials, and activity logs. For simplicity, we'll use a Microsoft Access database for our application to begin with. When working with Microsoft Access databases, usernames and passwords are not normally used to protect the data, so we'll skip those for now (although some databases, like Microsoft SQL Server, will almost certainly require you to supply a username and password to connect). So, all the information that is required for setting up our ODBC data source is the location of the Access database .mdb file.

The Access database .mdb file contains several database tables. Follow these steps to create an ODBC data source to the .mdb file:

1. Select Settings→Control Panel from the Start menu.

2. Double-click the 32-bit ODBC Control Panel icon.

3. Click on the System DSN tab.

4. Click the Add button.

5. You will see a list of available ODBC drivers. Select the Microsoft Access Driver and click Finish.

6. In the Setup box, select a name for the data source and enter it into the "Data Source Name" field. (We will use "Megabytes" for our example.)

7. In the Database section, click Select.

8. Browse for the .mdb file. Click OK to select it.

9. Click OK in the Setup dialog. The data source is now ready for use.

Note: Data source names (DSNs) are used by ODBC as a logical reference to a database. A DSN contains instructions on the type of database to connect to and a textual description for the data source. The DSN may also contain other data parameters that specify the location of the server and any usernames and passwords used to connect to the database server. The information required varies from driver to driver. DSNs are designated as "User," "System," or "File." A User DSN is accessible only by the current user logged into the computer; it is not shared in any way. A File DSN stores its connection data in a file on the drive. This file can be made accessible to other users and to users on other machines, assuming that they have the driver installed for the data source. A System DSN is available for any user to use on the current computer, including guests. This is necessary because when Internet users connect to our site, they use an anonymous user account to retrieve the files in the Web directory on our server. Since they also need access to the database, the System DSN allows them to do that since guests have that permission.

Storing the User Account Information

We are going to revisit the newuser.asp file. Recall that this is the file that we constructed in Chapter 3 that created a user account by setting cookie information on the user's browser. We want to extend that functionality to store that data in our database as well. This will make our data more permanent since a cookie can expire or be unexpectedly deleted by the user.

We first need to open a connection to the database. We accomplish this with the Open method. The first parameter to the method is a *connection string,* which is a semicolon delimited list of name–value pairs that are specific to the database we are connecting to. The username and password parameters are optional. As we said before, we will not require a username or password to gain access to our Access database. For our connection string, we simply provide the ODBC data source name (DSN), like this:

```
cnnUserInformation.Open "DSN=Megabytes"
```

The `cnnUserInformation` variable is a `Connection` object (`ADODB.
Connection`). The `DSN` parameter specifies which DSN to connect to.
Remember, this must be a System DSN in order for Active Server Pages to
work with the data source.

   Once we have established a successful connection to the database, we are
ready to add the account information from the form to the database. We can
do this by dynamically building an SQL `INSERT` statement and then executing
it using the `Execute` method of the `Connection` object.

   We begin by taking the string values for username, password, e-mail, and
street address and replacing any occurrences of a single quote (`'`) with two
single quotes (`''`):

```
username = Replace( username, "'", "''" )
password = Replace( password, "'", "''" )
email = Replace( email, "'", "''" )
staddr = Replace( staddr, "'", "''" )
```

The reason for this coding will become clear after we begin to build our SQL
statement. We will use an SQL `INSERT` statement to add a row to the table
`Users`:

```
sSQLStmt = "INSERT INTO Users ( username, password, email_addr, ⏎
street_address ) VALUES ( ⏎
'" & username & "', '" & password & "', '" & email & "', '" & staddr ⏎
& "')"
```

   In the first part of the SQL `INSERT` statement, we specify the table name
and the columns we wish to populate with data. Then, we want to "plug in"
the actual values using the strings contained in the procedure parameters
`username`, `password`, `email`, and `staddr`. Notice that each value is surrounded
by single quotes. What happens if one of the values contains a single quote?
The resulting SQL statement string will execute with a syntax error because
the database will think that the string value has ended and will not find a
comma directly preceding the quote. The calls to the VBScript `Replace()`
function handle this problem by "escaping out" the single quote with two single quotes. In this way, the database knows to treat the two quotes as a literal
single quote.

Executing the SQL Statement

With our SQL statement built, we are ready to execute it. We need to create an instance of the ADO `Connection` object, so we call `Server.CreateObject` to create one for us:

```
Set cnnUserInformation = Server.CreateObject( "ADODB.Connection" )
```

Then, we open the DSN for our database with the `Open` method:

```
cnnUserInformation.Open "DSN=Megabytes"
```

And then, we run our SQL statement using the `Execute` method and close the database connection with the `Close` method:

```
cnnUserInformation.Execute sSQLStmt
cnnUserInformation.Close
```

After our function returns, we display a short results page with a link to return the user to the main page.

Handling Exceptions in Your Code

We have foregone an important step in making the account creation script complete. What happens if an error occurs when we try to establish a connection to the database? What happens to the program if our SQL INSERT statement fails execution? In order for our script to be robust, we need a mechanism to trap errors from ADO objects. The `Err` object and the `Errors` collection of the `Connection` object allow us to do that.

Errors Object

If an error occurs in the data provider level when calling an ADO command, the error is added to the `Errors` collection. In order for us to be able to intercept an error, we need to instruct VBScript/ASP to override the default error-handling mechanism. By default, any time an error occurs in an ActiveX component, such as an ADO object, a runtime error message is sent to the user's browser. Here's an example of what a user might see if he/she failed to make a connection to the data source:

```
Microsoft OLE DB Provider for ODBC Drivers error '80004005'
[Microsoft][ODBC Driver Manager] Data source name not found and no
default driver specified
/Megabytes/newuser.asp, line 51
```

Clearly, we do not want the user to see this type of error. Not only is the error meaningless to the naïve user (not to mention that it takes away from the user "experience"), but also, execution of the script stops when this error is encountered. Our script contained some code to return the user to the main page. Since that would not be displayed, this error leaves the user in a state of doubt as to what to do next.

Trapping Errors

We can override this default error-handling mechanism by inserting the following statement at the beginning of our function:

```
On Error Resume Next
```

`On Error Resume Next` instructs VBScript to continue script execution when an error occurs in an ActiveX object. We can then determine whether an error occurred in an ActiveX object by checking the `Number` property of the intrinsic `Err` object. Subsequently, we can determine the exact ADO error that occurred by inspecting the `Errors` collection of the ADO `Connection` object.

Whenever you call `On Error Resume Next`, it is effective for the current procedure in which it resides. Once the procedure is exited, VBScript reverts back to its normal runtime error handling.

Let's modify our code a bit to add error checking. Here is how the `AccountCreate()` function looks with all the error handling in place:

```
cnnUserInformation.Open "DSN=Megabytes"
If Err.Number = 0 Then
cnnUserInformation.Execute sSQLStmt
        If Err.Number <> 0 Then
                ' Print out the detailed error message
                For Each vErr In cnnUserInformation.Errors
                        Response.Write "Error!! - " & vErr.Description ↵
& "<BR>"
                Next
                AccountCreate = Err.Number
                cnnUserInformation.Close
```

```
                   Set cnnUserInformation = Nothing
                   Exit Function
        End If

        cnnUserInformation.Close
Else
' error opening the database connection
        AccountCreate = Err.Number
        Set cnnUserInformation = Nothing
        Exit Function
End If
```

In the preceding code, we first check to see whether the connection to the database succeeded. We do this by checking the Err object's Number property. A nonzero value indicates an error has occurred. Since we just executed an ADO method on the Connection object, we loop through the Errors collection of the object using an ADO Errors object (the variable named vErr) as the iterator. In this example, we retrieve the Description property of the ADO Errors object. This contains the string of the error message, which will give us a description of any error that happened.

A complete list of the properties of the ADO Errors object with a description of each property is given in Table 4-2. These properties combined make for rich error reporting with ADO.

Table 4-2.   ADO Errors Object Properties

Property	Description
Description	The error message string from the ADO or data provider
HelpContext	The help file and topic (if any) associated with the current error
HelpFile	The help file path for the error
NativeError	Any provider-specific error message
Number	The number of the current error
Source	The name of the component in which the error occurred
SQLState	A five-character code indicating the error

The Close Method

When we have finished with querying and updating the database, it's always good practice to explicitly close the database connection so that system resources are properly freed. To close a database connection, issue the `Close` method, like this:

```
cnnUserInformation.Close
```

The `Close` method doesn't release the memory used by the `Connection` object, but it frees up a connection resource on the database server for use by another user. Most database management systems have a limit to the number of concurrent connections to the server. On high-traffic sites, freeing the connection immediately after use is imperative for smooth operation of the application. You will also want to set the object reference to `Nothing` to free the memory used by the connection (`Set cnnUserInformation = Nothing`).

Database Connection Pooling

As mentioned, it is important to free up a database connection immediately after use since we have a finite number of connections with which to work. There is a problem associated with this approach: When a connection is made with the `Open` method, significant resources on the database server are used. The constant processing involved in opening and closing databases can wreak havoc on the scalability of the application. To make efficient use of resources, the ODBC layer of data access uses connection pooling.

Connection pooling is the process of maintaining a finite number of open connections to the database. Connection pooling conserves system resources by keeping the database connection open for subsequent queries at a later time. In this way, when a `Close` command is encountered, the database doesn't have to incur the same overhead associated with a fully open operation without connection pooling. Pooled connections have a timeout period. This timeout period is the length that a pooled connection stays active. You can configure this value by using the ODBC Control Panel (see Figure 4-1). The time is expressed in seconds.

Here is another important fact to remember about persistent connections: Like any COM component, you have the ability to assign an ADO object to a session or an application variable. However, this is not recommended. If, for example, you place an ADO `Connection` object that contains an open connection in a `Session` or an `Application` object, you have just restricted other appli-

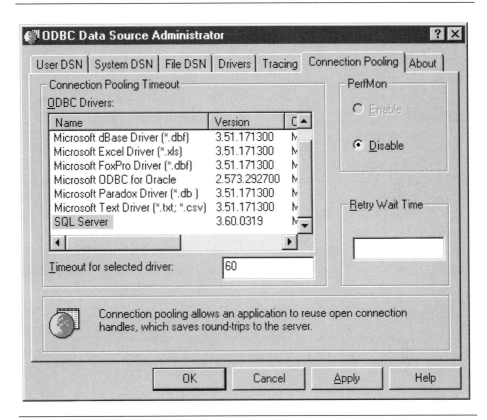

Figure 4-1. The OBDC control panel.

cations from using the connection you have open. Since the majority of the life-time of the object will be taken up by idle database activity, this limits the scala-bility of the application by eliminating the number of pooled connections.

Therefore, you should keep the time that a database connection is open to a minimum. Instead of placing the `Connection` object inside a `Session` or an `Application` object, just open and close the object from within the confines of the `.asp` file.

Database Transaction Processing

Relational databases must maintain the integrity of their data. Internal errors that occur inside a program can cause a particular database update to fail. If the program is not careful, it may continue to update other data in the database instead of properly aborting. To protect against such mishaps, database transactions are used. A *transaction* is defined as a series of steps that must succeed as a whole for the transaction to be considered successful. If one of the steps in a transaction fails, the changes made (if any) before the failure are "undone," and the database data is returned to its original state.

ADO provides a facility for transaction processing. The methods `BeginTrans` and `CommitTrans` control database transaction processing. When we wish to begin a new database transaction, we call the `BeginTrans` method. The `BeginTrans` method returns a nesting-level number. Whenever a transaction is initiated inside another transaction, the nesting level is incremented by 1. The "top-level" transaction is assigned to level 1. Each call to either `CommitTrans` or `RollbackTrans` affects the most recently open transaction. Each transaction must be processed sequentially, in a first-in, first-out fashion.

An example of how to use transactions is shown in Listing 4-1. The `TransactionTest` subroutine executes two SQL INSERT statements.❶, ❷ If one or the other fails (for the sake of example, the second statement will fail; notice the intentional syntax error),❷ the changes are not applied to the database.

Listing 4-1. Using Transactions (example4-1.asp)

```
<%
Sub TransactionTest()

        ' Allow us to trap errors ourselves
        On Error Resume Next

        ' Open the database
        Set cnn = Server.CreateObject( "ADODB.Connection" )
        cnn.Open "DSN=Megabytes"

        ' Start a new transaction
        cnn.BeginTrans

        ' Execute the first SQL statement
❶       cnn.Execute( "INSERT INTO Users ( username, password ) VALUES ↵
( 'Matt', 'passwd' )" )

        ' If an error occurred, rollback the transaction and exit the ↵
subroutine
        If Err.Number Then
                Response.Write "<FONT COLOR=red><B>Error!</B> - ↵
</FONT>" & Err.Description
```

```
                cnn.RollbackTrans
                Exit Sub
        Else
                Response.Write "First SQL statement successful!<BR>"
        End If


        ' The following SQL statement will force a fail execution.
❷       cnn.Execute( "INSURT INTO Users ( username, password ) VALUES ↵
( 'MattC', 'passwd2' )" )


        ' Since an error will occur here, undo the last SQL INSERT with ↵
a call to RollbackTrans
        If Err.Number Then
                Response.Write "<FONT COLOR=red><B>Error!</B> - ↵
</FONT>" & Err.Description
                cnn.RollbackTrans
                Exit Sub
        End If


        ' If we reached this point, both of our SQL INSERTs were ↵
successful.
        ' We will apply the changes to the database with CommitTrans
        cnn.CommitTrans


        ' Close the database connection


        cnn.Close
End Sub


Response.Write "<H1>Transaction Test</H1>"


TransactionTest
%>
```

Properties Object Properties

It is important to note that not all databases support transactions. If you are in doubt about whether or not your database can support transactions, you can verify this by checking for the existence of the "Transaction DDL" property in the `Properties` collection of the `Connection` object. The `Properties` collection also contains many more values, which can be used to determine the capabilities of your database. The `Properties` collection of the `Connection`

Table 4-3. Properties Object Properties

Property	Description
Name	String. The name of the property.
Type	Integer. Integer constant designating the property's data type.
Value	Variant. The property value.
Attributes	Long. Provider-specific info about the property.

object is actually a collection of objects, which is different from the collections you've worked with so far. Each object in the collection is a property object. See Table 4-3 for `Properties` object properties and descriptions.

So, to determine whether our Megabyte's database supports transactions, we could run the following function to check transaction compatibility:

```
Function TransactionsSupported( cnn )
        TransactionsSupported = False
        For Each sProp In cnn.Properties
                If sProp.Name = "Transaction DDL" Then
                        TransactionsSupported = True
                        Exit Function
                End If
        Next
End Function
```

This function shows how to iterate through the property objects in the `Properties` collection. If we find one matching "Transaction DDL," the function returns true, and transactions are supported by the connection. If we attempt to start a transaction with a driver that does not support them, an error will result.

Note: The `example4-1.asp` file contains a demonstration of the `TransactionSupported()` function.

Other Properties of the Connection Object

The `Connection` object contains several properties (see Table 4-4) that are used to get and set parameters for the connection. Most of these are advanced settings, and we will encounter some of them in our application.

Table 4-4.   Connection Object Properties

Property	Description
Attributes	Long. General characteristics for the object. Can be one of these constants: adXactCommitRetaining—Automatically create a new transaction upon a call to CommitTrans. adXactAbortRetaining—Automatically create a new transaction upon a call to RollbackTrans.
CommandTimeout	Long. How long to wait for a command to complete, expressed in seconds. Default is 30 seconds.
ConnectionString	String. A semicolon delimited string of name–value pairs specifying connection parameters for the database.
ConnectionTimeout	Long. Specifies how long to wait, in seconds, for a connection to be established to the database.
CursorLocation	Long. Sets which cursor library to use. Can be: adUseClient—Use cursor code library on the client (may provide additional cursor functionality). adUseServer—Use cursor code library on the client (default).
DefaultDatabase	String. Specifies the default database to use for the connection. (not all providers support this feature).
IsolationLevel	Long. A constant specifying how changes to the database data are visible in pending transactions. Possible values are: adXactUnspecified—Cannot determine isolation level. adXactChaos—Cannot override pending changes from another user. adXactBrowse—Allow viewing of uncommitted changes in other transactions.

(continued)

Table 4-4.   (continued)

Property	Description
	adXactReadUncommitted—Same as above.
	adXactCursorStability—Can read only committed changes in other transactions.
	adXactReadCommitted—Same as above.
	adXactRepeatableRead—Must requery the recordset to see changes.
	adXactIsolated—Complete isolation of transactions.
	adXactSerializable—Same as above.
Mode	Long. Constant that states the permissions for the connection. Can be:
	adModeUnknown
	adModeRead—Read only.
	adModeWrite—Write only.
	adModeReadWrite—Read/write.
	adModeShareDenyRead—Open connection with exclusive read permissions.
	adModeShareDenyWrite—Other users may not write to the connection while your connection is open.
	adModeShareExclusive—Exclusive open on the database.
	adModeShareDenyNone—Exclusive open with no permissions to anyone else.
Provider	String. Specifies the name of the data provider for the connection.

(continued)

Table 4-4. (continued)

Property	Description
State	Long. Returns a constant indicating whether or not the connection is opened or closed. adStateOpen—Connection is open. adStateClose—Connection is closed.
Version	Long. Returns the ADO version number.

Recordset Object

So far, the Megabyte's application has been adding only new records to the database. Obviously, we want to issue some SQL SELECT statements so that we can retrieve the contents of the database. With ADO, the results returned from an SQL SELECT statement are saved inside a Recordset object.

The Recordset object is roughly analogous to a database cursor. Recall that a database cursor is a sort of pointer that is used to traverse through a series of records returned by a database query. With recordsets, we have the ability to navigate through the returned rows, get the results, and even add to the results if we wish. Like a standard database cursor, a Recordset object refers to only one record at a time. The fields and the column values used in the query are stored in a collection.

Cursor Types

ADO recordsets support different types of cursors (see Table 4-5). The type of cursor that you choose depends on your application. Each cursor is optimized for the particular ways you wish to navigate through the result set. Also, each cursor has a different method of handling how changes to the database by other users affect the result set.

The recordset property CursorType controls the type of cursor to use. You must set this value before any results are returned. If you do not specify a cursor type, a forward-only cursor will be used as the default.

Table 4-5. ADO Recordset Cursor Types

Cursor Type	Supported Movements	Modification Visibility	Other Capabilities and Important Notes
Dynamic `adOpenDynamic`	Forward, backward	Row additions, row deletions, field value changes	Overall the most versatile cursor. Not all providers may support this type of cursor.
Keyset `adOpenKeyset`	Forward, backward	Field value changes only	
Static `adOpenStatic`	Forward, backward	None	Most versatile in terms of navigation. Good for generating reports.
Forward-only `adOpenForwardOnly`	Forward	Row additions, row deletions, field value changes	Provides fastest access when forward-only movement is required.

If you plan to make changes to the recordset, you need to specify a record-level locking method for the data provider to use. A locking method assures that another user cannot unexpectedly update a record while updates are being made to the database. The `LockType` property sets the locking method for the recordset. It must be set before the recordset is opened. ADO provides the lock types listed in Table 4-6.

Table 4-6. Cursor Lock Types

Lock Type	Description
Read-only (`adLockReadOnly`)	The recordset cannot be changed at all.
Pessimistic (`adLockPessimistic`)	Locks are applied as soon as a field value has been changed in the recordset.
Optimistic lock (`adLockOptimistic`)	Locks are applied only when the `Update` method is called.
Batch optimistic lock (`adLockBatchOptimistic`)	This lock type is required when performing batch updates.

Performing Queries with Recordsets

A recordset requires a connection to the database to perform the query. A Recordset object has the ability either to use an existing connection (a previously created Connection object) or to use a connection created "on-the-fly" by the Recordset object itself. If you need to perform queries or updates that require transactions, an explicitly declared Connection object is needed for the recordset since you need to call the transaction management method of the Connection object. When you allow the recordset to use its own connection, that Connection object's properties and methods are not available to you to use.

Take a quick look at the example of using recordsets shown in Listing 4-2. Afterward, we'll make additional modifications to newuser.asp in the Megabyte's application using our newly acquired knowledge of recordsets.

Listing 4-2. Using Recordsets

```
<!- #INCLUDE FILE="adovbs.inc" ->
<%
        Response.Buffer = True

        On Error Resume Next
        Dim rstUsers

        ' Create a new recordset object and have it use a static cursor
❶       Set rstUsers = Server.CreateObject( "ADODB.Recordset" )
        rstUsers.CursorType = adOpenStatic

        ' Open the recordset
❷       rstUsers.Open "SELECT username, street_address FROM Users", ⏎
"DSN=Megabytes",,,adCmdText
        If Err.Number Then
                Response.Write "Error occurred opening recordset"
                Response.End
        End If

        ' Retrieve and display the results
        Response.Write "<H1>Megabyte's Users Recordset ⏎
Demo</H1>Starting at the beginning, moving forward...<HR><PRE>"

❸       While Not rstUsers.EOF
❹               Response.Write rstUsers.Fields( "username" ) & vbTab ⏎
& rstUsers.Fields( "street_address" ) & vbCrLf
❺               rstUsers.MoveNext
```

```
        Wend

        Response.Write "</PRE>"

        Response.Write "<BR>Starting at the end, moving ⏎
    backward...<HR><PRE>"

        ' Move to the end
❻      rstUsers.MoveLast

        ' Display records again, moving in reverse this time
        While Not rstUsers.BOF
                Response.Write rstUsers.Fields( "username" ) & vbTab ⏎
    & rstUsers.Fields( "street_address" ) & vbCrLf
❼              rstUsers.MovePrevious
        Wend

        Response.Write "</PRE>"

        ' Flush the Response buffer
        Response.Flush

        ' Close the connection and clean up
        rstUsers.Close
        Set rstUsers = Nothing
    %>
```

Tip: Notice the top line of this script—the line

```
<!--#INCLUDE FILE="adovbs.inc"-->.
```

This file holds a series of constants that are used in ADO commands. You should always make a habit of including this file in your ASP pages that use ADO. It makes programming easier since you don't have to memorize, for example, that a static cursor (adOpenStatic) is represented by a value of 3. You can simply use the Const adOpenStatic. You can typically find the adovbs.inc file in your ..\Program Files\Common Files\System\ado directory. You'll need to move or make a copy of the file in a known virtual directory so that you can reference it with a relative or virtual path in the #include construct.

Beginning the Query Process

Preparing the Recordset

We start the example by creating a `Recordset` object directly.❶ Since this example is just a simple SQL `SELECT` query, we don't need to declare a `Connection` object for the recordset to use. The internal one to the recordset will suffice. We then designate the recordset to use a static cursor.

Opening the Recordset

The next section of code uses the `Open` method to open the recordset and run the query against the database.❷ The `Open` method has the following syntax:

```
rstObject.Open Source[variant], ActiveConnection[variant], ⏎
CursorType[long], LockType[long], Options
```

All of the parameters in the `Open` method are optional. *Source, ActiveConnection, CursorType,* and *LockType* correspond to the properties of the `Recordset` object of the same names.

The *Options* parameter is a constant specifying the type of parameter in *Source.* The *Source* parameter could be an SQL statement, a stored procedure, or a table name. Possible values are as follows:

`adCmdText`—*Source* is a SQL statement.

`adCmdTable`—*Source* is a table name in the database.

`adCmdStoredProc`—*Source* is a database stored procedure.

`adCmdUnknown`—The type of *Source* is not known. The provider will determine the *Source* type internally. If the *Options* parameter is left blank, it is defaulted to `adCmdUnknown`.

In our example, we know that the *Source* attribute will be an SQL statement, so we specify `adCmdText` in the *Options* parameter. The SQL statement queries the `Users` table in the Megabyte's database for the username and street address for all users. We have set the property for `CursorType` to `adOpenStatic`, and we are leaving the `LockType` parameter out since we are not updating records at this time. After we attempt to open the recordset, we check the `Err` object to see whether an error occurred while opening the recordset.

Retrieving the Results

If the recordset successfully opened, we are ready to retrieve our results. The result set will more than likely retrieve more than one record, so we set up a `While . . . Wend` loop to iterate through the results.❸ Notice the condition in the loop:

```
While Not rstUsers.EOF
  .
  .
  .
```

The `EOF` property (the acronym borrowed from flat-file lore, meaning *end of file*) is set to true if the recordset is already positioned on the last record in the result set. Inside the loop, we reference a collection of the `Recordset` object called `Fields`,❹ which contains the values of all the table columns we specified in the SQL statement. The name of the column in the SQL statement is the same name as the item in the collection.

   After we display the fields for the current record, we advance the cursor in the recordset to the next record by calling the `MoveNext` method.❺ If `MoveNext` attempts to move past the last record in the result set, the `EOF` property is set to true. At that point, the loop exits.

   As mentioned, we can move both forward *and backward* in our recordset. In the next section of code, we demonstrate how to move in the backward direction.

   When the script made its final call to `MoveNext`, the cursor moved past the last record. In order for us to navigate the recordset again, we need to position the cursor back inside the result set. Since we want to print the results in reverse order, we call `MoveLast`❻ and then perform a similar traversal as the first. The `MovePrevious` method,❼ moves us "back" one record in the result set. We know we've reached the end when the `BOF` property (meaning *beginning of file*) is reached.

Determining Recordset Capabilities

Depending on the type of cursor that you select for your recordset, ADO might restrict the type of operation you can perform on the recordset. For example, some recordsets allow for only one direction of cursor movement. Others may not allow updates to the data. Still others may not allow you to add new records. Use the `Supports` method to query for this compatibility information. The Supports method returns a true or false according to whether or not it supports the supplied cursor option. The following example checks to see whether our recordset supports the "approximate positioning" option:

```
If rstUsers.Supports( adApproxPosition ) Then
    ' Do something here
End If
```

You can check for support of the recordset options listed in Table 4-7.

Table 4-7. Recordset Options

Option	Description
adAddNew	Indicates that the recordset can accept new records by using the AddNew method.
adApproxPosition	The recordset allows for positioning of the cursor on a specific record, using the AbsolutePosition or AbsolutePage property.
adBookmark	Indicates the recordset can use an ADO bookmark, which functions as a record placeholder.
adDelete	Indicates that records can be deleted from the recordset using Delete.
adFind	Recordset can be searched using the Find method.
adHoldRecords	Indicates the ability of the recordset to retain changes made to the recordset even if more records are requested.
adMovePrevious	Recordset has the ability to move the cursor in reverse by using MovePrevious, MoveFirst, Move, or GetRows.
adNotify	Recordset will post events for various operations.
adResync	Recordset will allow the Resync method to be used to refresh the data.
adUpdate, adUpdateBatch	Recordset allows updating in single record or batch mode, respectively.

Making Updates to the Recordset

For updating the recordset, ADO provides the methods AddNew, Update, and Delete. By default, these operations affect the current record only, but some methods, such as Update and Delete, can affect multiple records.

The AddNew method is used to create a new record inside the current result set of the Recordset object. Delete will erase the current record of a series of records in the result set.

Let's modify the previous example with a demonstration of AddNew, Delete, and Update. After we retrieve our records, let's erase them and add some new ones. We will then display our new records. In order for us to use a recordset that accepts updates, we need to make some adjustments to the code where our CursorType is declared. Previously, we declared our CursorType as adOpenStatic. Since a static cursor cannot be updated, we will use a keyset cursor (adOpenKeyset) instead. We also need to set a record locking mechanism for the recordset. We will use optimistic locking, which will lock the records on execution of an Update call. Here's the code:

```
rstUsers.CursorType = adOpenKeyset
rstUsers.LockType = adLockOptimistic
```

After we display the contents of the recordset (both forward and backward), we begin with our code to delete a record. First, we make sure that our recordset can delete records. The Supports option adDelete can check for this:

```
If rstUsers.Supports( adDelete ) Then
    Response.Write "Recordset cannot support deletes"
    Response.End
End If
```

We then position the recordset on the last record and attempt to delete that record:

```
' Move to last record. This will be the one we delete
rstUsers.MoveLast

' Delete this record
Response.Write "Deleting account: " & rstUsers.Fields( "username" ) ⌐
& "<BR>"
rstUsers.Delete adAffectCurrent
```

```
If Err.number Then
    Response.Write "Error occurred on delete: " & Err.Description
    Response.End
End If
```

The `Delete` method takes an optional parameter that tells ADO which records are affected by the delete operation. In this case, we select `adAffectCurrent`. This states that only the current record should be deleted. Other options include `adAffectAll`, which deletes all records in the recordset, and `adAffectGroup`, which restricts the delete to records that meet the search criteria in the `Filter` property. We will explore filters soon in a future section. As a last step, we check for errors.

The next step in our code adds a new record to the recordset. We begin the process of adding a new record with a call to `AddNew`, which creates a new record and positions the cursor on that record:

```
rstUsers.AddNew
```

You can populate the fields in this newly created record by assigning values to the items in the `Fields` collection:

```
rstUsers.Fields( "username" ) = "newuser"
rstUsers.Fields( "street_address" ) = "123 Main St."
```

Finally, we call the `Update` method, which saves the changes to the recordset and updates the database:

```
rstUsers.Update
```

Incidentally, if any of the `Move` methods are called after modifications are made to the recordset, an `Update` is implicitly called for you.

Updating the Megabyte's Account Creation System

The Megabyte's login page has a limitation we need to address. Currently, there is no mechanism to check to see whether the account information that the user types in is unique. We don't want the user to type account information that already belongs to someone else, nor do we want the user to enter his/her account information multiple times.

To begin, let's make a function to check for account information based on the data the user enters on the form. Let's call the function `AccountLookup`. We declare it like this:

```
Function AccountLookup( username, ByRef nErrCode )

        ' the recordset to use to look up the ↵
        Dim rstUserRec
account information

        ' Let the function handle errors
        On Error Resume Next

        ' Create the recordset object and open it
        Set rstUserRec = Server.CreateObject( "ADODB.Recordset" )
        rstUserRec.Open "SELECT * FROM Users WHERE username = '" & ↵
username & "'", _
                        "DSN=Megabytes", adOpenKeyset, adCmdText

        ' Check for an error
        If Err.Number Then
                Set rstUserRec = Nothing
                nErrCode = Err.Number
                AccountLookup = False
                Exit Function
        End If

        ' No SQL error occurred
        nErrCode = 0

        ' Does account exist?
        If rstUserRec.RecordCount > 0 Then
                AccountLookup = True
        Else
                AccountLookup = False
        End If

        rstUserRec.Close
        Set rstUserRec = Nothing
End Function
```

The function passes in the username to look up as an input parameter. The function will return true if the account already exists and false if it doesn't. The function also returns an error code, which we check before the function's return value to see whether any internal errors occurred.

The guts of the function are straightforward. The function begins by creating a `Recordset` object using the `Server.CreateObject` method. The `Open` method is then invoked. We supply an SQL `SELECT` statement that queries the `Users` table for any records that have a username equal to the string passed in the username function parameter. The recordset will use a database connection that it creates internally using the ODBC connection string "DSN=Megabytes." The recordset will use a keyset cursor for the query. This will allow us to see the most recent changes to the record should it be modified at some point during the function call. The last parameter tells ADO that the *Source* parameter is an SQL statement so that it knows how to execute the command.

After checking for an execution error, we test for the existence of the account in the `Users` table. We know from the `WHERE` clause in our SQL statement that if the query matches any records, the account already exists. The `RecordCount` property tells us how many records were affected by the last query. If we matched anything, `RecordCount` will be greater than zero. The function returns a true/false value (along with an error code) indicating whether or not the account exists.

Note: In some instances, `RecordCount` will return an unexpected value; sometimes, the count could be incorrect or a count of −1 could be returned. This usually happens because of the cursor type you selected. Typically, `RecordCount` works well for static cursors. Other cursors will work if they support approximate positioning (check with the `Supports` method) or if the recordset has been fully populated. You can accomplish this by calling the `MoveLast` method. Here's how: After you call `Open` for your recordset, call the `MoveLast` method on the recordset to position the cursor at the end. This effectively forces ADO to visit every record in the result set, thus obtaining an accurate count.

Advanced Features of ADO

So far, we have shown how to perform basic database operations by working with the `Recordset` and `Connection` objects. ADO is very versatile and provides many advanced features designed to make common database programming tasks easier. Some of the features are new to ADO (v2.0), and we'll note those as we encounter them. Many of the "advanced" ADO commands are compatible across different versions of ADO (v1.0, 1.5, etc.).

Retrieving Recordsets into an Array

A single method call to `GetRows` can take all the record data in a recordset and copy it into an array. This array is a two-dimensional VBScript array. The fields in the recordset are placed in the first dimension, and the rows are placed in the second. This function is useful if you require high-speed access to the data in the recordset or if you plan to make several passes through the data. Since the results are kept in memory, access is extremely quick.

Note: You can find the complete `GetRows` example in the `example4-2.asp` file.

Here's how `GetRows` works: First, we create a recordset and query some data with it. We will use the default options for opening the recordset:

```
Set rstMyRecordset = Server.CreateObject( "ADODB.Recordset" )
rstMyRecordset.Open "SELECT * FROM Users", "DSN=Megabytes"
```

If no errors occur with our query, the next step is the call to `GetRows`:

```
aMyRecords = rstMyRecordset.GetRows
```

Our example calls the `GetRows` method without any parameters. This will cause `GetRows` to return all the rows in the recordset starting with the current record and ending with the last record. All fields in the recordset will be represented in the data returned. `GetRows` takes three optional parameters. Here's the syntax:

```
variant = obj.GetRows( rows, start, fields )
```

Rows is a long integer value representing the number of records to return. *Start* is a bookmark specifying from which position in the recordset to begin retrieving records (we'll investigate bookmarks soon). *Fields* designates which fields to return and can be either a string (representing a field name), a number (representing the ordinal position of the field), an array of strings (each element corresponding to a field name), or an array of numbers (representing ordinal positions of the desired fields). It's important to note that if you specify the field list as an ordinal or a string array, the sequence you specify is the order that the data will be returned in the result array. This may be different than the order specified in the command text or SQL statement.

The *Start* parameter can also accept the following predefined constants:

`adBookmarkCurrent`—Start retrieving data from the current record.

adBookmarkFirst—Start retrieving records from the beginning of the recordset.

adBookmarkLast—Retrieve records from the last record.

Moving along with our example, the next part of the script iterates through the two-dimensional array using two nested For . . . Next loops and displays the results to the browser. We have used the VBScript UBound function to determine the dimensions of the result array, aMyRecords:

```
nNumCols = UBound( aMyRecords, 1 )
nNumRows = UBound( aMyRecords, 2 )
Response.Write "<PRE>"
For nX = 0 To nNumRows
        For nY = 0 To nNumCols
                Response.Write aMyRecords( nY, nX ) & vbTab
        Next
        Response.Write vbCrLf
Next
Response.Write "</PRE>"
```

Retrieving Recordsets as Strings

GetRows is a good method for quickly retrieving the records in a recordset, but there is an even faster method. The GetString method can return records in a recordset just as GetRows can, but it puts the output of the retrieval into a pre-formatted string. This string could then be passed directly to Response.Write or to another command for additional processing.

Note: You can find the complete GetString example in the example4-3.asp file.

The syntax is as follows:

```
obj.GetString( stringFormat, numRows, colDelimiter, rowDelimiter, ↵
nullVal )
```

The *stringFormat* parameter is a constant that tells GetString what format to use for the string. In ADO v2.0, the only option is adClipString. The *numRows* parameter is the number of rows to return. The default is –1, which means to return all rows. The *colDelimiter* specifies the string to use to delimit each column and defaults to a tab character. The *rowDelimiter* specifies the string to use to delimit each row (record) and defaults to a carriage return. The *nullVal* indicates the string to use in substitution for null database values and defaults to an empty string.

We can modify the previous example to use `GetString` instead of `GetRows`. This will save us the coding work of iterating through the array, displaying each row to the browser. Here's the modified code:

```
rstMyRecordset.Open "SELECT * FROM Users", "DSN=Megabytes"
Response.Write "<TABLE BORDER=1><TR><TD>"
If Err.Number = 0 Then
Response.Write rstMyRecordset.GetString( adClipString, _
-1, "</TD><TD>","</TD></TR><TR><TD>", " " )
Else
          Response.Write "Error retrieving rows: " & Err.Description
End If
Response.Write "</TABLE>"
RstMyRecordset.Close
```

Notice how we shorten our data display code to just one line! We also played some HTML trickery with the row and column delimiters to get the data to display in an HTML table.

Searching Recordsets

We have demonstrated in previous sections how you can retrieve database data with a `Recordset` object and process the results. We used SQL statements to retrieve a specific subset of data from a database table by using a `WHERE` clause in the statement. There is an alternative form for querying data for specific values, and that method is the `Find` method of the `Recordset` object.

The `Find` method works by specifying a search expression that roughly corresponds to a SQL `WHERE` clause. There are some limitations as to the types of expressions you can use. The SQL `WHERE` expression may have only one term in it. For example, the expressions

```
FoodChoice = 'pizza'
OrderID > 655
LastName NOT LIKE 'Cro%'
```

represent valid expressions to use with the `Find` method. Any expression that contains more than one term, like

```
OrderID > 655 AND LastName NOT LIKE 'Cro%'
```

cannot be used with the `Find` method.

To demonstrate, the code fragment in Listing 4-3 will search the `Users` table in our database for any `username` that begins with the letter *m*. The code begins as usual with the creation of a `Recordset` object. The *Source* of our data will be the `Users` table, and we denote this in the *Options* parameter (with the `adCmdTable` constant).

Listing 4-3. Searching Recordsets (example4-3.asp)

```
<%
Response.Write "<h1>Find Demo</h1>"
Dim rstFindRecSect
Set rstFindRecSect = Server.CreateObject( "ADODB.Recordset" )

rstFindRecSect.Open "Users", "DSN=Megabytes", adOpenKeyset, _
                                    adLockReadOnly, adCmdTable
If Err.Number = 0 Then
        If rstFindRecSect.Supports( adFind ) Then
                Response.Write "This recordset supports the Find ↵
method.<BR>"
        Else
                Response.Write "No support for Find. Sorry<BR>"
                Response.End
        End If

        rstFindRecSect.Find "username LIKE 'm%'", 0, adSearchForward

        If Not rstFindRecSect.EOF Then
Response.Write "I found the record: <B>" & _
rstFindRecSect.Fields( "username" ) & "</B>"
        End If
Else
                Response.Write "Error retrieving recordset: " & ↵
Err.Description
End If
        rstFindRecSect.Close
%>
```

After checking for an error, we use the `Supports` method to test for the recordset's compatibility with the `Find` method. This is important since not all data providers support this method. If the `Supports` method successfully tests for `Find` compatibility, we issue the `Find` method:

```
rstFindRecSect.Find "username LIKE 'm%'", 0, adSearchForward
```

The Find method takes four parameters. The first parameter is the search criterion. As mentioned, the search criterion is typically a single SQL WHERE expression. For our query, we are asking ADO to position us on the first record where the username starts with an *m*. The second parameter, which is optional, is a number telling Find how many records to skip from the current cursor position. The third parameter tells in which direction Find should search for the record. Our choices are adSearchForward and adSearchBackward for searching forward and backward through the recordset, respectively. The last parameter, which we intentionally leave off, is an ADO bookmark used to indicate where to start the search.

When the Find method is executed, the cursor positions itself automatically according to the results of the search. If a record is found that meets the search criterion, the cursor is positioned on the first record that meets that criterion. If no record is found, the EOF property is set to true and the cursor is positioned at the end of the recordset.

After we execute the Find method, we check to see whether our search found any records. For this, we use the following code:

```
If Not rstFindRecSect.EOF Then
        Response.Write "I found the record: <B>" & _
                rstFindRecSect.Fields( "username" ) & "</B>"
End If
```

If the EOF property is not set to true, we know the cursor is positioned on a record in the recordset. This record is one that matched our search criterion. So, we display the results in our HTML output.

Filtering Recordset Records

We have mentioned the limitations of the Find method. With Find, you cannot perform any searches that involve expressions with multiple terms. We can overcome this limitation by using the recordset Filter property.

The Filter property does just what its name implies: It filters records in the recordset, making the filtered records invisible to you for the duration that the filter is active. With the Filter property, you have the ability to specify as many search criteria terms as you wish.

We will use filters in the Megabyte's Pizzeria example, but first let's take a quick look at the example code in Listing 4-4 to get familiar with the concepts. In this example, we perform another query of the Users table in our database. So, we open a Recordset object with the Users table as our *Source.*❶ We then clear any filters that may have been applied to the recordset with the command:❷

Listing 4-4. Using Filters (example4-4.asp)

```
<%
Response.Write "<h1>Filter Demo</h1>"
Dim rstFindRecSect
Set rstFindRecSect = Server.CreateObject( "ADODB.Recordset" )

rstFindRecSect.Open "Users", "DSN=Megabytes", adOpenKeyset, _
                adLockReadOnly, adCmdTable
If Err.Number = 0 Then
        rstFindRecSect.Filter = adFilterNone
        If Not rstFindRecSect.EOF Then
        Response.Write _
  "<TABLEBORDER=1><CAPTION><B>NoFiltering</B></CAPTION><TR><TD>" & _
  rstFindRecSect.GetString( _ adClipString, _
                        -1, "</TD><TD>", _
                        "</TR><TR><TD>", "" )
            Response.Write "</TABLE>"
        End If
        rstFindRecSect.Filter = "username LIKE 'm%' OR phone_number ↲
        LIKE '708%'"              ' We are returned to the top of the
newly filtered recordset
        If Not rstFindRecSect.EOF Then
        Response.Write _
  "<TABLE BORDER=1><CAPTION><B>Recordset Filtered</B></CAPTION><TR><TD>" ↲
  & rstFindRecSect.GetString( _adClipString, _ -1, "</TD><TD>", _
  "</TR><TR><TD>", "" )
        End If
        Response.Write "</TABLE>"
Else
        Response.Write "Error retrieving recordset: " & Err.Description
End If
rstFindRecSect.Close
%>
```

```
rstFindRecSect.Filter = adFilterNone
```

Here, `adFilterNone` is an ADO constant to signal that no filtering is to be done on the recordset. It also clears any previously applied filter. We could also use an empty string instead of the `adFilterNone` constant to clear the filter. We would then call the `GetString` function to return the recordset data and display it with the `Response.Write` call.❸

We are now going to filter the recordset and display that subset of data. Suppose we want to show records that have a `username` that begins with the letter *m* or records that are in the 708 area code.❹ We use the following filter:

```
rstFindRecSect.Filter = "username LIKE 'm%' OR phone_number LIKE '708%'"
```

When this filter is applied, the recordset's cursor is taken back to the top of the newly filtered recordset.❺ We call `GetString` again to display our filtered results:

```
Response.Write _
"<TABLE BORDER=1><CAPTION><B>Recordset Filtered</B></CAPTION><TR><TD>" ↵
& _
rstFindRecSect.GetString( adClipString, 115-1, "</TD><TD>", _
 "</TR><TR><TD>", "" )
```

The Megabyte's Pizzeria application will allow guests to browse the restaurant's menu online. The food selections are stored in our database in a table called `MenuItems`. We want the Browse Menu feature to be flexible, so we will allow the user to customize the selections he/she sees in the list. For instance, if the user is interested only in what the daily specials are, the list can be limited to just those items. We can save the type of list the user sees in a cookie so that, upon returning, the user doesn't need to check the boxes again if he/she wants to see the same list. A system such as this is a good candidate for a recordset filter. The ASP block of code that is used to display the list appears in Listing 4-5.

Listing 4-5. Filtering and Displaying Menu Items

```
<%
Dim rstMenu
Dim sFilterStr
```

```
    Dim sFormElement
    Dim aMenuItems
    Dim nNumRows
    Dim nNumCols
    Dim sOutput
    Dim nX, nY

    sOutput = ""
    ' Create the recordset object for the menu table
    Set rstMenu = Server.CreateObject( "ADODB.Recordset" )

    ' Open the recordset which contains the rows to the MenuItems table
❶ rstMenu.Open "SELECT DISTINCT item_name, item_desc, price, food_type
    FROM MenuItems", "DSN=Megabytes", adOpenStatic, adLockReadOnly

    ' Get the values of the checkboxes so we can build our filters. The
    ' Forms collection will contain items only if the user selected
    ' the "Refresh List" button

❷ If Request.Form( "items_specials" ) = "on" Then
        sFilterStr = "food_type = 'Special'"
    Else
        sFilterStr = ""
    End If

    ' Apply the filter
    rstMenu.Filter = sFilterStr

    ' Retrieve the records
❸ aMenuItems = rstMenu.GetRows( adGetRowsRest, , _
                        Array( "item_name", "item_desc", "price" ) )

❹ nNumRows = UBound( aMenuItems, 2 )
    nNumCols = UBound( aMenuItems, 1 )
    Response.Write "<TABLE BORDER=0><TR BGCOLOR=yellow><TD COLSPAN=" & _
                        nNumCols + 1 & _
                        " BGCOLOR=yellow><B>Items</B></TD></TR><TR ⏎
    BGCOLOR=silver>"
❺ For nX = 0 To nNumRows
            For nY = 0 To nNumCols
            sOutput = sOutput & "<TD BGCOLOR=silver>" & aMenuItems( nY, ⏎
    nX ) & _
                                    "</TD>"
```

```
Next
sOutput = sOutput & "</TR><TR>"
Next
sOutput = sOutput & "</TR></TABLE>"

Response.Write sOutput
' Close the recordset
rstMenu.Close
Set rstMenu = Nothing
%>
```

The HTML form that is part of `menu.asp` contains a checkbox that states whether we display all the menu items or just the specials. We start by opening a `Recordset` object with an SQL statement that returns the menu item names, the menu item description, and the price of the item:❶

```
rstMenu.Open "SELECT DISTINCT item_name, item_desc, price, food_type ↵
FROM MenuItems", "DSN=Megabytes", adOpenStatic, adLockReadOnly
```

When the `Open` method is called, the recordset's cursor will be positioned on the first record in the table. We are retrieving the recordset using a static, read-only cursor, which gives the best performance if we don't need to do any updates.

The next step is to check the `Request` collection to see whether the `items_specials` checkbox was marked. Based on whether or not this box is checked, we set a filter that extracts the records that are marked as specials. That is, the `food_type` field is set to "Special":❷

```
If Request.Form( "items_specials" ) = "on" Then
    sFilterStr = "food_type = 'Special'"
Else
    sFilterStr = ""
End If
```

If the checkbox was not checked, no filter for the recordset will be set (recall that an empty string designates this). We apply the filter in the usual manner by setting the `Filter` property to our filter string `sFilterStr`:

```
rstMenu.Filter = sFilterStr
```

With the recordset's cursor now positioned on the first record of the filtered recordset, we call GetRows to retrieve the recordset data into a two-dimensional array:❸

```
aMenuItems = rstMenu.GetRows( adGetRowsRest, , _
          Array( "item_name", "item_desc", "price" ) )
```

We are using GetRows a little differently than we did in our previous examples. Instead of invoking the default behavior of returning all fields in the recordset query, we pass an array of field names in the *Fields* parameter of GetRows. The adGetRowsRest constant states that all remaining rows should be retrieved from the current record. We use the VBScript function Array to construct and return a one-dimensional array with the strings "item_name", "item_desc", and "price" as the elements.

Looping through the aMenuItems array generates the output for the menu. First, the upper bounds of the x–y dimensions of the aMenuItems array are calculated using the VBScript UBound function.❹ Then, the For . . . Next loop marches through the array, appending the table and formatting HTML tags and record data to the output string sOutput.❺ Finally, the contents of sOutput are written to the browser with a call to Response.Write.

Dynamic Queries with the Command and Parameter Objects

There is another method with which we can query for a certain set of records. The Command and Parameter objects allow us to specify query criteria by inserting placeholder values in the SQL statement and dynamically replacing them with values specified in a collection. The Command and Parameter objects are also useful for passing parameters to database stored procedures. The main advantages to using the Command and Parameter objects over the Connection object to execute queries are execution speed and the ease of construction of complex queries. The performance boost arises because ADO is not continually referring to default values of the Connection object since the statement is constructed once and reused multiple times.

To use the Command object, we first must create a new ADO Command object and set the initial CommandText to an SQL statement or stored procedure. For our example, we will use an SQL statement:

```
Dim rstMyRecSet
Dim objParam
Dim cmdMyCmd
```

```
Set cmdMyCmd = Server.CreateObject( "ADODB.Command" )
cmdMyCmd.CommandText = "SELECT * FROM Users WHERE username = ?"
cmdMyCmd.Prepared = True
cmdMyCmd.ActiveConnection = "DSN=Megabytes"
```

Note: You can find the complete `Command` and `Parameter` object demo in
the `example4-5.asp` file.

The `CommandText` property contains the SQL statement to execute. Notice
that the value for `username` has been assigned to a question mark (?). The
question mark signals ADO that a value will be substituted in that place by the
addition of a parameter to the `Command` object. The `Prepared` property is set to
true, which tells the provider to save a compiled version of the SQL statement. If your application plans on executing the query set in `CommandText`
many times, setting `Prepared` to true will give your application a performance
boost since the provider is not parsing the SQL statement for each execution.
We also specify what connection the `Command` object should use. In this case,
we use our usual connection string.

The next step is to create a parameter for the `Command` object. We call the
`CreateParameter` method to do this:

```
Set objParam = cmdMyCmd.CreateParameter( "Username", adBSTR, ⏎
    adParamInput, Len( "mcrouch" ), "mcrouch" )
```

The first parameter of the `CreateParameter` method is the name we give to
the parameter. We will call it "Username" (an arbitrary name). The second
parameter is a constant representing the data type of the parameter. The constant `adBSTR` tells `CreateParameter` that the value for the parameter is a Unicode string or BSTR (more on BSTRs in Chapter 7). The next parameter is
the direction of the parameter—that is, if the data is being passed in or out (or
both). The constant `adParamInput` indicates that the parameter is input-only
(no data will be returned in the parameter). Next, we specify the length of the
parameter's value, and then the value itself.

After successful creation of the parameter, we append the parameter
to the `Parameters` collection of the `Command` object. Then, we execute the
compiled SQL statement and retrieve the records from the returned
recordset:

```
cmdMyCmd.Parameters.Append objParam
Set rstMyRecSet = cmdMyCmd.Execute( n )
```

```
While Not rstMyRecSet.EOF
       Response.Write "Record retrieved: " & rstMyRecSet.Fields↵
( "username" ) & "<BR>"
       rstMyRecSet.MoveNext
Wend
rstMyRecSet.Close
Set rstMyRecSet = Nothing
Set cmdMyCmd = Nothing
Set objParam = Nothing
```

Exporting Recordset Records to Files

With the release of ADO v2.0 came the capability to export the contents of a recordset to a file. The Save method of the recordset provides this capability. Save is useful when you wish to export data for use in other programs. See Listing 4-6 for a sample of the Save method.

Listing 4-6. Using the Save Method (example4-6.asp)

```
<!- #INCLUDE FILE="adovbs.inc" ->
<%
    Set obj = Server.CreateObject( "ADODB.Recordset" )

    obj.Open "SELECT * FROM Users", "DSN=Megabytes", adOpenStatic

    obj.Save "exported.dat"

    obj.Close
    Response.Write "Saved Recordset"
    Set obj = Nothing
%>
```

Querying for Database Schema Information

In some instances, you may want information about the database itself, rather than the records in the tables. For example, if you are creating an ad hoc reporting tool, you will need to retrieve the names of the database tables and the columns in those tables. Perhaps you are creating a Web-based database creation tool that has a facility to create tables, referential constraints, foreign keys, and other database attributes. Since such a tool will require access to this information, ADO must provide a facility for this. The OpenSchema method of the Connection object can access all of this information and a great deal more.

The OpenSchema method queries for two types of information—catalogs and schemas. A *schema* is a collection of database objects that are grouped together by a user called the *owner*. The schema may include tables, indexes, keys, and other data relevant to the database. A *catalog* is a listing of schemas. Often, a catalog and a schema are the same thing, as in the case of Microsoft Access and SQL Server.

To query for database data using OpenSchema, you first must establish a connection to the data source using the Connection object. Once the connection is established, you call the OpenSchema method.

Note: You can find the OpenSchema sample in the example4-7.asp file.

The OpenSchema method has the following syntax:

```
Connection.OpenSchema( SchemaQuery, Restrictions, SchemaID )
```

SchemaQuery is a constant that indicates what type of data to retrieve. Table 4-8 lists the possible values for *SchemaQuery*. Some are for advanced use, and we'll show some examples with the most common types of queries.

Not all queries are supported by all drivers, and some don't apply to the data source to which you are connecting. For instance, it doesn't make sense to query for stored procedure information on an ISAM database such as Excel, dBase, or other flat-file source. Check with the documentation on the provider to see whether a particular query is supported.

Suppose we want to list all the table names in the Megabyte's database. For this type of query, we would specify adSchemaTables as the *SchemaQuery* parameter to OpenSchema. We need to open a connection to the data source and then issue a call to the OpenSchema method:

```
Set cnn = Server.CreateObject( "ADODB.Connection" )
cnn.Open "DSN=Megabytes"
Set rst = cnn.OpenSchema( adSchemaTables )
```

OpenSchema returns a Recordset object with the requested data. Each type of query returns a recordset with a different Fields collection. This Fields collection is used to reference the information retrieved by the query.

Table 4-8. Schema Properties

QueryType	Description
adSchemaAsserts	Assertions for the catalog
adSchemaCatalogs	Available catalogs and their descriptions
adSchemaCharacterSets	Character sets supported by the catalog
adSchemaCheckConstraints	Valid values for each column in the catalog
adSchemaCollations adSchemaColumnPrivileges	How the catalog sorts data Security privileges for each column
adSchemaColumns	The column information for each table in the catalog
adSchemaColumnsDomainUsage	Domains
adSchemaConstraintColumnUsage	Columns used for constraints and assertions
adSchemaConstraintTableUsage	Tables used for constraints and assertions
adSchemaForeignKeys	Foreign keys used in the schema
adSchemaIndexes	Indexes defined in the catalog
adSchemaPrimaryKeys	Primary keys used by tables in the schema
adSchemaProcedureColumns	Table columns used in procedures
adSchemaProcedureParameters	Parameters used for defined stored procedures
adSchemaProcedures	The stored procedures defined for the schemas
adSchemaProperties adSchemaProviderTypes	Data types supported by the data provider
adSchemaReferentialContraints	Referential constraints used by tables in the schema
adSchemaSchemata	Schemas owned by a particular user

(continued)

Table 4-8. (continued)

QueryType	Description
adSchemaSQLLanguages	The ANSI SQL conformance levels for the catalog
adSchemaStatistics	Catalog statistics
adSchemaTableConstraints	Referential table constraints in the schema
adSchemaTablePrivileges	User privileges for tables
adSchemaTables	Tables in the catalog
adSchemaTranslations	Available character translations in the catalog
adSchemaUsagePrivileges	User-level privileges
adSchemaViewColumnUsage	Columns used in catalog views
adSchemaViews	Views in the catalog
adSchemaViewTableUsage	Tables used in views

The method is no different than a recordset whose source data comes from an SQL query:

```
Response.Write "<PRE>"
While Not rst.EOF
        Response.Write rst.Fields( "TABLE_NAME" ) & vbTab & _
                                rst.Fields( "TABLE_TYPE" ) & "<BR>"
        rst.MoveNext
Wend
Response.Write "</PRE>"
```

Among the fields in the `adSchemaTables` query are TABLE_NAME and TABLE_TYPE, which give the name of the table and table type, respectively. TABLE_TYPE can be assigned to "SYSTEM TABLE", which indicates that the table is used internally by the database, or "TABLE", which designates that the table is one created by the user. If we were interested in just user tables, we could apply a filter on the recordset before we retrieved the records, like this:

```
rst.Filter = "TABLE_TYPE = 'TABLE'"
```

Chapter Review

Let's review the key points in this chapter.

■ ADO is Microsoft's strategy for what it refers to as "Universal Data Access." ADO evolved from previously released data access technologies like ODBC. OLE-DB provided a COM interface to ODBC, which was C/C++ only. The OLE-DB object model was simplified, and DAO and RDO functionality was combined into what is now ADO.

■ ADO is composed of the `Recordset`, `Connection`, `Command`, `Parameter`, and `Errors` objects. Each plays a critical role in ADO.

■ ADO can support database transactions. Transactions allow us to keep data integrity by "undoing" changes made to the database during a series of database updates. Not all providers support transactions.

■ The `Recordset` object holds results returned from queries. We have the ability to traverse through these results in forward and backward directions (if supported by the provider) and also make modifications to the recordset data. We can also add new rows to the result set and save those changes to the database. Recordsets are roughly equivalent to database "cursors," which are used in other DBMS programming environments.

■ Different types of cursors can be used for recordsets. They differ by their ability to search records forward or in reverse, how updatable the rows are, and how row-level locking is implemented.

■ ADO provides high-level routines to manipulate recordsets. With a single command, we can read the results in a recordset into a two-dimensional array. We can also retrieve the recordset data and convert it to a single, formatted string for displaying in one call to `Response.Write`.

■ The `Find` method provides a way to search for individual values in a recordset.

■ Recordset filters allow us to display records that match the filter's criterion only. The filtered records become invisible to any ADO commands.

■ The `Parameter` and `Command` objects allow us to build a dynamic query with actual values substituted for parameter placeholders. Prepared statements are "compiled" by the DBMS and often execute faster than when we just run the statement by itself.

- ADO can export the results of a recordset to an external file using the Save command. Future versions of ADO will allow direct export of recordset data to XML or HTML.

- The OpenSchema method has the ability to query the database for column, type, and database schema information using formal ADO conventions.

What's Next

We will begin investigating the real magic behind Active Server application—the use of COM components inside Active Server Pages. We'll provide a high-level architectural view of COM objects and give explanations of properties and methods. We'll discover some tips on how to best use COM objects in our Active Server Pages. And, we'll learn how we can leverage off of third-party COM objects to add functionality to the Megabyte's application.

■ Further Reading

- *Universal Data Access Site*—http://www.microsoft.com/data. This site contains information on all of Microsoft's data access technologies, with links to download the latest Data Access Components (contains the latest version of ADO). You can also learn about ADO's exciting new features, like data shaping and disconnected recordsets. Check it out!

- *Windows NT Option Pack 4.0*—This package contains many other ADO samples that you can use or borrow from. Look in the IISSamples subdirectory of your Option Pack installation.

Using COM Objects in Active Server Pages

Introduction

Utilizing COM objects in your Web application is the key to making powerful Web applications. Whether you need to incorporate advanced business logic processing or control the output of the Web server, COM objects are the way to make it all happen. In Chapter 5, we'll expand on our existing knowledge of COM objects (the ASP intrinsic objects) and extend it to include some other useful COM objects that ship with IIS and ASP.

From Object-Oriented Code to COM

Throughout your programming career, you've no doubt heard about how object-oriented languages make developing software easier for the programmer. In traditional structured programming, code modules are grouped into functions, and data structures are segregated from those functions. The object-oriented approach is meant to group those functions and the data structures together into a single unit. The object's functions then perform operations on itself (the data). For example, a "car object" data structure could contain elements such as make, model, color, and so on. The type of functions to perform on the car could include `StartEngine`, `StopEngine`, `Accelerate`, `Brake`, `TurnLeft`, `TurnRight`, and so on. The functions and the corresponding data structure make up the object.

Encapsulation

The goal of object-oriented programming is to facilitate the practice of code reuse through a practice called *encapsulation.* If we need to perform a particular function in an application, say, e-mailing a message, we might create a "mail object" for this purpose. Our mail object could have a data structure that contains the recipient's name, the sender's name, and the text of the message. Included in our object would be a function to deliver the message. The e-mail function is generic enough to be used by many applications. Once the object is implemented, another programmer would take the code for the object and compile it into his/her project. The user of an object doesn't have to be concerned with how the internals of the object actually work, but only with how to access the object and perform its operations. This is the essence of encapsulation.

Obstacles to Code Reuse with C++

C++ is the language that most programmers will think of when they hear the term *object-oriented programming*. Depending on your experience with the language, you may have had varying degrees of success in reusing your classes. Here are some obstacles to effective code reuse with C++:

- C++ classes are designed with source-code reuse in mind. They can be used only inside their original implementation context. That is, C++ classes can be used only inside C++ programs. This would make a highly functional C++ class written in C++ useless in, say, a Visual Basic program.

- Although many C++ classes are distributed in source-code form, they can be distributed in compiled form (as Windows DLLs), just as they are in COM objects. Before the days of COM, this meant exposing member functions of a class as simple, C-style functions. Therefore, once exposed in this manner, a class could not be used in an object-oriented way if the DLL was loaded dynamically from another program.

Enter the Component Object Model

The Component Object Model (COM) was designed to address the shortcomings of conventional object-oriented languages like C++ and traditional binary software distribution of code. COM is not about a particular type of software, but rather a philosophy of programming. This philosophy is manifested in the COM specification. The specification explicitly states how a COM object should be constructed and what behaviors it should have. COM objects are roughly equivalent to normal classes, but COM defines how these objects interact with other programs at the binary level. By *binary,* we mean compiled code, with all the methods and member variables of the class already built into an object. This "binary encapsulation" allows us to treat each COM object as a "black box." We can call the black box and utilize its functionality without any knowledge of the inner workings of the object's implementation. In the Windows environment, these binary objects (COM objects) are packaged as either dynamic link libraries (DLLs) or executable programs (EXEs). COM is also backed by a series of utility functions that provide routines for instantiating COM objects, process communication, and so on.

Using COM Objects in ASP

Creating COM Object Instances

How are COM objects used in Active Server Pages? It should come as no surprise that you have already used them in the Megabyte's application and in the other code examples. The ADO objects themselves are COM objects. The intrinsic ASP objects (`Request`, `Response`, `Server`, etc.) are as well. With the exception of the intrinsic objects, we instantiate COM objects by calling the `CreateObject` method of the `Server` object, like this (using the ADO Connection object as an example):

```
Set cnnMyConnectionObj = Server.CreateObject( "ADODB.Connection" )
```

COM components are made up of *properties* and *methods.* You can think of properties as the member variables of the class. Properties describe characteristics of the object. Methods are the operations to perform on the object. In VBScript, properties and methods have the following syntax:

```
Obj.Property = value          ' (assigning a property a value)
value = Obj.Property          ' (retrieving the value of a property)
```

To call a method,

```
ReturnValue = Object.Method( param1, param2, …, param n)
Object.Method param1, param2, …, param n
```

The first method example shows the method being called as a function. It returns a value that is stored in `ReturnValue`. When you call the method in this manner, parentheses must be used around the parameters. The second example shows how to call a method when the return value is not important.

When you call the method in this manner, it is the same manner as calling a subroutine.

Cleaning up COM Object Instances

When we create a COM component, COM allocates memory for the object. In order for our application to make efficient use of memory, we need to free the memory used by the object once we are finished with it. We do this by assigning the object to the VBScript constant `Nothing`, as in

```
Set obj = Nothing
```

You should release an object in this manner as soon as you have performed all of your operations on it. Releasing the object saves precious system resources, especially in a multiuser environment.

It is best not to create an instance of a COM object and put it in a session or application variable. While this may be convenient as first, it decreases the scalability of the application because the resources used by the component stay in use for the lifetimes of the `Session` and `Application` objects in which they are contained. This approach becomes especially problematic if ADO objects, like the `Connection` object, are placed in session and application variables. Since many database management systems have a finite amount of connections available, the process of opening a connection to the database and placing it in an application variable uses up one of the database connections in the pool. This prevents other processes or users from using a connection that would otherwise have been available had the connection been closed after use. This approach may seem inefficient as first since most client/server applications open the database connection once and use it for the lifetime of the application. On the Web, there is no application persistency or state (in the traditional sense). Web applications are also more likely to have higher levels of concurrent users. Since you will be opening and closing database connections many times, ODBC connection pooling will manage those expensive processes most efficiently.

Now that you have been briefed on how COM components are used in ASP, let's move on to some code examples showing the use of the IIS/PWS standard components.

Using the Built-in Scripting Objects

The `Scripting` components are a series of COM objects that are shipped with the Microsoft Scripting Runtime. Our discussion will deal with VBScript v4.0;

hence, the objects covered are those that shipped with that version. They are designed to give elementary file access and I/O as well as provide a few other utility functions that are very valuable.

Dictionary Object

The `Dictionary` object is used to store keyed name–value pairs. Strings are used as key values (the name), and any data type, except arrays, can be stored for the value. Essentially, the `Dictionary` object is a collection, just like the ones you've been working with that are part of the `Response` and `Request` objects. The difference is that the `Dictionary` object is a collection that you create. The `Dictionary` object is a good way of implementing a fast lookup table for a short list of values. If you require fast access to data that you access many times, you may want to use a `Dictionary` object to do the work. Using a database might prove unacceptably slow for this purpose. The properties and methods of the `Dictionary` object are given in Table 5-1 along with brief explanations of each item.

Onward with the code! We create the `Dictionary` object in the usual way:

```
Set objDict = Server.CreateObject( "Scripting.Dictionary" )
```

We will first add some name–value pairs to the `Dictionary` object we created. This is done using the `Add` method. The `Add` method takes two parameters: `key` and `value`. Let's add a series of values to the `Dictionary` object:

```
objDict.Add "Name", "Matt Crouch"
objDict.Add "Age", "24"
objDict.Add "Favorite Color", "green"
objDict.Add "Favorite Food", "pizza"
```

The `Dictionary` object does not allow you to add two keys with the same value; they must all be unique. An attempt to do this will generate a runtime script error.

We can get the number of items in the dictionary by referring to the `Count` property, like this:

```
Response.Write "There are " & objDict.Count & _
       " items in the dictionary.<BR><BR>They are:<BR><BR>"
```

Table 5-1.   Dictionary Object Properties and Methods

Property	Description
CompareMode	The string comparison method. Set to either **vbBinaryCompare** (for case-sensitive comparisons) or **vbTextCompare** (for case-insensitive compares).
Count	Get the number of name–value pairs in the dictionary.
Item	Get or set the value of a key in the dictionary.
Key	Get or set a key name.

Method	Description
Add	Add a key–value pair to the dictionary.
Exists	Check for the existence of a key in the dictionary.
Items	Return the item for each key in the dictionary into an array.
Keys	Return all the keys in the dictionary into an array.
Remove	Remove the specified key from the dictionary.
RemoveAll	Remove all keys from the dictionary.

If you want to perform iterative tasks with a **Dictionary** object, you can dump the keys and values of the dictionary to an array. Use the **Keys** method to first get the keys of the dictionary. Then, use these keys to get to the items of the dictionary:

```
Dim aKeyArray
aKeyArray = objDict.Keys
```

Here, **aKeyArray** is a single-dimensional array containing all the keys in the dictionary. We can then use the following code to get all the key–item pairs in the dictionary:

```
sOutputString = ""
For Each sKey In aKeyArray
```

```
        sOutputString = sOutputString & sKey & ": " & _
            objDict.Item( sKey ) & "<BR>"
Next
Response.Write sOutputString
```

If we want to perform a lookup of a value in the dictionary, we can use the Exists method:

```
If objDict.Exists( "Favorite Food" ) Then
        Response.Write "<BR>I found your favorite food and it's <B>" & _
                        objDict.Item( "Favorite Food" ) & "</B>"
Else
        Response.Write "I haven't a clue what you like to eat."
End If
```

Be careful when using dictionaries to ensure that the CompareMode is set appropriately for your application. By default, CompareMode is set to vbBinaryCompare. In other words, any string comparisons will be case-sensitive. The CompareMode property must be set prior to placing any values in the dictionary since several of the dictionary's methods perform comparisons internally.

We can change the name of a key with the Key property. Simply reference the Key property with the current key name and set it to the new key name, like this:

```
objDict.Key( "Favorite Food" ) = "Special"
```

Now, when you want to retrieve the key, use the new name to reference it, as in this example:

```
Response.Write "<BR>New key name: " & objDict.Item( "Special" )
```

You can remove items from the dictionary using either Remove to remove a single key or RemoveAll to delete all the keys:

```
objDict.Remove "Special"
objDict.RemoveAll
```

Note: You can find the complete Dictionary object sample in the example5-1.asp file.

FileSystemObject Object

The `FileSystemObject` object is useful for gaining access to the computer's file system. You can copy, move, delete, rename, create, and get file/folder information, plus read and write text files. Information about the drives installed on the computer is also accessible. Let's take a quick look at what's available to us in terms of functionality. The properties and methods of `FileSystemObject` are given in Table 5-2.

File and Folder Objects

The `File` object contains information about the file that it references, like name, size, type, modification times, and so on. Normally, a `File` object or `Folder` object is obtained by calling the `GetFile` or `GetFolder` method of `FileSystemObject`. When the call succeeds, we can query for the above-mentioned information, or we may move, copy, delete, or perform other operations. We can also get and set file/folder attributes, just as we do in Windows Explorer. The same properties for the `File` object are available in the `Folder` object. Table 5-3 provides a complete list of the `File` and `Folder` objects' methods and properties.

The `Attributes` property deserves some explanation. Each file in Windows has a series of *attributes.* Attributes can be read-only or can be set by your application. Table 5-4 gives the names and values.

To set up a complete attribute specification, you can logically `Or` each attribute together. For example, if you wish to set a file to have read-only access and to set the file for archive, you can use this statement:

```
myFile.Attributes = 32 Or 1
```

where `myFile` is a valid `File` object.

Drive Object

In addition to files and folders, `FileSystemObject` can get information on drives connected to the computer. With this feature, we can query for data such as space available, the total capacity of the drive, the volume name, and so on. This data is made available through the properties shown in Table 5-5.

Table 5-2. FileSystemObject Methods

Method	Parameters	Description
BuildPath	(string)*path*, (string)*filename*	Concatenates *filename* onto *path*, appending backslashes as needed.
CopyFile	(string)*source*, (string)*destination*, (Boolean, optional)*overwrite*	Copies a file from *source* to *destination*. Both parameters must be full pathnames. If *overwrite* is true, file will be copied even if *destination* already exists.
CopyFolder	(string)*source*, (string)*destination*, (Boolean, optional)*overwrite*	Copies the *source* folder and all its contents (including subfolders) into the *destination*. If *overwrite* is true, folder will be copied even if *destination* already exists.
CreateFolder	(string)*folder*	Creates the folder *folder* (must be a full path). If the folder exists, an error will be generated.
CreateTextFile	(string)*filename*, (Boolean, optional)*overwrite*, (Boolean, optional)*unicode*	Creates a new text file *filename*. File will be overwritten if *overwrite* is true. If *unicode* is true, then the file will accept Unicode characters. If false, then file will be ASCII only. Returns a TextStream object.
DeleteFile	(string)*filename*, (Boolean, optional)*force_delete*	Deletes *filename*. If *force* is true, then file is deleted even if it is read-only.

(continued)

Table 5-2. (continued)

Method	Parameters	Description
DeleteFolder	(string)*foldername*, (Boolean, optional)*force_delete*	Deletes *foldername*. If *force* is true, then folder is deleted even if it is read-only.
DriveExists	(string)*drive_spec*	Returns true if *drive_spec* exists.
FileExists	(string)*filename*	Returns true if *filename* exists.
FolderExists	(string)*foldername*	Returns true if *foldername* exists.
GetAbsolutePath Name	(string)*pathname*	Returns the fully qualified pathname for *pathname*.
GetBaseName	(string)*pathname*	Returns the base name of *pathname*.
GetDrive	(string)*drive_spec*	Returns a **Drive** object for the drive *drive_spec*.
GetDriveName	(string)*drive_spec*	Returns the name of the drive specified by *drive_spec*.
GetExtensionName	(string)*pathname*	Returns the file extension for *pathname*.
GetFile	(string)*pathname*	Returns a **File** object for the file specified by *pathname*.
GetFileName	(string)*pathname*	Returns the filename part of *pathname*.
GetFolder	(string)*pathname*	Returns a **Folder** object.

(continued)

Table 5-2.   (continued)

Method	Parameters	Description
GetParentFolder Name	(string)*pathname*	Returns the parent folder of the current file in *pathname*.
GetSpecialFolder	(const)[SystemFolder, TemporaryFolder, WindowsFolder]	Returns the pathname of the computer's system folder, temp folder, or Windows folder.
GetTempName		Generates a random filename used for temporary files.
MoveFile	(string)*source*, (string)*destination*	Moves a file from *source* to *destination*. If *destination* exists or if *destination* is a folder, an error occurs.
MoveFolder	(string)*source*, (string)*destination*	Moves a folder and its contents from *source* to *destination*. If *destination* is an existing file or folder, an error occurs.
OpenTextFile	(string)*filename*, (integer, optional)*mode*, (Boolean, optional)*create*, (integer, optional)*format*	Opens the text file *filename*, returning a TextStream object. If *create* is true and the file doesn't exist, it is created. *format* is either TristateTrue (-1, Unicode), TristateFalse (0, ASCII), TristateUseDefault (-2). *mode* is 1 (reading), 2 (writing), 8 (appending).

Table 5-3. File and Folder Objects' Methods and Properties

Method	Parameters	Description
Copy	(string)*destination*, (Boolean, optional)*overwrite*	Copy the file to *destination*, overwriting if *overwrite* is true.
Delete	(Boolean, optional)*force*	Delete the file; ignore read-only attribute if *force* is true.
Move	(string)*destination*	Move the file to *destination*.
OpenAsTextStream (File object)	(integer)*mode*, (integer)*format*	Open the file for reading and writing using *mode* and *format*.
CreateTextFile (Folder object)		

Property	Type	Description	(R)ead/ (W)rite
Attributes	Integer	Bitwise values indicating file attributes	R/W
DateCreated	String	Date when file was created	R
DateLastModified	String	Date when file was last modified	R
Drive	String	Drive that the file resides on	R
Name	String	Name of the file	R/W
ParentFolder	String	Folder that the file resides in	R
Path	String	Pathname of the file	R
ShortName	String	Short name (MS-DOS 8-3 style) of the file	R
ShortPath	String	Short path (with directory names truncated to 8 characters	R
Size	Long	Size of the file in bytes	R
Type	String	File type of the file (same as Type column in Windows Explorer)	R

Table 5-4. File Attributes

Name	Numeric Value	Description	(R)ead/ (W)rite
Alias	64	File is a shortcut.	R
Archive	32	File is to be archived, changed since last backup.	R/W
Compressed	128	File is compressed.	R
Directory	16	File is a directory.	R
Hidden	2	File is invisible in directory listings.	R/W
Normal	0	File is normal.	—
ReadOnly	1	File is read-only.	R/W
System	4	File is a system file.	R/W

Table 5-5. Drive Object Properties

Property	Type	Description
AvailableSpace	Long	Amount of used space on the drive, expressed in bytes
DriveLetter	String	The letter assigned to this drive
FileSystem	String	The type of file system in use on the disk (can be CDFS, FAT, FAT32, NTFS)
FreeSpace	Long	The amount of free space available for the user
IsReady	Boolean	Indicates whether or not the device is available, useful for removable media drives (CD-ROMs, etc.)
Path	String	Path to the local or remote drive
RootFolder	String	The root folder of the drive
SerialNumber	String	The serial number of the drive
ShareName	String	For use with connecting to remote drives, the network name of the drive
TotalSize	Long	The total capacity of the drive in bytes
VolumeName	String	The name of the disk volume

Files, Folders, and Drives Collections

`FileSystemObject` and the `Folder` object both contain collections. `FileSystemObject` contains a collection called `Drives`. This is a collection of `Drive` objects, and each drive accessible from the computer (both local and networked) is represented. The `Folders` collection contains a series of `Folder` objects. The `Folder` object's `SubFolder` property is used to obtain a `Folders` collection. The `Folder` object also contains a collection called `Files`, which is a collection of `File` objects. Using these three collections, you can write routines to traverse the directory structure of your disk.

Listing 5-1 provides a demonstration of using the `FileSystemObject` object's properties, methods, and collections. First, we list the available drives on our system, all the directories on the root level of the `"c"` drive, and the contents of `"c:\My Documents"`.

Listing 5-1. Using FileSystemObject (example5-2.asp)

```
    ' Create a FileSystemObject
❶  Set objFile = Server.CreateObject( "Scripting.FileSystemObject" )

    Response.Write "<B>The drives on this system:</B> <BR>"
    ' List each item in the Drives collection, each separated by a space
❷  For Each sDrive In objFile.Drives
            Response.Write sDrive & " "
    Next
    Response.Write "<BR><BR><B>The folders at the root level:</B> <BR>"

    ' Get a Drive object for the c:\ drive
❸  Set myDrive = objFile.GetDrive( "c" )

    ' Set up the root folder so we can iterate the contents (the ⏎
    sub-folders)
❹  Set myRootFolder = myDrive.RootFolder

    ' Print out the name of each sub-folder on a separate line
❺  For Each sFolder in myRootFolder.SubFolders
            Response.Write sFolder & "<BR>"
    Next

    Response.Write "<BR><BR><B>Files in c:\My Documents</B><BR>"

    ' Get a folder object for the "My Documents" folder
❻  Set myFolder = objFile.GetFolder( "c:\My Documents" )
```

```
' List all the files in this folder
❼ For Each sFile In myFolder.Files
        Response.Write sFile & "<BR>"
Next

' Clean up
Set myDrive = Nothing
Set myFolder = Nothing
Set objFile = Nothing
```

We start any file system manipulation with a call to create a new
Scripting.FileSystemObject component:❶

```
Set objFile = Server.CreateObject( "Scripting.FileSystemObject" )
```

Next, we traverse the Drives collection and display the drives in use on
the computer. A For Each . . . Next loop is convenient for accomplishing
this:❷

```
Response.Write "<B>The drives on this system:</B> <BR>"
For Each sDrive In objFile.Drives
        Response.Write sDrive & " "
Next
```

To display the folders in the root directory of the "c" drive, we must obtain
a Drive object for the root folder.❸ We use the RootFolder property,
which returns a Drive object to the root folder, to get that information.❹
We set a new Folder object from the Folder object retrieved from
RootFolder:

```
Set myDrive = objFile.GetDrive( "c" )
Set myRootFolder = myDrive.RootFolder
```

Just like before, we use a For Each . . . Next loop to traverse through collection items. The collection is the SubFolders collection, which is a property of
the Folder object:❺

```
For Each sFolder in myRootFolder.SubFolders
        Response.Write sFolder & "<BR>"
Next
```

To display the files in the folder "c:\My Documents", we first call the GetFolder method of FileSystemObject to return a Folder object for our folder:❻

```
Set myFolder = objFile.GetFolder( "c:\My Documents" )
```

And then, we traverse the collection:❼

```
For Each sFile In myFolder.Files
    Response.Write sFile & "<BR>"
Next
```

TextStream Object

Although not common in ASP projects since most storage of data will be in databases, you may still require the need to read and write text files. FileSystemObject provides functions for this as well. To begin reading or writing from a text file, we need to have a reference to a File object (by referencing a File object in an existing Files collection), or we need to call the OpenTextFile method of FileSystemObject. File I/O with the TextStream object works by much the same principles as file I/O in other programming languages. Access to the file is sequential only. A file pointer is used to track your position in the file. You can read one character at a time, a line at a time, and you may position the file pointer ahead any number of positions in the file. Table 5-6 lists the TextStream object's methods and properties.

Listing 5-2 shows some "quick-and-dirty" code that opens the **config.sys** file and displays the contents of it. Since we are just displaying the entire contents of the file, we can use the convenient ReadAll method to grab the entire contents of the file in one go.

Listing 5-2. Using TextStream (example5-3.asp)

```
<%
Set objFile = Server.CreateObject( "Scripting.FileSystemObject" )
Set objStream = objFile.OpenTextFile( "c:\config.sys" )
Response.Write "<PRE>" & objStream.ReadAll & "</PRE>"
objStream.Close
Set objFile = Nothing
%>
```

Let's look at another example of TextStream. In this example, we'll modify an existing file and append some text to it. Suppose we wanted to add some

Table 5-6.   TextStream Object Methods and Properties

Method	Parameters	Description
Close		Closes the stream.
Read	(integer)*num_chars*	Reads *num_chars* characters from the stream, returns as string.
ReadAll		Reads the whole file into a string.
ReadLine		Reads characters until the end of the line, returns in a string.
Skip	(integer)*num_chars*	Moves the file pointer over *num_chars* positions.
SkipLine		Skips a line in the file.
Write	(string)*str*	Writes the string *str* to the file.
WriteBlankLines	(integer)*num_lines*	Writes *num_lines* blank lines to the file.
WriteLine	(string)*str*	Writes the string *str* to the file with a new line character appended to the string.
Property	**Type**	**Description**
AtEndOfLine	Boolean	True if file pointer is at the end of the current line in the file.
AtEndOfStream	Boolean	True if file pointer is at the end of the file.
Column	Integer	Position of the file pointer on the current line, with the first character at position 1.
Line	Integer	The number of the line the file pointer is positioned on, first line starting with 1.

commands to our `autoexec.bat` file. This requires us to open the file for appending. In our previous example, we used none of `OpenTextFile`'s optional parameters. We need to override those defaults. So, we open the file as shown in Listing 5-3. Notice that `objStream` is a stream to `config.sys` that is open for writing in append mode in ASCII. We use the `WriteLine` method to add a new line of text to the new file. (It is recommended that you not use your `config.sys` file for this script! You have been warned. . . .)

Listing 5-3. Another Example of TextStream (example5-4.asp)

```
<%
Set objFile = Server.CreateObject( "Scripting.FileSystemObject" )
Set objStream = objFile.OpenTextFile( "c:\config.sys",8,False,False )
objStream.WriteLine "REM adding something to config.sys"
objStream.Close
Set objFile = Nothing
Response.Write "config.sys has been modified."
%>
```

Using the Standard IIS Components

In addition to the `Scripting` objects, IIS/PWS also ships with a series of COM components that make Web-related programming tasks easier. We will make use of some of these components in Megabyte's Pizzeria. These components are included in the default installation of IIS/PWS, and some are available from the IIS Resource Kit as a download from Microsoft.

AdRotator Component

Many commercial Web sites feature graphical advertisements that are embedded in its pages. In order to provide maximum coverage for the site's many sponsors, the advertisements, often called *banner ads,* are displayed in a random order. So, upon each visit to a page, a user may see a different banner ad displayed than was displayed on a previous visit.

The `AdRotator` component works by retrieving advertisements from a formatted text file stored on the Web server. The file is in two "parts." The first part is formatted like this:

```
REDIRECT redirectionASPScript
WIDTH widthOfAdvertisement
HEIGHT heigthOfAdvertisement
BORDER widthOfAdvertisementBorder
*
```

where REDIRECT is an ASP script that handles the navigation to the advertiser's home page (or a page appropriate to the ad), WIDTH is the width in pixels to display each advertisement graphic, HEIGHT is the height of each advertisement graphic, and BORDER is the width of the border in pixels to display around the graphic. The asterisk (*) indicates the beginning of the advertisement data.

Here's a sample of what might be in the data portion of the advertisement file: Each advertisement in the rotation file has four lines. The first line is a URL for the image to display. The second line is the URL that the AdRotator component will send in the query string to the REDIRECT URL. The third line is the alternate text that is displayed in place of the image if the user has images turned off in his/her browser. The fourth line is the advertisement weight parameter. The number is a long integer, with values from 0 to 4,294,967,295. The higher the weight an advertisement has, the more frequently it will appear on the page. For example, if all advertisements had the same weight value, they would all display equally as often. Here's an example entry:

```
http://www.hostname.com/images/ad.gif
http://www.hostname.com/
Alternate text to display for browsers with images turned off
20
```

Now, let's look briefly at the properties and methods of the AdRotator component. They are listed in Table 5-7.

Table 5-7. AdRotator Properties

Property	Description
Border	Integer. The border width around the image in pixels. Can be used to override the BORDER setting in the rotation file. Default is 1.
Clickable	Boolean. Makes the advertisements into hyperlinks or displays them as regular images. Default is true.
GetAdvertisement(*path*)	Returns the image of the next advertisement in the file *path*.
TargetFrame	String. Indicates the frame in which the advertisement image will be loaded. Default is NO FRAME, which indicates that the advertisement will display in the current frame.

We must make sure two elements are in place for the ad rotator to work. First, we need to construct the rotation file with all the advertisement data. This file must be accessible from the Web file space; the path can be a relative or absolute path. We also need to write the code for the REDIRECT script. This is an .asp file that performs a browser redirect (with the Response.Redirect command). We'll need to specify the URL to this script for the REDIRECT parameter in the rotation file. A minimal redirection script can consist simply of a single line, such as this:

```
Response.Redirect( Request.QueryString( "url" ) )
```

To get the ad rotator to display a banner, we can put in the following ASP code. To make things interesting, let's add the AdRotator code to our Megabyte's Welcome Page (welcome.asp). In this way, we'll inform our visitors of any new happenings at Megabyte's as soon as they enter the site. We'll place the AdRotator code just above the area where the main body of the document lies:

```
<%
        ' Create a new AdRotator component
Dim objAdRot
        Set objAdRot = Server.CreateObject( "MSWC.AdRotator" )

        ' Display the banner ad
        Response.Write objAdRot.GetAdvertisement(
"/mega/content/adrot.txt" )

        Set objAdRot = Nothing

%>
<BR><TABLE border=0 cellPadding=1 cellSpacing=1 width=75%>
        <TBODY>

        <TR>
            <TD NOWRAP vAlign=top bgcolor=antiquewhite>
                <P><FONT><IMG alt=""
src="..\..\..\TEMP\Images\Image3.gif"
                ><FONT face=Arial><A href="menu.asp">Browse ⏎
Menu</A></FONT></FONT></P>
                <P><FONT face=Arial><FONT></FONT></FONT><FONT> ⏎
</FONT></P>
                <P><FONT face=Arial>
```

```
                    <FORM action="" id=FORM1 method=post
name=FORM1><FONT></FONT></FORM><FONT><IMG alt=""
              src="Images\Image4.gif"
              ></FONT></FONT><FONT><FONT face=Arial><A
href="Content/menu.asp">Order Online</A></FONT></FONT></P>
              <P><FONT><FONT face=Arial><IMG alt=""
              src="Images\Image5.gif"
(remaining file edited for length)
```

Here is the rotation file (`adrot.txt`) that is used by the `AdRotator` component. Notice that each advertisement has equal weight:

```
REDIRECT /mega/content/redirect.asp
WIDTH 50
HEIGHT 40
BORDER 1
*
/mega/images/banner1.gif
/mega/content/ad1.htm
Ad Number 1
10
/mega/images/banner2.gif
/mega/content/ad1.htm
Ad Number 2
10
/mega/images/banner3.gif
/mega/content/ad1.htm
Ad Number 3
10
```

If you investigate the code that the `AdRotator` component spits out when retrieving an ad, you will see something like the following. Note that it is the output of calling this VBScript statement:

```
Response.Write objAdRot.GetAdvertisement( "/mega/content/adrot.txt" )
```

```
(output)
<A
HREF="/mega/content/redirect.asp?url=/mega/content/ad1.htm&image=/mega/
images/banner1.gif" ><IMG SRC="/mega/images/banner1.gif" ALT="Ad Number
1" WIDTH=440 HEIGHT=40 BORDER=1></A>
```

There are a few interesting things about this output that was generated by the `AdRotator` component. First, our `redirect.asp` script contains two query string parameters: `url` and `image`. The `url` parameter contains the URL to which the redirect script should navigate. The HTML `<IMG SRC . . .>` tag acts as a hyperlink to the redirection script. The `image` parameter contains the URL to the advertisement banner graphic.

Both of these parameters can be used in a number of creative ways in the `redirect.asp` file. The most common task is to log the user's click of the banner ad. From the `url` parameter, we know which advertisement was clicked. We can then increment a permanently stored counter that corresponds to the ad. This information can be used to gauge the effectiveness of the ad. However, all that we really require of the redirection script is that the user be taken to a page that represents the content behind the ad. So, our file contains the bare minimum code to accomplish this:

```
<%
' the URL is contained in the "URL" variable in the query string
' we can add additional code here (ex. logging the URL to a database)

Response.Redirect( Request.QueryString( "url" ) )
%>
```

Browser Capabilities Component

When a Web server receives a request from a browser, many different kinds of data are sent along with the request. One very useful piece of information is contained in the HTTP variable `USER_AGENT`. This variable contains specially formatted information that describes what browser the user is using (Internet Explorer, Netspace Navigator, etc.), what CPU platform the user's computer is (Windows, Mac, UNIX, etc.), the version number of the browser, and other information. This information is useful for several reasons:

1. Identifying the browser being used to view the site enables us to determine the most popular browser used to view the site.

2. Given the browser type, we can tailor the content of our Web pages to display items that are appropriate for that browser to display. For instance, Netscape Navigator cannot use ActiveX controls (without third-party software), but, for users of Internet Explorer, we want to display those ActiveX controls to give the user the most interactive Web experience possible.

3. We can return feedback to the user that a particular browser is needed to view the site.

When the browser request arrives at the server, the USER_AGENT header contains the information about the user's Web browser environment. We can write a small ASP script to get this header:

```
<%
    Response.Write "HTTP_USER_AGENT variable contains: " &
        Request.ServerVariables( "HTTP_USER_AGENT" )
%>
```

Here is some possible output:

```
Mozilla/4.0 (compatible; MSIE 4.01; Windows 95)
```

What does this mean? We might be able to decipher it and conclude that I am running Microsoft Internet Explorer v4.01 on Windows 95. But many different browsers are running out there on the Internet. How do we programmatically determine the exact user environment from this information?

This is where the Browser Capabilities component comes in. Its function is twofold: (1) We can parse out all the version information in the HTTP_USER_AGENT header, and (2) we can determine what browsers are capable of in terms of displaying content.

The Browser Capabilities component is rather simple, actually. It works by looking up the capabilities of a browser from a flat file called browscap.ini, which is a large file that is constantly maintained to include information from many vendors that supply browsers. A snippet from the file looks like this:

```
[IE 4.0]
browser=IE
Version=4.0
majorver=4
minorver=0
frames=TRUE
tables=TRUE
cookies=TRUE
backgroundsounds=TRUE
vbscript=TRUE
javascript=TRUE
javaapplets=TRUE
```

```
ActiveXControls=TRUE
Win16=False
beta=False
AK=False
SK=False
AOL=False
crawler=False
cdf=True


;;ie 4 beta 1
[Mozilla/4.0 (compatible; MSIE 4.0b1; Windows 95)]
parent=IE 4.0
platform=Win95
beta=True
cdf=False
```

Notice that each entry is marked at the beginning by the HTTP_USER_AGENT in brackets. Following the user agent are the browser capabilities. Each line identifies a capability of the browser. The parent entry indicates that the system inherits the properties from the browser version specified. The other entries are almost self-explanatory.

Each browser capability is a property of the MSWC.BrowserType component. For example, if we want to test to see whether the browser supports tables, we can say the following:

```
<%
    If browser.Tables Then
        Response.Write "i do tables"
    End If
%>
```

Keep in mind that your browscap.ini file may become outdated sometime during the lifetime of your application. So, it's a good idea to keep it updated as much as possible. You can get new versions of the browscap.ini file from various online sources (like http://www.browscap.com). At the top of browscap.ini, a line with the date of the file's last modification is listed.

Content Linking Component

The Content Linking component is used to manage a list of related relative URLs. The Content Linking component has several uses. The component is handy if you are designing a site in which the user is to navigate a series of URLs in sequence. The `Content Linking` component can iterate through a series of URLs sequentially, or a URL can be retrieved by using an index to it in an ordered list. The `Content Linking` component is also useful for generating tables of contents (which we will demonstrate shortly).

The component works by looking up URLs in a text file that you create and that is on the Web server. The file, called a *list file*, is a tab-delimited file with the following format:

```
URL          Link Text          Comments
```

where `URL` represents a relative URL. Only relative URLs are supported by the component. `Link Text` represents the text to make into a hyperlink for the URL. The `Comments` field contains any comments that you wish to add about the URL.

The `Content Linking` component can access the URLs in the list file either sequentially or by using an ordinal index (starting with 1). The complete list of object properties is given in Table 5-8.

Table 5-8. Content Linking Component Properties

Property	Description
GetListCount	Returns the number of items in the list file.
GetListIndex	Returns the current list index number.
GetNextDescription	Returns the description of the URL following the current list index.
GetNextURL	Returns the formatted HTML-formatted link for the URL following the current list index.
GetNthDescription	Returns the description at index N.
GetNthURL	Returns the formatted HTML-formatted link for the URL at index N.
GetPreviousURL	Returns the formatted HTML-formatted link for the URL previous to the current index.
GetPreviousDescription	Returns the formatted description for the URL previous to the current index.

A sample list file might contain something like this (we'll call this file content.txt):

```
/mega/content/asp1.htm    ASP File #1    description of #1
/mega/content/asp2.htm    ASP File #2    description of #2
/mega/content/asp3.htm    ASP File #3    description of #3
/mega/content/asp4.htm    ASP File #4    description of #4
/mega/content/asp5.htm    ASP File #5    description of #5
/mega/content/asp6.htm    ASP File #6    description of #6
/mega/content/asp7.htm    ASP File #7    description of #7
/mega/content/asp8.htm    ASP File #8    description of #8
```

We can construct hyperlinks for each of these URLs as shown in the code of Listing 5-4.

Listing 5-4. Content Linking (example5-5.asp)

```
<%
Set contentLink = Server.CreateObject( "MSWC.NextLink" )
n = contentLink.GetListCount( "content.txt" )
Response.Write "<H1>Table of Contents</H1><UL>"
For i = 1 To n
        Response.Write "<LI><A HREF=""" & contentLink.GetNthURL( _
"content.txt", i ) & """>" & _
contentLink.GetNthDescription( ⏎
"content.txt", i ) & _
"</A>"
Next
Response.Write "</UL>"
Set contentLink = Nothing
%>
```

Each of the Content Linking component's properties takes the name of the list file as the first parameter. Make sure that the list file is available somewhere in your Web directory space.

Chapter Review

Let's review the key points in this chapter.

- COM is a specification for reusable, binary software components. It expands on many of the philosophies of traditional object-oriented programming, like encapsulation and polymorphism. The objects are not source code, like C++ objects. They are compiled code that can be used by any language that supports COM.

■ COM components can be used inside Active Server Pages and calls using VBScript (or any other ActiveX Scripting language).

■ COM objects are made up of properties and methods. Properties are roughly analogous to class member variables in C++, and methods are the member functions that operate on the data contained in the properties.

■ Objects are created using the `CreateObject` method of the `Server` object. It has the general form

```
Set obj = Server.CreateObject( "ProgID.Class" )
```

■ The syntax for accessing properties and methods follows the "dot" convention (e.g., `Obj.MyMethod`).

■ Objects instances are cleaned up by using the VBScript statement `Set` (e.g., `Set obj = Nothing`).

■ The `Dictionary` object is used to store lists of name–value pairs. Each name is unique for a given dictionary.

■ The `FileSystemObject` object is used to manage files on the server (i.e., copying, moving, deleting, etc.). We can also use `FileSystemObject` to open text files for reading and writing. Some of the `FileSystemObject` methods return object references to `File`, `Folder`, and `Drive` objects. The `File`, `Folder`, and `Drive` object properties can be used to obtain information about the files and folders referenced by the object.

■ The `AdRotator` component is used to display pictures in the browser window from URLs listed in a text file. According to the frequency level specified for a particular URL in the file, it will be displayed more or less often than the other pictures.

■ The `Browser Capabilities` component is used to identify the browser type from which a request originated and also to determine various features of that browser.

■ The `Content Linking` component is used to manage a list of related relative URLs. It is used for managing a list of URLs that need to be accessed in a particular sequence. It can also be used to generate tables of contents for a Web site.

What's Next

In Chapter 6, we are going to look at the details of the Component Object Model (COM) and the Active Template Library (ATL). We will build our first COM component using Visual C++ and the ATL COM Wizard. We will also investigate the features of the ATL, which provides wrapper classes around much of the COM API. The ATL strives to make C++ COM programming as easy as Visual Basic while still retaining the power and flexibility of C++.

■ Further Reading

■ *VBScript Documentation*—http://msdn.microsoft.com/scripting. This site contains a downloadable form of the VBScript documentation. Included in this documentation is a complete object reference for the components covered in this chapter.

Introduction to COM Architecture and the Active Template Library

Introduction

We are arriving at the most exciting part of this book—the point where we start to explore the *Component Object Model* (COM) and the *Active Template Library* (ATL). You've already seen COM in action when you used objects like ADO and the intrinsic ASP objects. Adding rich program functionality to your application turns into an almost trivial affair. To really appreciate the beauty of COM and all it has to offer, we need to take our learning to the next level. In Chapter 6, we'll briefly explore the most important COM concepts, and then we'll discuss how to use the ATL to make our own COM objects for use in our projects.

The Benefits of Creating COM Objects

In Chapter 1, we talked about all the virtues of using COM objects in Active Server Pages. It's a great way to add functionality to your application by using code from somewhere else. We have seen that COM provides us with a clean, object-oriented way of accessing the functions of the object. COM becomes increasingly important as our Web application grows in size. A common design mistake that many beginning ASP developers make is to code the entire logic of the application using server-side script. This makes for a lot of code to maintain and also makes the code difficult to read. We need to come up with a solution to increase the readability of our code as well as address the performance degradation issues incurred with executing large amounts of script code. Remember that our scripts are interpreted, and, by definition, that makes overall execution time slower. It also keeps our application's source code in plain view to just about anyone (with administrative access to the Web server) since it is just text inside ASP files. Not only could this reveal the trade secrets of your company, but this also makes it all too easy for someone, ill-intentioned or not, to make changes to the script code.

Making COM objects for use in your application is beneficial on several fronts. Once your script code is compiled into COM objects, you can further increase the performance of your application by running them in the Microsoft Transaction Server (MTS) context. If your VBScript code contains *business logic* (rules set by your organization that govern business process), that functionality is a good candidate for a COM object. You can then use that functionality outside of Active Server and deploy it in another application. The Megabyte's application has several areas that we can make into COM objects, and we'll investigate that in the coming sections.

Overview of COM Architecture

In Chapter 5, we took a look at COM from a very high level perspective. We noted that COM objects are roughly equivalent to classes in object-oriented languages. In that sense, they have members (properties) and functions (methods). They are in compiled form. An instance of a COM object is created by a command issued in your program (known as the *client*) before properties and methods are called. After we are finished with the object, we release it. But how does all this work? What is going on "under the hood"? What is a COM object, really?

A COM object (on the Windows operating system) can exist in three different forms. The first is an in-process server implemented as a *dynamic link library* (DLL). DLLs are used throughout Windows. They are compiled code files that are loaded into the program's memory space that uses them. DLLs are useful because an application can be field-upgraded by replacing DLL files with updated ones, rather than by shipping the entire application. Another advantage of DLLs (both COMs and regular DLLs) is that multiple programs can use a single instance of a DLL in memory, rather than loading the code into memory for every program that uses it. DLLs reduce the size of the main executable program since program functions in the DLL are not statically linked into the main executable file.

The second form a COM object can take is an out-of-process server implemented as an *executable* (EXE) file. EXE COM objects behave very much like other executable programs; Windows gives them their own memory space to run in, along with its own process. EXE COM objects are generally slower than their DLL counterparts since the operating system incurs some overhead during the program's launch. However, we gain robustness since a problematic COM object in an EXE cannot crash the client application because the two do not share memory spaces. The third form is an *NT service*—a special kind of EXE that executes in the background with special privileges. This book deals only with the first type of COM object—the in-process server (DLL).

Making a COM Component with the Visual C++ ATL COM Wizard

Fortunately for us, Visual C++ does a lot of the hard work associated with making a COM component. Visual C++ comes with a cool feature called the *ATL COM Wizard*. The ATL COM Wizard is one of many automatic code generators that ship with Visual C++. The wizard generates much of the "housekeeping" code required for the framework of the object. The wizard simply asks a few questions about your implementation, and it creates a skeleton code framework for you. Once the framework is in place, you can begin your implementation.

We are now going to construct a fully functional COM component. After the COM component is created, we will test it out in some sample ASP files. As we walk through the steps of the ATL COM Wizard, you may see code generated that may not be clear to you. Likewise, we'll select options in the wizard dialogs that you may not understand at the moment. Not to worry: Each of these items will be explained in detail after we build the component. The objective in these exercises is to familiarize you with the steps of creating a component.

Creating the Project

Let's begin by constructing a simple COM component, as follows:

1. Start the process by launching Visual C++ 6.0 from the Windows Start menu.
2. Select New from the File menu.
3. The New dialog appears. Click on the Projects tab if it is not already selected. The listing you see is all of the available Visual C++ project wizards. Highlight the selection that says "ATL COM AppWizard." (See Figure 6-1.)
4. In the "Project name" box, type the name of our project. For this exercise, name the project "Pizza."

5. You may choose a location for this project from the "Location" box. Visual C++ will create the project in a new directory by default. Make sure the "Create new workspace" radio button is highlighted.

6. Click OK.

7. A wizard dialog will appear. For our exercise, select "Dynamic Link Library" for the server type. Make sure the other checkboxes are unchecked. (See Figure 6-2.)

8. Click Finish.

9. The next dialog that appears is a confirmation dialog asking you to confirm the settings you selected for the ATL COM AppWizard. Click OK to generate our ATL COM framework code. (See Figure 6-3.)

That's it! The ATL COM AppWizard has finished generating the code for our project. Now it's your turn.

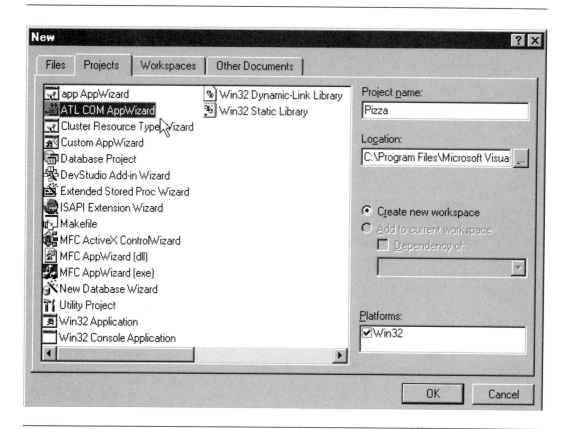

Figure 6-1.   The New Project dialog.

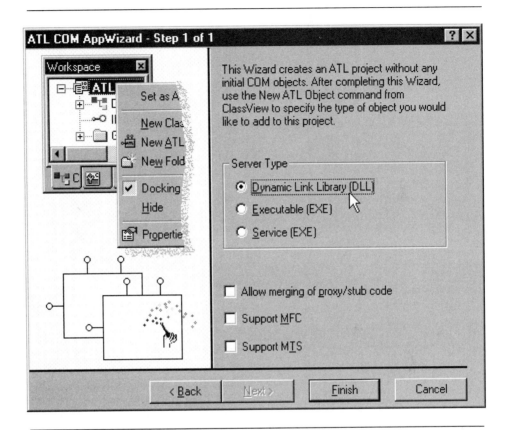

Figure 6-2.   The AppWizard dialog.

Adding a New ATL Object

Let's add some COM objects to the code and add the implementation, as follows:

1. On the left side of your screen is the Visual C++ project view. Below you will see different tabs for the view mode. Click on the Class View tab if it is not already selected. You will quickly see that our project does not have any classes yet. We need to add one, and this class will become our COM object.

2. Right-click on the "Pizza classes" item, and select "New ATL Object" from the menu. (See Figure 6-4.)

3. Visual C++ will then ask you what type of ATL object you wish to add. There are several choices; each has its own special purpose. For our example, highlight the "Simple Object" option, and click Next. This option is for a "plain vanilla" COM object. (See Figure 6-5.)

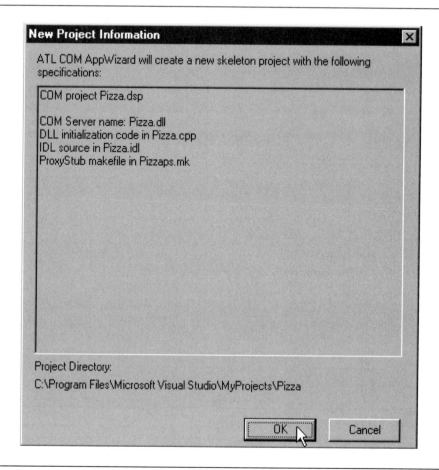

Figure 6-3.   The confirmation/information dialog.

4. The next dialog asks you about what to name files, classes, and variables in the generated C++ source code. Begin by typing the name "PizzaSample" in the Short Name box. Visual C++ will automatically fill out the other boxes; the Prog ID box should read "Pizza.PizzaSample." This will be the name that you will use to refer to the completed object in your VBScript code. (See Figure 6-6.)

5. Click on the Attributes tab.

6. You will want to accept the defaults for this dialog. One exception: Check the box labeled "Support ISupportErrorInfo." (See Figure 6-7.)

7. Click OK.

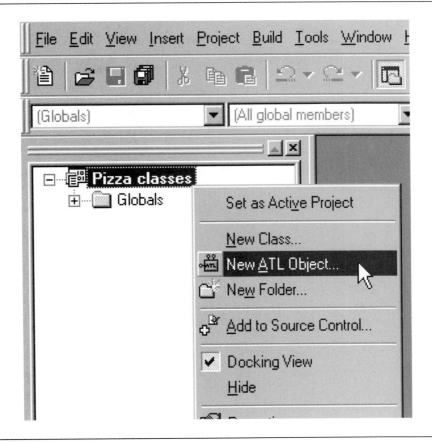

Figure 6-4. Step 2 for adding a new ATL object.

The code for our object class is now generated. If you look in the class view, you will see our class in the hierarchy. Several member functions for the class have been generated, as well as some utility code for the DLL. Figure 6-8 shows the expanded view.

Adding Methods to the COM Object

Now let's add some methods to our COM object, as follows:

1. Locate the "IPizzaSample" item in the tree view at the level of "Pizza classes." (See Figure 6-9.) Right-click on the item, and select "Add Method. . . ."

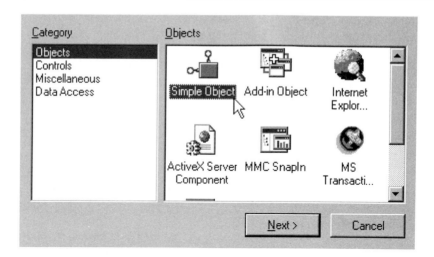

Figure 6-5. Step 3 for adding a new ATL object.

2. The Add Method to Interface dialog appears. Type in "RollDough" for the name of our method. In the Parameters box, type in "[in] short nDiameter." We can also add a help string for this method to provide assistance to the developer using the object. To add the help string, click on the Attributes button. (See Figure 6-10.)

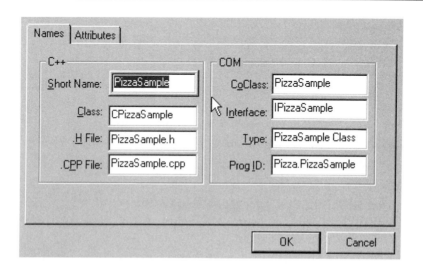

Figure 6-6. The Names dialog.

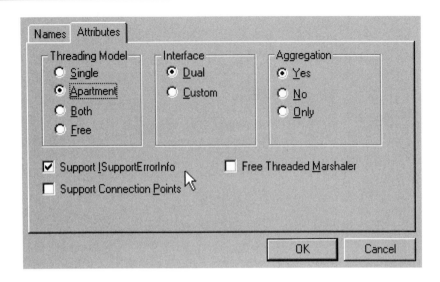

Figure 6-7. The Attributes dialog.

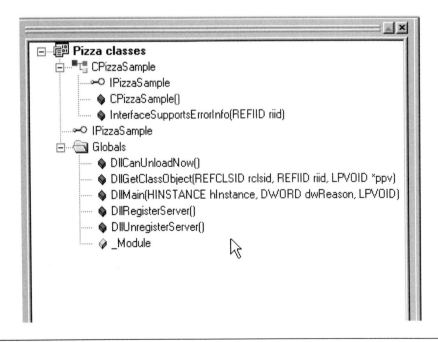

Figure 6-8. Expanded view.

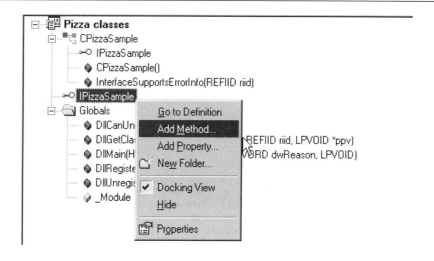

Figure 6-9. Step 1 for adding methods to the COM object.

3. The Edit Attributes dialog appears. Click to highlight the value for the help string. Edit it with the text shown in Figure 6-11.

4. Click OK.

5. Click OK once more to add the method.

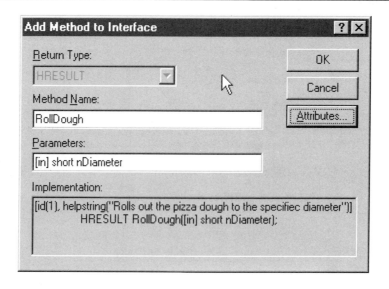

Figure 6-10. The Add Method to Interface dialog.

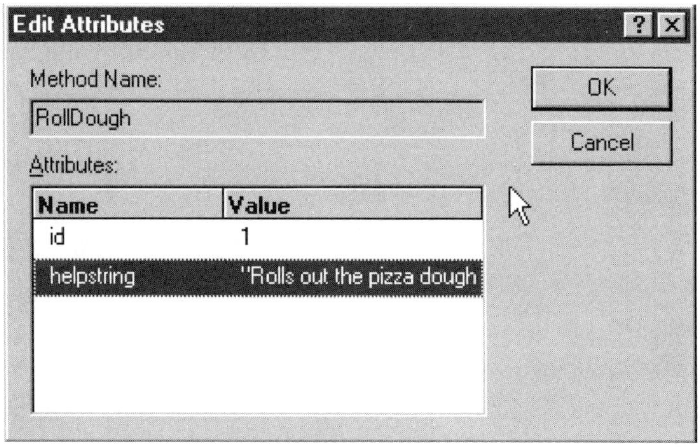

Figure 6-11.   The Edit Attributes dialog.

Repeat steps 1–5 to create another method. Call it "PrepareToppings." This method takes no parameters.

Create one final method called "Bake." For the parameters to this method, refer to Figure 6-12 and fill out the information as shown.

You may be wondering what all the parameters are in the "Parameters" field, so we'll briefly explain them. BSTR is a special type of COM-compatible

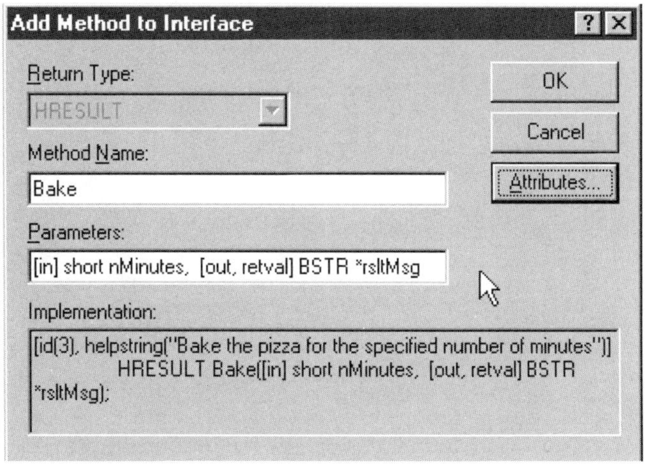

Figure 6-12.   Parameters for the Bake method.

string data type. The `out, retval` clause states that this string value will be modified by the function and that it is returned as the value of the function. The `in` clause states that the `nMinutes` parameter will be used for input only (the value is passed to the function, but it cannot be altered). We'll cover COM data types and parameters in greater detail in later sections and chapters.

You should now have an object with three methods defined: `RollDough()`, `PrepareToppings()`, and `Bake()`.

Adding Properties to the COM Object

Our COM object also needs to implement some properties. In our code, properties are just like any other method but with a slightly different implementation. Visual C++ creates the necessary function declarations for properties just as it did for our methods. Creating a property is a two-step process, as outlined next.

The first step is to create a member variable for our class, `CPizzaSample`. To do this, simply right-click on the class, and select "Add Member Variable" from the menu. The dialog that appears is shown in Figure 6-13.

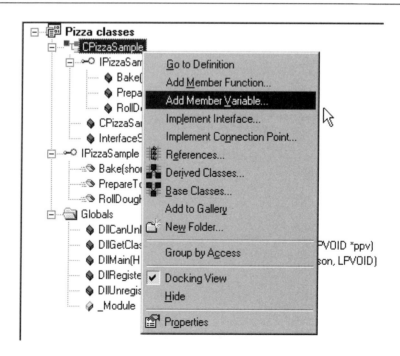

Figure 6-13. First step in adding a member variable.

Our variable will have a type of "short." Name our variable "m_Diameter." For the access, click Private to make our variable a private member of the class. (Remember data encapsulation and information hiding!) Click OK, and the code for our variable declaration is added. (See Figure 6-14.)

Now, on to the second step in creating a property. We proceed as follows:

1. Right-click on the "IPizzaSample" item in the class view at the level of "Pizza classes." Select "Add Property" from the menu.

2. The Add Property to Interface dialog appears. For Property Type, select "short." This should be the same type as the type you selected for the member variable you created earlier. For Property Name, enter "Diameter." The property name is the name by which the user of the completed object will refer to the property. In general, you will want to make the name of the property and the corresponding member variable similar to reduce confusion in your code. Leave the default selections for Function Type intact. (See Figure 6-15.)

3. Click on the Attributes tab to add the help string for the property. This works just the same as before.

4. When you have entered all the data, click OK to create the "method."

Take a look at the class view again. Figure 6-16 shows a fully expanded view of all the code that was added by the wizard and added by us.

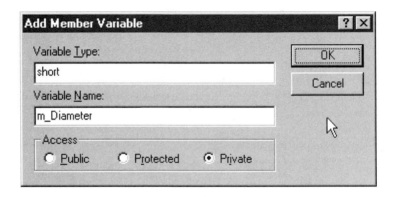

Figure 6-14. The Add Member Variable dialog.

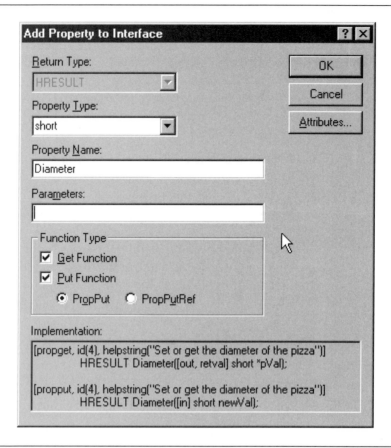

Figure 6-15.   The Add Property to Interface dialog.

Adding Implementation Code for Methods and Properties

Our object now has properties and methods defined for it. However, we still do not have an implementation for these properties and methods. It's our responsibility to add implementation for these functions. To begin, let's look at the property, Diameter, that we created.

In the class view for the CPizzaSample class, you will see two member functions called get_Diameter() and put_Diameter(). The "get" function is responsible for returning the value of the property, and the "put" function sets the value of the property. If you double-click on these items, Visual C++ will open the source-code window and position the cursor inside the implementations of these functions.

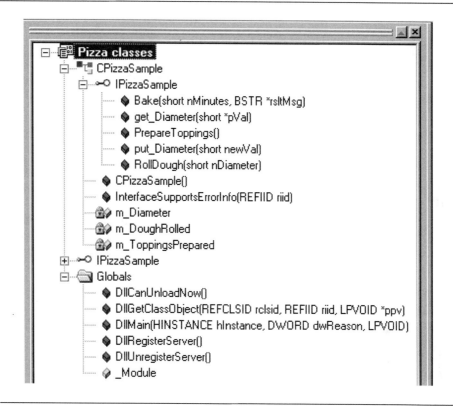

Figure 6-16. Fully expanded view of properties and methods.

Here's the code that was generated for `get_Diameter()`:

```
STDMETHODIMP CPizzaSample::get_Diameter(short *pVal)
{
    // TODO: Add your implementation code here
    return S_OK;
}
```

The TODO comment reminds us of where we need to add code to the implementation. The parameter to `get_Diameter` is a pointer to a short. Since the user of our object will expect to receive the value of this property, we just assign this parameter to the value in our class's member variable `m_Diameter`, like this:

```
*pVal = m_Diameter;
```

Now our code for the get_Diameter function should read as follows:

```
STDMETHODIMP CPizzaSample::get_Diameter(short *pVal)
{
    // TODO: Add your implementation code here
    *pVal = m_Diameter;
    return S_OK;
}
```

That's all that is required for this function.

The implementation for put_Diameter() is similar. We are simply assigning our m_Diameter class member variable to the value passed into the function:

```
STDMETHODIMP CPizzaSample::put_Diameter(short newVal)
{
    // TODO: Add your implementation code here
    m_Diameter = newVal;
    return S_OK;
}
```

Now our methods need some implementation. Double-click on the Bake() function (above the get_Diameter() function in the class view). We are then placed inside the function for this method. Add the code listed under the TODO comment:

```
STDMETHODIMP CPizzaSample::Bake(short nMinutes, BSTR *rsltMsg)
{
    // TODO: Add your implementation code here

    CComBSTR bstrReturnMsg1( _T( "Your pizza is done!" ) );
    CComBSTR bstrReturnMsg2( _T( "You need to bake it longer than ↵
that!" ) );

    if ( nMinutes < 10 )
    {
        *rsltMsg = bstrReturnMsg2.Copy();
    }
```

```
    else
    {
        *rsltMsg = bstrReturnMsg1.Copy();
    }
    return S_OK;
}
```

The actual implementation of the `Bake()` method isn't very exciting.
The method takes one parameter, `nMinutes`, which is the number of
minutes to bake the pizza. We decide that 10 minutes is too short of a
time to fully bake a pizza, so we will return a message string telling the
user this. Otherwise, we return the other string.

Note: A new class that we have not yet worked with is used here.
`CComBSTR` is a wrapper class for the BSTR data type. It provides us a
convenient method with which to manipulate BSTRs. We'll look at more
of this later.

The other two methods are similar in nature. They use two class
member variables, which we did not define yet, `m_DoughRolled` and
`m_ToppingsPrepared`. Be sure to add them in the class (data type is short,
and access is private). Their implementations are very simple and are left
as an exercise for the reader to make things a little more interesting:

```
STDMETHODIMP CPizzaSample::RollDough( short nDiameter )
{
    // TODO: Add your implementation code here
    m_Diameter = nDiameter;
    if ( m_DoughRolled != 1 )
    {
        m_DoughRolled = 1;
    }
    return S_OK;
}
STDMETHODIMP CPizzaSample::PrepareToppings()
{
    // TODO: Add your implementation code here
    if ( m_ToppingsPrepared != 1 )
    {
        m_ToppingsPrepared = 1;
    }
    return S_OK;
}
```

Compiling the Project

We now need to compile and link our component so that we can test it in some Active Server Pages. To build the DLL, select Build Pizza.dll from the Project menu. In the output window, you will see several compilation status messages scroll by. The build is complete when you see that no errors have been encountered. Part of the build process is *registration* (explained next). If registration is successful, we are ready to use our component!

COM Component Registration

Before any COM component can be used, it must be registered. When a COM component is installed on the user's system, a special registration program called `regsvr32` marks the name of the component in the Windows Registry. At design time, the COM object is assigned a *globally unique identifier,* or *GUID* (pronunciation rhyming with "squid"). A GUID is a very large number made up of 128 bits (that makes 2^{128} possible values) that are generated using a special algorithm that guarantees the global uniqueness of the number. This is done by using the computer's network card ID, the current system time, and other data and passing it through a complex algorithm in order to generate the GUID. Internally, when we call a COM object, this GUID is used to refer to the object. The `regsvr32` program extracts the embedded GUID from the COM object and stores it in the Registry along with the *progID*.

The ASP `Server` object method, `CreateObject`, takes a progID as its parameter. The progID is a logical name that is used to refer to a unique COM object. Sometimes, the progID string is suffixed with a version number (e.g., `ADODB.Connection.1`). This ensures that, if two COM objects with the same progID get installed on the machine, name conflicts can be alleviated. This progID is stored in the Registry upon object registration.

Calling a COM Component from an ASP Page

We are ready to call our component from an ASP page. Now that the component is registered, all we need to do is to create an instance of it using the `CreateObject` method. We can then call the methods of the object. Here's an example:

```
<%

' Declare our pizza COM object
Dim objPizza
```

```
' Create the pizza COM object
Set objPizza = Server.CreateObject( "Pizza.PizzaSample" )

' Set the diameter of our pizza. This actually calls put_Diameter()
objPizza.Diameter = 14

' Roll out the dough
objPizza.RollDough 14

' Prepare the toppings
objPizza.PrepareToppings

' Inform the user what the size of the pizza is. The reference to the
' value of the Diameter property is retrieved using get_Diameter()
Response.Write "You rolled a " & objPizza.Diameter & " inch pizza<BR>"

' Finally, bake the pizza for 15 minutes
Response.Write objPizza.Bake( 15 )

' Release our pizza object
Set objPizza = Nothing
%>
```

If all goes well, you should see the following output:

```
You rolled a 14 inch pizza
Your pizza is done!
```

Under the Hood of COM and ATL

We've seen how easy it is to create a COM component using the ATL COM AppWizard. Visual C++ takes most of the work out of this task. To make this happen, a lot of "plumbing" code was added. But what does this code do exactly? More importantly, what parts of this code are most relevant to you, the component designer?

To help clear this up, we are going to dive into some of the specifics of the COM architecture. We will not tread too deeply into COM waters since our focus is ATL, which simplifies most of the raw COM API. Nonetheless, it helps to have a basic understanding of how everything works. Along the way, we'll identify relevant sections of the ATL COM AppWizard-generated code and explain them in further detail.

Interfaces

Although COM is language neutral, the COM API and the object architecture have their roots in C++ (on the Windows platform). COM leverages off of the object-oriented nature of C++, with its classes and data encapsulation capabilities, to form the underlying architecture of COM. *Encapsulation* is the process of packing up object implementation and hiding it from the programmer, and it is used extensively in the COM programming model. In fact, C++ classes and COM objects closely mirror each other in terms of structure. COM, however, needs to have a mechanism in which the client program (regardless of what language it was written in) can have access to the methods and properties of the class. It does this via an interface.

An *interface* is the bridge that is used to gain programmatic access to a COM object. In C++, a COM interface is itself a class. The members of this class do not have an implementation defined for them yet. Each of the class members is a pure virtual function. Recall from C++ that a *pure virtual function* is a function in a class that has no implementation defined for it at the time of its declaration. When all of the members of a class are made up of pure virtual functions, that makes the class an *abstract base class* (ABC). Later, we will create a class that derives from the interface class that implements the pure virtual functions defined in the interface class.

A Simplified Interface Class

To illustrate some fundamental COM concepts, we're going to adapt the `IPizzaSample` interface class from `pizza.h` (generated by the ATL COM AppWizard) and strip it of most of its detail, Here's the "simplified" class called `IPizza`:

```
class IPizza
{
    virtual void RollDough( int nDiameter ) = 0;
    virtual void PrepareToppings( void ) = 0;
    virtual void Bake( int nMinutes, BSTR *rsltMsg ) = 0;
}
```

This class will be the start of our COM interface. COM follows a naming convention for interfaces. Traditionally, they all begin with an uppercase *I,* as in `IMyInterface`, `IFooBar`, and `IAmAnInterface`. This styling helps us to identify an interface at a glance from other classes.

The rule of thumb behind interfaces is that, once one is defined, it cannot be modified in any way. There are a couple of reasons for this. First, it simplifies the client code. A client can always depend on the interface being there, with all its methods and properties intact. So, the risk of the client code's breaking due to a COM object's changing implementation is minimized. Second, COM interfaces are a very specific memory structure, which depends on the physical ordering of the functions in the interface class. This structure is called a *vtable*. If any methods are added or taken away, this ordering will be adversely affected and cause the COM object not to function correctly.

An Implementation Class

So far, we have shown that a COM object begins with an abstract base class that contains pure virtual functions that define the object's methods. Since we are just defining the way that the object will expose itself to the client program, it is convenient to forego the implementations of these methods for now. Most importantly, separating interface from object implementation allows us to enforce object encapsulation since the interface class is the only way for the programmer to get to the methods of the object. Remember that the interface does not define implementation. This separation allows us to swap out the implementation at will and also allows the component to scale when new features are added (new methods will be defined by a new interface).

We now need our object to do something, so we must define some implementation for it. We can do this by creating a new class that derives from the interface class, as in the following example:

```
Class CPizza : public IPizza
{
     void RollDough( int nDiameter )
     {
          // Implementation code for rolling the dough
     }
     void PrepareToppings()
     {
          // Implementation code for preparing the pizza toppings
     }
     void Bake( int nMinutes, BSTR *rsltMsg )
     {
          // Implementation code for baking the pizza
     }
}
```

Calling the Methods of the Implementation Class

In this class, we actually provide some implementation code for the pure virtual functions we defined in the interface class. We now have all the pieces in place to call the methods on our object. We do this by calling a function (yet to be implemented) that gets an interface pointer to the implementation class object (this function is yet to be defined). Once we have that pointer, we can begin calling the methods by using the C++ $\rightarrow$ operator on the interface pointer. Here's an example:

```
void MakePizza()
{
    BSTR *bstrReply;
    IPizza *pPizza = GetPointerToOurClassObject();
    pPizza->RollDough( 12 );
    pPizza->PrepareToppings();
    pPizza->Bake( 45, &bstrReply );
}
```

Creating a New Interface

Now suppose we wanted to expand our object with some new capabilities. After examining the requirements of the modification, the programmer determines that new methods to the object are required. We can't violate the COM ruling about modifying existing interfaces, so we have to create a new interface with new pure virtual functions. The new interface must support all the methods of the old interface. To do this, we just inherit from the old interface, like this:

```
Class INewPizza : public IPizza
{
    virtual void TossPizzaInAir( int nHeight ) = 0;
}
```

INewPizza now has all the methods of IPizza, plus the new method TossPizzaInAir. Calling our new method will work much the same as in the earlier example except that now we use a pointer to our new interface:

```
void MakePizza()
{
    INewPizza *pNewPizza = GetPointerToOurClassObject();
    BSTR *bstrReply;
    pNewPizza->RollDough( 12 );
```

```
                pNewPizza->TossPizzaInAir( 3 );
                pNewPizza->PrepareToppings();
                pNewPizza->Bake( 45, &bstrReply );
}
```

As you can see, making the object accessible through the interface enables only existing code to continue to use the old interface, `IPizza`. For programmers who want to take advantage of the new functionality of `TossPizzaInAir()`, they simply use the new interface, `INewPizza`.

When a call to a method is made on the object through one of its interfaces, it finds the address of the method's function through a vtable (an array of pointers to functions in the class). An entry in the vtable is made for each virtual function in the class. In COM, all functions are pure virtual functions, so they get an entry in the vtable.

What happens when we call a method? In our example, we make calls like

```
pPizza->Bake( 45, &bstrReply );
```

which dereferences the `pPizza` pointer. Then, the internal vtable pointer is dereferenced, and the index is located for the pointer to the function in `CPizza` that performs the action. That function is then called.

So far, we have a mechanism that we can use to call the methods of a class through an interface. This is the fundamental principle of COM. However, we are not quite at the point of a full COM implementation. We still need to figure out a few things. The issues to be addressed are as follows:

■ The implementation for our stubbed-out function, `GetPointerToOurClassObject()`, is not defined yet. We need to know how the object is actually going to be created. We need to know how to get to the different interfaces of the object in case we have to call a method in that interface.

■ We need to know how to obtain an interface pointer.

■ We need to manage memory used by the object. So far, we have not discussed how this is done.

The IUnknown Interface

For the classes that we created to truly be COM objects, they must support the "standard" COM interface called `IUnknown`. `IUnknown` contains the following methods:

1. `AddRef()` and `Release()` are responsible for maintaining the reference count for interfaces and objects. The *reference count* is a numeric value that is incremented by `AddRef()` each time an interface is used and is decremented when `Release()` is called. Reference counting is an important mechanism in maintaining the amount of memory used by the object. In a multiuser environment, it is not memory efficient for instances of objects to remain in memory for long periods. Too many object instances can quickly exhaust system memory. If the reference count for an interface or an object reaches zero, a special function is called that releases the memory used by the object or interface.

2. `QueryInterface()` is responsible for getting to the other interfaces of the object, assuming, of course, that we already have a pointer to some interface of the object.

In addition to the fact that all COM objects must support the `IUnknown` interface, any subsequent interface that you create must derive from `IUnknown`.

Interface Definition Language (IDL)

The *Interface Definition Language* (IDL) is a language used to define interfaces for COM. You might ask why we need to "define" an interface when we seemed to do this already with our C++ class definitions. In our C++ interface class, we defined parameters to the functions just as you are normally used to doing with C++. If we were simply using the object on our computer, within the same memory space as the client program, this approach would work perfectly. But COM is designed not to have any machine or process boundaries in regard to calling mechanisms. The COM object could be located anywhere, including on another server. We need a mechanism to transmit data across these boundaries. That process is called *marshalling*, and the IDL assists with implementing the marshaling code.

IDL is a language with syntax similar to C++. Microsoft Visual C++ contains an IDL "compiler," which does not output compiled binary code, but C++ source code. The source code produced by the IDL compiler allows the development system to produce this marshalling code.

IDL allows us to associate a GUID with interfaces and objects. When the COM object is registered, the GUIDs from the IDL are written to the Registry. When we wish to create an instance of a COM object, the object-creation routine looks up the progID in the Registry and retrieves the location of the DLL file (or EXE file for out-of-process servers). The code is loaded at this point. Later on, we'll look at the functions of COM that actually create an instance of the component.

The IDL language looks something like the following. This snippet from the IDL file of our `Pizza` COM object shows our interface definition:

```
// Pizza.idl : IDL source for Pizza.dll
//

// This file will be processed by the MIDL tool to
// produce the type library (Pizza.tlb) and marshalling code.

import "oaidl.idl";
import "ocidl.idl";
        [
❶              object,
❷              uuid(5F649750-D3DE-11D2-8369-006097ADC885),
               dual,
               helpstring("IPizzaSample Interface"),
               pointer_default(unique)
        ]
❸       interface IPizzaSample : IDispatch
        {
               [id(1), helpstring("Rolls out the pizza dough to the spe-
cific diameter")] HRESULT RollDough([in] short nDiameter);
               [id(2), helpstring("Prepare the toppings for the pizza")]
HRESULT PrepareToppings();
               [id(3), helpstring("Bake the pizza for the specified num-
ber of minutes")] HRESULT Bake([in] short nMinutes, [out, retval] BSTR
*rsltMsg);
               [propget, id(4), helpstring("Set or get the diameter of
the pizza")] HRESULT Diameter([out, retval] short *pVal);
               [propput, id(4), helpstring("Set or get the diameter of
the pizza")] HRESULT Diameter([in] short newVal);
        };
    [
        uuid(5F649741-D3DE-11D2-8369-006097ADC885),
        version(1.0),
        helpstring("Pizza 1.0 Type Library")
    ]
library PIZZALib
{
        importlib("stdole32.tlb");
        importlib("stdole2.tlb");
```

```
        [
                uuid(5F649751-D3DE-11D2-8369-006097ADC885),
                helpstring("PizzaSample Class")
        ]
        coclass PizzaSample
        {
                [default] interface IPizzaSample;
        };
};
```

Looking at the top of the IDL file, we see a bracketed code block with the `object` keyword.❶ This block of code tells us that we are defining an interface for an object. The `dual` keyword tells us that the interface is a dual interface;❷ that is, the `IPizzaSample` interface inherits from another interface called `IDispatch`. Below this code block is the IDL definition of our interface.❸ Each one of the properties and methods that we defined in the wizard is represented here. Each method and property contains information about the parameters and how they are handled.

Let's look at the `Bake()` method as an example:

```
[id(3), helpstring("Bake the pizza for the specified number of ⌐
minutes")] HRESULT
                        Bake([in] short nMinutes, [out, retval] BSTR ⌐
*rsltMsg);
```

Recall that our `Bake()` method took two parameters, one of which was the number of minutes to bake the pizza, and a returned string value. We also defined a help string for the method. In IDL, the `[in]` construct is used to indicate that the parameter will be supplied by the user as input. This value is not modified by the method itself. The `[out, retval]` construct indicates that the specified parameter is returned by the method as output.

In the examples that follow, we will see how to call our `Pizza` object from within a C++ program. This is an important exercise because the other COM object that we build in coming sections will be calling other COM objects, like ADO. Since VBScript takes all of the hard work out of COM, the C++ way of working with COM objects may seem difficult at first. However, the conventions used in C++ share some common elements with those used in VBScript.

Instantiating Objects

The COM API provides functions for *instantiating* objects—that is, retrieving a reference to a COM object so that we can call its methods. We will be using one of two ways to create instances of objects in our code.

CoCreateInstance()

The first way is to call the COM API function `CoCreateInstance()`. Let's look at the syntax of this function and discuss exactly what happens when we call this function:

```
HRESULT CoCreateInstance( REFCLSID rclsid,
                          IUnknown *pUnkOuter,
                          DWORD dwClsCtx,
                          REFIID riid,
                          void **ppv )
```

where `rclsid` is the GUID of the COM object we want to create; `pUnkOuter` is the parameter used for aggregation (but not used by us, so `NULL` goes here); `dwClsCtx` is the locality of the class (we will use `CLSCTX_ALL` as our default); `riid` is the GUID ID of the interface we want to return; and `ppv` is a handle to the desired interface.

The first parameter to `CoCreateInstance()` is the GUID of the class we wish to create. Recall that this value is stored in the Registry along with the human-readable progID. If you open the Registry Editor, you will see all of the classes installed on your computer under the `RKEY_CLASSES_ROOT` (see Figure 6-17). Each progID is assigned a key, and underneath that key is a key that contains a value that is the CLSID (GUID ID). `CoCreateInstance()` uses this CLSID internally to create an instance of the class.

The next parameter of concern to us is `riid`. Like the `rclsid` parameter, `riid` is a GUID ID. This is the GUID of the interface we want to return. Unlike the CLSID, which is stored in the Registry, the interface ID for the `Pizza.PizzaSample` component comes from the "compiled" IDL code. Remember that the IDL compiler produces the marshalling code as well as the GUIDs of the object and its interfaces. So, we need to `#include` those files in the source file that contains calls to `CoCreateInstance()`. We'll look at more of this later.

The last parameter is the pointer to the desired interface. The returned pointer will be cast to `void **`. Once we have this pointer, we can then begin

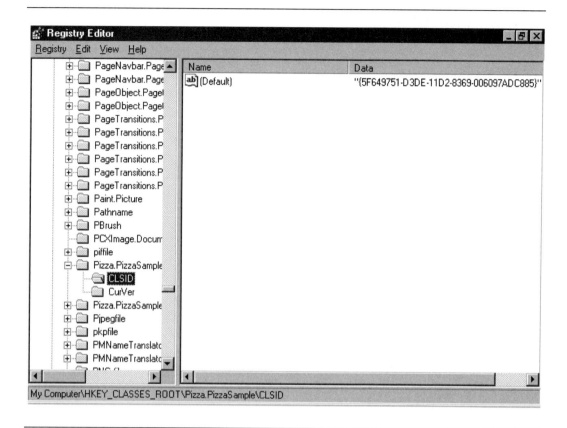

Figure 6-17. The Registry Editor dialog showing Pizza.PizzaSample CLSID.

to call the methods on the object through the interface pointer. Here's an example that starts from the beginning. It's a simple Win32 console application:

```
// We include the standard IO header and the wide-character string
// header. The COM routines are defined in windows.h
#include "stdafx.h"
#include <windows.h>
#include <stdio.h>
#include <tchar.h>


// point these to the locations of the pizza_i.c and pizza.h files
#include "C:\Program Files\Microsoft Visual
Studio\MyProjects\Pizza\pizza_i.c"
```

❶

```
❷  #include "C:\Program Files\Microsoft Visual
    Studio\MyProjects\Pizza\pizza.h"

    // -------------- MAIN PROGRAM --------------
    int main(int argc, char* argv[])
    {
        // Initialize the COM library.
❸      CoInitialize( NULL );
        // These variables hold the size of the pizza
        // and the message returned from Bake().
❹      BSTR msg;
❹      short nSize;

        // Declare an interface pointer to the PizzaSample object's
    //interface
❹      IPizzaSample* pPizza = NULL;

        // Create the object
❺      HRESULT hr = CoCreateInstance( CLSID_PizzaSample,
                            NULL, CLSCTX_INPROC_SERVER,
                            IID_IPizzaSample,
                            ( void **)&pPizza )

        // Set the diameter of the pizza to 21 inches
❻      hr = pPizza->put_Diameter( 21 );

        // Retrieve the diameter into the nSize variable
❻      hr = pPizza->get_Diameter( &nSize );

        // Print the diameter
❼      _tprintf( _T( "The pizza has a diameter of %d inches.\n" ), nSize );

        // Bake the pizza
        hr = pPizza->Bake( 13, &msg );
        // Check the HRESULT returned to see if the method
❽      // call succeeded.
        if ( SUCCEEDED( hr ) )
        {
            // Print the message
            _tprintf( _T( "Pizza status: %ls\n" ), msg );
        }

        // Free the object
❾      pPizza->Release();
```

```
          // Uninitialize the COM library
❿         CoUninitialize();

          return 0;
    }
```

At the beginning of our program, we bring in the definitions and implementations for the IPizzaSample interface class that are inside the pizza.h and pizza_i.c files.❶, ❷ These were the files that were generated by the IDL compiler. If we investigate the files in more detail, we see the identifiers used by our sample application. Here's what the pizza_i.c file looks like:

```
/* this file contains the actual definitions of */
/* the IIDs and CLSIDs */

/* link this file in with the server and any clients */

/* File created by MIDL compiler version 5.01.0164 */
/* at Sun Mar 07 14:46:58 1999
 */
/* Compiler settings for C:\Program Files\Microsoft Visual ⏎
Studio\MyProjects\Pizza\Pizza.idl:
      Oicf (OptLev=i2), W1, Zp8, env=Win32, ms_ext, c_ext
      error checks: allocation ref bounds_check enum stub_data
*/
//@@MIDL_FILE_HEADING( )
#ifdef __cplusplus
extern "C"{
#endif

#ifndef __IID_DEFINED__
#define __IID_DEFINED__

typedef struct _IID
{
    unsigned long x;
    unsigned short s1;
    unsigned short s2;
    unsigned char c[8];
} IID;

#endif // __IID_DEFINED__
```

```
#ifndef CLSID_DEFINED
#define CLSID_DEFINED
typedef IID CLSID;
#endif // CLSID_DEFINED

const IID IID_IPizzaSample =
{0x5F649750,0xD3DE,0x11D2,{0x83,0x69,0x00,0x60,0x97,0xAD,0xC8,0x85}};

const IID LIBID_PIZZALib =
{0x5F649741,0xD3DE,0x11D2,{0x83,0x69,0x00,0x60,0x97,0xAD,0xC8,0x85}};

const CLSID CLSID_PizzaSample =
{0x5F649751,0xD3DE,0x11D2,{0x83,0x69,0x00,0x60,0x97,0xAD,0xC8,0x85}};

#ifdef __cplusplus
}
#endif
```

The items in boldface are the ones we are concerned with at the moment. They are constants that represent the GUIDs of the class (CLSID_PizzaSample) and interface (IID_IPizzaSample) for our PizzaSample object. Instead of supplying a *ProgID.ClassName* combination as we do in VBScript, we used the constants generated by the MIDL compiler that are in the pizza_i.c file.

At the beginning of the main() function, we call the COM API function CoInitialize() to initialize the COM library routines.❸ Next, we define the following variables:❹

```
IPizzaSample* pPizza;
BSTR msg;
short nSize;
```

The first variable declares a pointer to an **IPizzaSample** interface. **IPizzaSample** is defined in pizza.h. The following fragment from the pizza.h file shows the class declaration for the **IPizzaSample** interface:

```
EXTERN_C const IID IID_IPizzaSample;

#if defined(__cplusplus) && !defined(CINTERFACE)

    MIDL_INTERFACE("5F649750-D3DE-11D2-8369-006097ADC885")
    IPizzaSample : public IDispatch
```

```
    {
    public:
        virtual /* [helpstring][id] */ HRESULT STDMETHODCALLTYPE ↵
RollDough( /* [in] */ short nDiameter ) = 0;

        virtual /* [helpstring][id] */ HRESULT STDMETHODCALLTYPE ↵
PrepareToppings( void) = 0;

        virtual /* [helpstring][id] */ HRESULT STDMETHODCALLTYPE Bake(
            /* [in] */ short nMinutes,
            /* [retval][out] */ BSTR __RPC_FAR *rsltMsg) = 0;

        virtual /* [helpstring][id][propget] */ HRESULT ↵
STDMETHODCALLTYPE get_Diameter(
            /* [retval][out] */ short __RPC_FAR *pVal) = 0;

        virtual /* [helpstring][id][propput] */ HRESULT ↵
STDMETHODCALLTYPE put_Diameter(
            /* [in] */ short newVal) = 0;
    };
```

We now call the CoCreateInstance() function. The IPizzaSample pointer variable will hold the interface returned by CoCreateInstance():❺

```
// Create the object
HRESULT hr = CoCreateInstance( CLSID_PizzaSample,
                    NULL, CLSCTX_INPROC_SERVER,
                    IID_IPizzaSample,
                    ( void **)&pPizza )
```

HRESULTs

Notice that the CoCreateInstance() function returns an HRESULT. What kind of variable is this? An HRESULT is a 32-bit number that uses its arrangement of bits to indicate the status returned by the function. All COM methods return an HRESULT. It is the mechanism that is used to report errors to the calling program. Table 6-1 lists some of the standard HRESULT codes used in COM. You can find a complete list in the file winerror.h.

If we succeed with getting an interface pointer to our objects, we can start to call their methods. As before, we use the → notation to get at the methods of the object. Here is the code for setting the diameter of our pizza:❻

Table 6-1. Some Standard HRESULT Codes

Code	Description
S_OK	The method successfully executed.
E_FAIL	A general failure occurred.
E_OUTOFMEMORY	Memory could not be allocated for the requested operation.
E_INVALIDARG	The parameter(s) to the method is (are) of the wrong type.
E_NOINTERFACE	The interface is not supported. QueryInterface() returns this code when it tries to get a nonexistent interface.
E_POINTER	This indicates an invalid pointer.
E_NOTIMPL	The requested feature is not implemented.
E_ABORT	The operation is aborted.
E_ACCESSDENIED	The required security permission is not present.

```
hr = pPizza->put_Diameter( 21 );
hr = pPizza->get_Diameter( &nSize );
_tprintf( _T( "The pizza has a diameter of %d inches.\n" ), nSize );
```

The odd-looking code for retrieving and setting the value of the Diameter property is very different from the calling convention used in VBScript. At first glance, these look like methods rather than properties as we know them in VBScript, but put_Diameter and get_Diameter are, in fact, methods. They are the methods that COM calls "under the hood" when we set and get properties. put_Diameter works in a straightforward manner. get_Diameter does a call-by-reference to retrieve the diameter since the function itself is already returning a value, the HRESULT.

The _tprintf() function is used for our output.❼ Since COM deals mainly with wide-character strings, this version of printf() is necessary to generate correctly formatted output. Of course, our COM objects do not have a user interface, nor do the applications that we will be writing use standard input/output.

Back to our example: We then call the `Bake()` method.❽ This method returns the message regarding the results of the baked pizza. It gets returned in the parameter `msg`:

```
hr = pPizza->Bake( 13, &msg );
```

SUCCEEDED and FAILED Macros

The `SUCCEEDED` macro is used to check the `HRESULT` return codes. `SUCCEEDED` will evaluate to true if its value is `S_OK`. Always use the macro when checking for success. This ensures that you catch any type of failure since `SUCCEEDED` checks the most significant bit of the `HRESULT` to determine a success or a failure. In other words, don't say something like `if (hr == S_OK)` because this may not yield the expected outcome. The `FAILED` macro is used to check for any values that indicate a failure, including the values in Table 6-1 that are prefixed with an *E*.

Release()

After we are through with the object, we should free it so that our program does not leak memory. Since the `IPizza` interface inherited the methods of the `IUnknown` interface (just like all COM interfaces), we can call the `Release()` method easily.

At this point in our code, we are done with the COM object instance. We should destroy it so that its resources can be used again. We call the standard `IUnknown` method, `Release()`, to do this:❾

```
pPizza->Release();
```

Remember that each call to `Release()` must be balanced by a call to `AddRef()`. You may be wondering why we are calling `Release()` when there does not seem to be a call to `AddRef()` anywhere. Well, there is, but it's hidden from you. `CoCreateInstance()` actually calls `AddRef()` inside its implementation, so calling `AddRef()` yourself is not necessary.

Finally, the call to `CoUninitialize()` cleans up after COM library usage.❿

Calling COM Objects Using ATL Smart Pointers and Type Libraries

There are actually many ways in which you can create an instance of a COM object and call its methods. The preceding method relied on using predefined constants for interfaces and classes defined in the code produced by the IDL compiler. In most cases, you may not have this code available to you. If you are using a third-party component, which ships with just the runtime binary file, you will not have the header and C files for the interfaces and GUID definitions. In addition, if you are in a non-C/C++ development environment (such as VBScript), you are in trouble as well. Even if you have these files, you're out of luck because they are not in the native language of the development system you're using. Thus, we need a way to get the interface and type information of the COM object without having to resort to the header and C file definitions. That's the job of type libraries.

Type Libraries

A *type library* is essentially a "tokenized" form of IDL. A type library can be contained inside a file (`.tlb` or `.olb`), or it can be stored as a resource inside a compiled DLL. In the case of third-party components, the common practice would be to query for the type library information inside the DLL file. In order for you to find out the type library's name of the COM object you are using, you can use the handy OLE/COM Object Viewer that is included in Visual Studio.

To find out type library information for a COM object,

1. Open the OLE/COM Object View from the Visual Studio Program Group.
2. From the File menu, select View TypeLib.
3. Select a file with type library information, such as a COM object's DLL. Try `pizza.dll`, which is the DLL for our example COM object.

As Figure 6-18 shows, a listing of all the available interfaces and classes (coclasses) appears in a tree layout. At the top of the tree is the name of the type library. This is the name that you use inside your code when specifying where to get type library information (`PIZZALib`).

Using the #import Directive

How do you specify a type library to be used for your code? Microsoft Visual C++ comes with a compiler directive called `#import` for this purpose. Its job is to generate ATL wrapper classes for the COM object's interfaces. The wrapper classes provide several advantages over using the MIDL-generated files.

```
ITypeLib Viewer                                                          _ □ ×
File  View

PIZZALib (Pizza 1.0 Type Library)    // Generated .IDL file (by the OLE/COM Object Viewer)
  coclass PizzaSample                //
    IPizzaSample                     // typelib filename: Pizza.dll
      Methods                        [
        m  RollDough                   uuid(5F649741-D3DE-11D2-8369-006097ADC885),
        m  PrepareToppings             version(1.0),
        m  Bake                        helpstring("Pizza 1.0 Type Library")
        m  Diameter                  ]
        m  Diameter                  library PIZZALib
      Inherited Interfaces           {
        IPizzaSample                     // TLib :       // TLib : OLE Automation : {00020430-0000-
          m  RollDough               0000-C000-000000000046}
          m  PrepareToppings             importlib("StdOle2.Tlb");
          m  Bake
          m  Diameter                    // Forward declare all types defined in this typelib
          m  Diameter                    interface IPizzaSample;
          Inherited Interfaces
  dispinterface IPizzaSample             [
  interface IPizzaSample                   uuid(5F649751-D3DE-11D2-8369-006097ADC885),
                                           helpstring("PizzaSample Class")
                                         ]
                                       coclass PizzaSample {
                                           [default] interface IPizzaSample;
                                       };

                                       [
                                         odl,
                                         uuid(5F649750-D3DE-11D2-8369-006097ADC885),
                                         helpstring("IPizzaSample Interface"),
                                         dual,
                                         oleautomation
                                       ]
                                       interface IPizzaSample : IDispatch {
                                           [id(0x00000001), helpstring("Rolls out the pizza dough
Ready
```

Figure 6-18. Type library information.

1. *COM object properties can be used as data members.* Instead of using a function call to assign and retrieve values of the properties of a COM object, as in get_Propname(&foo) and put_Propname(foo), the → operator is overloaded to handle these functions like data members of the class (e.g., PPizza→Propname = 3).

2. *No reference counting is required.* The wrapper classes handle calling AddRef() and Release() for you. When an object is declared, its reference count is increased automatically. Once the object falls out of the scope in which it was created, the object is Release()ed, and the count is decremented. For example, we can create a standard C++ try . . . catch sequence to detect exceptions thrown by COM. We can place the call to create the object inside the try block and call some methods. After all of the code in the try block executes or a failure occurs along the way, the object gets released.

3. *There are convenient wrapper classes for the VARIANT and BSTR data types.* COM requires that many of its non-numeric data types that are marshaled be either VARIANT or BSTR. The wrapper classes include functions for creation and initialization of these types, as well as some miscellaneous utility functions. BSTRs are very important in COM since Visual Basic and C++ clients require them when dealing with string data. You most commonly see the following type of declarations when dealing with BSTRs:

■ BSTR is the "base" data type. It is a wide-character string (Unicode-compatible).

■ _bstr_t is a compiler COM support class that wraps the BSTR data type. The definition is located in comdef.h. It contains some useful member functions for string manipulation.

■ CComBSTR, like _bstr_t, also wraps the BSTR data type. It is part of the Active Template Library (ATL). It contains some enhanced functionality over _bstr_t.

In Chapter 7, we will investigate BSTRs in more detail and learn about the methods of the wrapper classes.

4. *There is more robust error reporting.* COM methods always return an HRESULT as a return condition of their execution. C++ programmers might prefer the more familiar try . . . catch mechanism for handling errors. Since the wrapper class provides this, checking the HRESULTs of methods is not necessary.

Overall, the #import method of calling COM objects from C++ provides the most straightforward way of creating, calling, and releasing COM objects. In many ways, it closely resembles VBScript with its CreateObject call. In an upcoming example, we'll do a side-by-side comparison of creating an object using #import, calling some methods, and releasing the object and then show the equivalent code in VBScript.

Let's look at another sample Win32 console application. We want to change things around a bit so that we are not using the MIDL-generated headers and C files. So, here's what we have:

```
// pizzaconsole.cpp : Defines the entry point for the console ↵
application.
//


#include "stdafx.h"
#include <stdio.h>
```

```
#include <tchar.h>

#import "C:\Program Files\Microsoft Visual ⏎
Studio\MyProjects\Pizza\Debug\Pizza.dll"

int main(int argc, char* argv[])
{
    CoInitialize( NULL );
    try
    {
        // just like Server.CreateObject( "Pizza.PizzaSample" ).
        // We are declaring a smart pointer
        PIZZALib::IPizzaSamplePtr pPizza( __uuidof(
                    PIZZALib::PizzaSample ) );

        pPizza->Diameter = 16;
        pPizza->RollDough( 16 );
        pPizza->PrepareToppings();

        tprintf( _T( "Pizza diameter is: %d\n" ), pPizza->Diameter );

        // pPizza->Bake() returns a _bstr_t class. The wchar_t *
        // cast is an overloaded
        // operator to return a wide-character version of the
        // string for printing
        _tprintf( _T( "Pizza status: %ls\n"),
                    ( wchar_t *)pPizza->Bake( 3 ) );
    }
    catch( _com_error e )
    {
        // add error handling here
    }

    CoUninitialize();

    return 0;
}
```

❶ CoInitialize(NULL);
❷ try
❸ PIZZALib::IPizzaSamplePtr pPizza(__uuidof(
❹ pPizza->Diameter = 16;

Note: Make sure you replace the path to the file in the #import directive to the location of the DLL of our Pizza COM object.

We begin by initializing COM with CoInitialize(), just as we did with the previous example.❶ Then, we start a C++ try block.❷ This will allow us to trap any errors we encounter with code inside the `try` block. If the error relates to COM, the `_com_error` exception will be thrown. We can put our error-handling routine in this area.

The `_com_error` object contains error-related information about a COM-related exception that was thrown. Among the information that is included are the `IErrorInfo` interface functions (the same ones that we've seen with the VBScript `Err` object), like `Description`, `HelpContext`, `Source`, and so on.

The ATL Smart Pointer

The Active Template Library is a series of thin wrapper classes for COM. These classes enable us to syntactically treat the objects that we create by ATL means in much the same way as objects created in VBScript.

The first statement declares a smart pointer to the `Pizza` interface.❸ A *smart pointer* is a special ATL template class (named `_com_ptr_t<>`) that wraps up our interface definition class so that we can use the → operator to get at all of the functions of the object. We mentioned earlier that COM class properties can be accessed in this manner—that is, treating the properties like object members and not methods. That's part of the job of the smart pointer. The smart pointer also manages its own memory (freeing interface pointers with `Release()`). The smart pointers are constructed from a special macro in the type library header file. This file is generated automatically when the `#import` directive is used. The macro is called `_COM_SMARTPTR_TYPEDEF()`. It takes two parameters: the interface name and the GUID of that interface. The file `Pizza.tlh`, the type library header file, shows this function:

```
// Created by Microsoft (R) C/C++ Compiler Version 12.00.8168.0
(354d06d0).
//
// Pizza.tlh
//
// C++ source equivalent of Win32 type library C:\Program
Files\Microsoft Visual Studio\MyProjects\Pizza\Debug\Pizza.dll
// compiler-generated file created 03/07/99 at 15:12:39 - DO NOT EDIT!

#pragma once
#pragma pack(push, 8)

#include <comdef.h>

namespace PIZZALib {
```

```
//
// Forward references and typedefs
//

struct /* coclass */ PizzaSample;
struct __declspec(uuid("5f649750-d3de-11d2-8369-006097adc885"))
/* dual interface */ IPizzaSample;

//
// Smart pointer typedef declarations
//

_COM_SMARTPTR_TYPEDEF(IPizzaSample, __uuidof(IPizzaSample));

//
// Type library items
//

struct __declspec(uuid("5f649751-d3de-11d2-8369-006097adc885"))
PizzaSample;
    // [ default ] interface IPizzaSample

struct __declspec(uuid("5f649750-d3de-11d2-8369-006097adc885"))
IPizzaSample : IDispatch
{
    //
    // Property data
    //

    __declspec(property(get=GetDiameter,put=PutDiameter))
    short Diameter;

    //
    // Wrapper methods for error-handling
    //

    HRESULT RollDough (
            Short nDiameter );
    HRESULT PrepareToppings ( );
    _bstr_t Bake (
            short nMinutes );
    short GetDiameter ( );
    void PutDiameter (
            short pVal );
```

```
        //
        // Raw methods provided by interface
        //
        virtual HRESULT __stdcall raw_RollDough (
                short nDiameter ) = 0;
        virtual HRESULT __stdcall raw_PrepareToppings ( ) = 0;
        virtual HRESULT __stdcall raw_Bake (
                short nMinutes,
                BSTR * rsltMsg ) = 0;
        virtual HRESULT __stdcall get_Diameter (
                short * pVal ) = 0;
        virtual HRESULT __stdcall put_Diameter (
                short pVal ) = 0;
};


//
// Wrapper method implementations
//


#include "Pizza.tli"


} // namespace PIZZALib
#pragma pack(pop)
```

This macro then generates the smart pointer that has the same name as the interface with a "Ptr" appended to the end.

Now we create an object. Here's the code for that:

```
PizzaLIB::IPizzaPtr pPizza( __uuidof( PizzaLIB::Pizza ) );
```

This code declares a smart pointer, pPizza. The parameter to the constructor is the GUID of the class (obtained by using the __uuidof() statement), and the constructor automatically queries for the proper interface. The __uuidof() statement obtains the GUID of the Pizza class. This is the same GUID for the class that is written to the Registry using regsvr32.

The next few lines are already familiar to us. We just call the methods as we normally do:❹

```
pPizza->Diameter = 16;
pPizza->RollDough ( 16 );
pPizza->PrepareToppings();
```

The variables will fall out of scope when the program exits. This is the point where the memory occupied by the smart pointer is released.

Using a Namespace

A *namespace* is a logical container for all of a COM object's identifiers. In our code that declares our smart pointer, we prefixed the name of the class with the `Pizza` object's namespace `PizzaLIB`. We could have alternately declared what namespace to use right after the `#import` statement by saying:

```
using namespace PizzaLIB;
```

This would make the inclusion of the *namespace::smartpointerclass* unnecessary. We could simply specify the smart pointer class in our object creation. This condensed form may be easier to read:

```
IPizzaPtr pPizza( __uuidof( Pizza ) );
```

Using ADO with Visual C++ and Smart Pointers

Since the Megabyte's application heavily utilizes ADO, it is only appropriate to include a section devoted to using it within C++. The ADO objects behave in much the same way as other COM objects, but there are some exceptions. We will be outlining those along the way. We will also be creating our first business object. We will be taking the functionality of the account creation VBScript functions and encapsulating them into a COM object.

We first need to import the type library for the ADO DLL. The file of interest is called `msado15.dll`. The following statement shows the pathname to this file on the author's system. The actual location of the DLL for your installation may vary. If necessary, perform a file search using Windows Explorer to determine the location:

```
#import "C:\Program Files\Common Files\System\ado\msado15.dll" ↵
no_namespace rename( "EOF", "adoEOF" )
```

The `no_namespace` keyword tells Visual C++ not to use a namespace when `#import`ing the DLL. This is done so that we do not have to scope the ADO names. Also, ADO defines a constant called `EOF` (end of file) that happens to be a reserved word in many C++ implementations. To work around this problem, the **rename** keyword is used to redefine the name to something unique (adoEOF).

Here's another console application to demonstrate how to perform a simple query using a **Recordset** object:

```
int main(int argc, char* argv[])
{

        VARIANT id;
        long numrecs;

        CoInitialize( NULL );

        try
        {
                _RecordsetPtr pMyRecSet( __uuidof( Recordset ) );

                pMyRecSet->Open( "SELECT username FROM Users",
                                "DSN=Megabytes",
                                adOpenStatic, adLockOptimistic, 0 );

                numrecs = pMyRecSet->RecordCount;

                while ( pMyRecSet->adoEOF == VARIANT_FALSE )
                {
                                id = pMyRecSet->Fields->
                                Item[ _variant_t( 0L ) ]->Value;
                                _tprintf( "%ls\n", id.bstrVal );
                                pMyRecSet->MoveNext();
                }

                pMyRecSet->Close( );
                _tprintf( "Number of records is: %ld\n", numrecs );
        }
        catch ( _com_error e )
        {
                // Add error-handling code here
        }

        CoUninitialize();
        return 0;
}
```

Using ADO with Visual C++ and VBScript

There are some differences between calling methods in ADO objects and the COM objects that we created ourselves. First, the smart pointer classes for the objects have different names; for example, notice that the `Recordset` object has the name `_RecordsetPtr`. This is contrary to the way that Visual C++ named our interfaces and classes. Second, the parameters that we are passing to the object need some special handling. They require some typecasts in order for the object and the marshaller to correctly handle the data. Most of these concepts will be covered in detail in the coming chapters. For now, the best way to illustrate what's going on with the preceding program is to show the equivalent program in a language that we are intimately familiar with—VBScript.

Let's start with the variable declarations. The variables `id` and `numrecs` are going to be used by the application to hold the value of the database field queried and the number of records returned by the query, respectively:

```
VARIANT id;
long numrecs;
```

The `id` variable is a variant, so we can treat it like any number of data types. In C++, the `VARIANT` is a type union. The `numrecs` variable will be used to hold the number of records returned by the query. Declaring these variables in VBScript is straightforward:

```
Dim id
Dim numrecs
```

Next, we create a `Recordset` object. Our C++ code uses the smart pointer constructor, which receives the GUID of the `Recordset` class:

```
_RecordsetPtr pMyRecSet( __uuidof( Recordset ) );
```

In VBScript, we just use the normal `Server.CreateObject` function:

```
Set pMyRecSet = Server.CreateObject( "ADODB.Recordset" )
```

Now, we open our recordset with an SQL statement that selects all the usernames from the `Users` table. In C++, we usually do not have the option to skip parameters to the method call that are optional, so, in this example, we make sure we fill one in for each:

```
pMyRecSet->Open( "SELECT username FROM Users",
            "DSN=Megabytes",
            adOpenStatic, adLockOptimistic, 0 );
```

In VBScript, this operation is just as simple:

```
pMyRecSet.Open "SELECT username FROM Users", "DSN=Megabytes",
            adOpenStatus, adLockOptimistic
```

We can see an example of properties being treated like class member variables when we retrieve the record count from the `pMyRecSet` object. We retrieve it into the `numrecs` variable:

```
numrecs = pMyRecSet->RecordCount;
```

Obviously, the VBScript equivalent looks almost the same:

```
numrecs = pMyRecSet.RecordCount
```

Next, we start a `while` loop to begin retrieving all of the records. The `while` loop keeps checking for the end of the recordset:

```
while ( pMyRecSet->adoEOF == VARIANT_FALSE )
```

When we imported the ADO DLL using the `#import` statement, we used the `rename` keyword to rename the constant `EOF`, which is defined in the type library, to `adoEOF`. We now use that as the `EOF` property of the ADO object so that we can continue to use `EOF` as an identifier in other C++ routines. `VARIANT_FALSE` is the constant to use to check against the value returned by the `pMyRecSet->adoEOF` expression. Expressed in VBScript, this statement becomes

```
While Not pMyRecSet.EOF
```

The next statement is a little more difficult, but only because some of the parameters require some typecasting. This function retrieves the value of the username field in the current record:

```
id = pMyRecSet->Fields->Item[ _variant_t( 0L ) ]->Value;
```

We index the `Fields` collection using an enumerated value for the `Item`. Each item in the collection is numbered sequentially, starting with zero. Our `Fields` collection will have only one item, the username. So, we retrieve the value by passing a long zero (cast to a variant class, `_variant_t`, as the function expects) and accessing the `Value` property of that item. Here's the VBScript for that function call:

```
Id = pMyRecSet.Fields( "username" )
```

Our VBScript references the item by name instead of by the index number in the C++ example.

Inside the loop, we advance to the next record using `MoveNext`. When we exit the loop, the recordset is closed using the `Close` method. Then, the COM library is uninitialized. In VBScript, we need to perform a `Set pMyRecSet = Nothing` since VBScript does not free the resources of the object as ATL does when the object falls out of scope.

Chapter Review

Here are the key points of this chapter relating to COM.

- COM components make Web application development easier. Using prebuilt components that perform a particular task frees us from having to write the code ourselves, which is a very time-consuming task.

- COM components integrate well with ASP since much of the application functionality that is implemented in script can be compiled into a COM object. These COM objects are commonly referred to as *business objects* since they carry out the logistics of business applications. The component nature of COM objects makes the main application easier to upgrade since the components need only be swapped.

- The COM objects we create are called *COM servers,* and we call them from programs we create called *clients.* In ASP, the scripting engine and IIS are the clients.

- Many COM objects in ASP are in-process DLLs. They share the memory space and resources used by the Web server, which makes them faster than components that execute out-of-process (COM objects implemented as EXEs).

■ The Visual C++ ATL COM Wizard makes it easy for us to create a skeleton for our object. The "plumbing" code for the object is automatically generated, leaving us to fill in the details for the object's implementation.

■ COM objects are fully *encapsulated,* which means that the details of their implementation are completely hidden from the client. The only way to access the object is through a special abstract base class called an *interface.* All communication to the object happens through this interface. An interface also acts as a contract with the client program. The definition of the interface cannot change over time. If new functionality is required that goes beyond the capabilities of the existing interface, a new interface must be created.

■ All COM objects implement a standard interface called `IUnknown`. The `IUnknown` interface has three methods: `AddRef()`, `QueryInterface()`, and `Release()`. The `AddRef()` and `Release()` methods are responsible for object reference counting. Reference counting keeps track of how many instances of an object are active. `Release()` decrements the counter, and `AddRef()` increments it. If the counter reaches zero, this signals that the DLL can be unloaded from memory. `QueryInterface()` is responsible for obtaining a pointer to another interface of the object. The `IUnknown` interface must be implemented in order for the object to be a fully COM-compliant object.

■ All COM interfaces inherit from the `IUnknown` interface. So, the three methods of `IUnknown`—`AddRef()`, `QueryInterface()`, and `Release()`—are accessible from any interface.

■ The Interface Definition Language (IDL) is a C-like language that is used to define COM interfaces. It describes the manner in which data is marshaled by the COM object. The IDL code is then translated into C++, which handles the implementation of the marshalling.

■ The `CoCreateInstance()` function is a COM API function that is used to instantiate a COM component. You call it by passing the GUID of the class and the desired interface of the class. Internally, the class factory creates the object, the interface is obtained from `QueryInterface()`, and the reference count is incremented. A pointer to the interface is then returned.

■ Almost all COM methods return a value called an `HRESULT`. An `HRESULT` is a 32-bit number indicating the success or failure of a COM method. The exact reason for the failure can be determined by the position of the bits in the value. Constants for common `HRESULT` values are defined in the `winerror.h` file. Constants prefixed with an *E* indicate a failure.

■ For each property we add to the ATL class, the ATL COM Wizard adds skeleton code to get and set the values of the properties. They follow the form `get_Property` and `set_Property`. These methods are not available by directly using VBScript.

■ The `SUCCEEDED` and `FAILED` macros are used to evaluate `HRESULT`s. `SUCCEEDED` returns true if the `HRESULT` code indicates success. `FAILED` returns true if a failure occurred.

Here are the key points of this chapter relating to ATL.

■ The ATL can make use of type libraries, which are tokenized forms of IDL. We can bring a type library into our source code by using the `#import` compiler directive. Type libraries come from type library files (`.tlb`) or from the compiled DLL.

■ Type libraries eliminate the need for the "compiled" IDL files. Definitions for types used by the COM object, including any interface and class GUIDs, are contained in the type library.

■ The OLE/COM Object Viewer (OLE View) is useful for finding out type library names of COM objects, including any class IDs, interface IDs, and so on. It can also be used to browse the properties and methods of the object.

■ When a type library is `#imported`, Visual C++ generates wrapper classes for the interfaces. This enables us to treat properties as data members and make classes for data types used for methods. It also eliminates the need for reference counting and facilitates better error reporting.

■ Namespaces allow us to scope the identifiers used in a COM object in our code. This eliminates the need to fully qualify the name of an identifier, as in `IPizzaPtr`, which becomes `PizzaLIB::IPizzaPtr`.

Here are the key points of this chapter relating to ADO from C++.

■ ADO can be accessed from C++ just like any other COM object, with some modifications to how we use namespaces.

■ The `EOF` property needed to be redefined due to a name conflict with C++.

What's Next

This chapter explained the fundamentals of COM and also demonstrated how to build COM components using the Active Template Library. In the coming chapters, we'll continue our exploration of COM components and ATL. We will focus in greater detail on creating properties and methods. We will pay particular attention to the variable types used in the parameters to methods. Error reporting will also be explored, which will allow us to pass richly formatted error messages back to the caller of the object. Collectively, these concepts are known as *automation*.

We'll also explore supplemental technologies to ASP, like Transaction Server, Microsoft Message Queuing, and Active Directory Services Interface. Keep reading!

■ Further Reading

- ■ *Essential COM* by Don Box, Addison-Wesley, 1998—The mother of all COM books. Get it, read it, be one with it.

- ■ *The C++ Programming Language, Third Edition* by Bjarne Stroustrup, Addison-Wesley, 1997—A very good C++ book. You can't get much more authoritative since the author is also the inventor of C++!

CHAPTER 7

Advanced COM: Exploring Automation, COM/ATL Data Types, and Error Reporting

Introduction

So far, we've used the intrinsic objects of ASP and the COM objects that are included with VBScript. We've explored COM fundamentals and its structural foundations. We then put this knowledge to use and (with a little help from the ATL COM Wizard) built a COM object that we used inside ASP. Hopefully, you've begun to see the potential of creating applications using this methodology.

So, where does all this leave us now? Well, we've received only a taste of COM and ATL. There are still some skills to cover that will be of great help to you in making COM components. As an introduction to the material in Chapter 7, let's look at some things you'll need to learn and implement that will help you build solid COM components using C++/ATL.

1. *The method-invoking mechanism*—We've seen how to call methods of a COM component using C++ and VBScript. This chapter will provide you with some background on *automation*, the mechanism behind how COM methods get called from clients such as VBScript.

2. *COM/ATL data types*—This is a very important topic. Many of the COM components that you will construct will work with many different types of data (as parameters to methods and return types). The key is how to manipulate these types of data. ATL provides some wrapper classes for many of these data types, which provide functions for copying, initializing, and converting data types.

3. *Error reporting*—What happens if something goes wrong in your COM object code? How does the caller of the COM object trap the

error? This chapter will show you COM/ATL's method of reporting errors back to the client.

The title of this chapter is "Advanced COM. . . ," but *advanced* is a rather ambiguous term. Its use here means that these topics are covered in more depth than what has been done thus far. Among COM and ATL gurus, this is considered toddler-level material. But, we are beginners in this arena, and a more in-depth discussion of the basics of these topics will allow you to quickly grasp a firm understanding of them.

A Review of COM

As our introduction to automation, let's outline the key points of what we've learned regarding COM objects and their construction.

- COM provides an architectural framework to facilitate the use (and reuse) of object-oriented, binary code objects. The objects can be written in any language that can provide an implementation of a pointer to functions in order to create the abstract base classes needed for defining and implementing COM properties and methods.

- The Visual C++ ATL COM Wizard automatically generates much of the support code needed to provide COM functionality to the object. Objects built using this wizard can then be used in many different programming environments, including ASP.

- COM objects expose themselves through an interface, and the standard IUnknown interface allows us to query for additional interfaces that the object may implement using the QueryInterface() method.

- ATL provides wrapper classes for "raw" COM that enable us to use COM objects in C++ more in the fashion of how they are used in Visual Basic. The main benefit is the overloaded → operator that allows us to treat properties as data members of the class.

- Type libraries make using prebuilt COM objects easier by allowing us to retrieve type and interface information through a tokenized form of IDL. This frees us from having to rely on the "compiled" code generated by the IDL compiler to get type and interface information.

A lot of the work we have done with creating COM objects and calling them from client programs has been in the C++ environment. Since the native language of COM is C++ (at least the Microsoft implementation), we've seen the tight relationship between C++ classes, vtables, abstract base classes, and so forth, and how the combination of these elements forms the basis of COM. However, since the Microsoft COM implementation is very much tied to C++, we still need a way for other languages (like VBScript) to use these objects. That's where automation comes into play.

Defining Automation

The term *automation* is an historical one and dates back to the early days of Windows. Developers wanted the ability for Windows applications to exchange data with one another. For example, the ability to embed a spreadsheet document inside a word-processing document (and have that embedded spreadsheet updated automatically) enabled applications to become object-oriented. This technology was called *Object Linking and Embedding* (OLE). Later, this term was extended to *OLE Automation*. OLE started to mature, and the ability to add OLE "controls" (like buttons, checkboxes, dials, and such) that each had state and behavior made construction of applications possible from prebuilt components. The Windows world back then was 16-bit, and, over time, the OLE technologies were superseded by technologies built on the Component Object Model. OLE controls gave way to lightweight ActiveX controls and "controls" that did not provide a user interface (COM objects). Complete applications could then be built by combining the functionality of all these objects and *automating* them using a programming language.

Static versus Dynamic Invocation

COM objects can be invoked using two different methods, both of which we've briefly explored during our studies of COM objects. We see a glimpse of this invocation when we add an ATL object to our code using Visual C++.

As shown in Figure 7-1, we have two options under "Interfaces"—Dual and Custom. The Dual option is the default, and, thus far, we have built our ATL objects using this option. Choosing a dual interface allows the object interfaces to inherit from a special interface called `IDispatch`. The `IDispatch` interface is the workhorse behind automation and *dynamic invocation*.

Let's look at the differences between dynamic invocation and static invocation. In Chapter 6, we investigated two different ways to instantiate a COM object and call its methods, and we built two C++ console applications to illustrate these points. Those two methods were

1. The `#include` method—In our source code, we included the `_i.c` and `.h` files that were generated by the IDL compiler (MIDL). These two

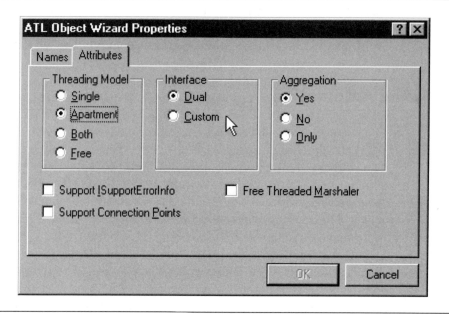

Figure 7-1. Choosing the Dual option.

files contain the interface and class GUIDs that were required by `CoCreateInstance()`, which was used to create an instance of the COM object.

2. The `#import` method—The type library embedded in the DLL file of the COM object was extracted to obtain the interface and class information.

Each of these methods used *static invocation* to call methods of the COM object, but this is not always a versatile solution. In each case, we knew exactly what the class IDs, COM interfaces, and methods were that were available to us. Both the MIDL-generated files and the type library told us that information. Often, however, we run into a situation where the MIDL-generated files are not available to us. For example, commercially made COM objects won't contain these files as part of the COM object software distribution. Another problem is that we may be working in a development environment, such as interpreted VBScript/ASP, that has no concept of importing a type library. Since VBScript is not compiled, it cannot determine types, GUIDs, or other necessary information like our sample C++ programs. With these interpreted languages, we're "flying blind" because we won't know whether the types and

identifiers that we are using are correct until either our method calls succeed
or we generate a runtime error.

It's also important to remember that a programmer of a COM object is
under no obligation to implement the IDispatch interface. One of the disadvantages to using IDispatch is that using it as the conduit to call other interface methods adds overhead. For this reason and to decrease the size of the
code, a programmer may opt not to add support for automation to the COM
object and just use custom interfaces that he/she writes.

When we use an interpreted language, as in VBScript, we've stated that
you cannot do any compile- or design-time checking for the types of parameters used in method calls. Typically, if an incorrect data type is used, the system will return an error message from the automation layer. We know,
however, that our COM object expects to have certain types passed to its
methods (as the IDL defines for us). VBScript is not a strongly typed language. In fact, if you recall from Chapter 2, the only supported variable type is
VARIANT. This may sound like a design problem, but it really isn't because the
Universal Marshaler knows how to handle variant-type data. So, in effect, if
the data you are passing in your parameters can be contained in a variant, the
data will be correctly marshaled. This data includes any kind of alphanumeric
string, date, number, or object.

IDispatch and Dispinterfaces

What makes up the IDispatch interface, and how does it implement automation? Basically, a method of the IDispatch interface is used to call methods of a
dispinterface (which is short for "dispatch interface"). A dispinterface is a COM
interface that has methods that are callable through automation with
IDispatch. In other words, a dispinterface is an interface that inherits the
IDispatch interface. If you look at the IDL for our Pizza object, you'll see this:

```
[
    object,
    uuid(5F649750-D3DE-11D2-8369-006097ADC885),
    dual,
    helpstring("IPizzaSample Interface"),
    pointer_default(unique)
]
interface IPizzaSample : IDispatch
{
    [id(1), helpstring("Rolls out the pizza dough to the specific ⌐
diameter")] HRESULT RollDough();
```

```
    [id(2), helpstring("Prepare the toppings for the pizza")]
HRESULT PrepareToppings();
    [id(3), helpstring("Bake the pizza for the specified number of
minutes")] HRESULT Bake([in] short nMinutes, [out, retval] BSTR
*rsltMsg);
    [propget, id(4), helpstring("Set or get the diameter of the
pizza")] HRESULT Diameter([out, retval] short *pVal);
    [propput, id(4), helpstring("Set or get the diameter of the
pizza")] HRESULT Diameter([in] short newVal);
};
```

The IPizzaSample interface (shown in boldface) shows that it inherits from IDispatch. So, by definition, that makes it a dispinterface. Inside the interface block are all the methods of the interface. Notice that each method contains an id() next to it. Each of these identifiers is called a DISPID (which is short for "dispatch ID"). These DISPIDs serve as an index for the IDispatch "dispatching" method Invoke(), which actually makes the call to our method. This process of getting a DISPID and calling its corresponding method is in contrast to the way methods are invoked on custom interfaces, which index the vtable directly and then make the method call.

Behind the Scenes with Invoke()

When we want to call a method on a COM object, such as our PizzaSample object, we need a mechanism to find out the DISPID of the method that we wish to call. This is necessary since, in our ASP VBScript code, we reference our object methods using textual names. IDispatch contains a method called GetIDsOfNames() for just that purpose. This is what the method looks like:

```
GetIDsOfNames( REFIID riid,
               LPOLESTR *rgsznames,
               UINT cNames,
               LCID lcid,
               DISPID *rgDispId )
```

The first parameter is always IID_NULL. The second parameter is an array of method names for which we want to retrieve DISPIDs. Each element in the array is expressed as an LPOLESTR (a wide-character string). The third parameter, cNames, is the number of elements in the rgsznames array.

An important feature of automation is its multilingual support. This is necessary since there may be some non-English-speaking programmers using your objects. These programmers would express the names of methods in their native language. For this purpose, we have the ability to specify a locale ID, which is the fourth parameter. In most situations, a constant will be placed here (LOCALE_SYSTEM_DEFAULT), which tells GetIDsOfNames() to use the locale that the client program is using. The last parameter, the return value, is an array of DISPIDs for the methods specified in rgsznames. Notice that our PizzaSample property, Diameter, shares the same DISPID for the get and put methods. In most cases, DISPIDs are unique to an interface, but properties are the exception. We see how to handle this perceived ambiguity in our discussion of Invoke(), the magical method of IDispatch.

Invoke()

You can say that Invoke() does the real work behind automation. It is the IDispatch method that "dispatches" or calls methods on our interface. The DISPID method is one item that we need for our call to Invoke(). Let's look at the parameters to Invoke() to see what we'll need to make the call:

```
Invoke( DISPID dispIdMember, REFIID riid, LCID lcid, WORD wFlags,
DISPPARAMS* pDispParams, VARIANT* pVarResult, EXCEPINFO* pExcepInfo,
UINT* puArgErr)
```

The dispIdMember is the ID of the method we wish to call. Again, this is the number in the IDL that is listed as id(x). The second parameter is reserved in the current implementation of Invoke(), so you should pass the constant IID_NULL for this parameter. The lcid indicates the locale ID that the client is using. The object can use this value to return messages back to the client in the appropriate language.

The wFlags parameter deserves some explanation. You may have noticed that our Diameter property of the PizzaSample object is read/write capable. So, it follows that the property has two methods: get and put. In the IDL, Visual C++ assigns each of these methods the same DISPID. We need to be able to tell the Invoke() parameter about the way that we are using the method specified in the DISPID parameter. Since the DISPIDs are the same for the Diameter method, we can distinguish between the types of usage, or context, by specifying one of the following constants in the wFlags parameter:

DISPATCH_METHOD—Used when calling a normal "method." The method can return a value.

DISPATCH_PROPERTYGET—Used when the method gets the value of a property.

DISPATCH_PROPERTYPUT—Used when the method sets the value of a property.

DISPATCH_PROPERTYPUTREF—Used when the method sets a property's value by reference.

The DISPPARAMS Structure

The pDispParams is a pointer to the structure DISPPARAMS, which is used to specify the parameters to the method that we are calling. The DISPPARAMS structure is versatile because we can package the parameters in a universal way. The definition of the structure is as follows:

```
typedef struct tagDISPPARAMS
{
     VARIANTARG* rgvarg;
     DISPID* rgdispidNamedArgs;
     UINT cArgs;
     UINT cNamedArgs;
} DISPPARAMS;
```

VARIANT, VARIANTARG*, and Such

The first member of the structure, VARIANTARG, is an array of variants. A VARIANTARG is actually the same as a VARIANT (it is typedefed to a variant). And what is a VARIANT exactly? In VBScript, we know it is a general-purpose data type into which we can put all kinds of data. "Under the hood" in C++, a VARIANT is a discriminated union. The discriminator is vt. Visual C++ contains a series of constants that you can use to set the type of data that is contained in the variant.

To construct a VARIANTARG array, we can use the C++ new keyword to create a new array of a specified size like this:

```
VARIANTARG* pMyArgArray = new VARIANTARG[1];
```

This will create a VARIANT array of one element.

We must now initialize each variant in the array and set the discriminator to the types that are required by the method that we wish to call. Our example will lead up to us calling the Bake() method of the PizzaSample object. The Bake() method takes a single short parameter, the number of minutes to bake the pizza. To initialize the VARIANT array, we use the VariantInit() function to prepare the first element of the array for accepting data. The

VARIANTARG array, like most arrays in C/C++, is zero-based, so we initialize the first (and only) variant like this:

```
VariantInit( &pMyArgArray[0] );
```

Next, we set the discriminator, vt, to a short. We use the constant VT_I2 for this purpose. This constant is part of a long list of constants that represent all the different types of data that can be contained in a variant. We'll list all of them in a moment. Let's show the code to initialize the variant. In the example, we'll set the variant value to 15 (for 15 minutes):

```
pMyArgArray[0].vt = VT_I2;
pMyArgArray[0].iVal = 15;
```

Next, we need to specify the number of arguments that we are passing in the structure. This is where we manipulate the pDispParams structure. We'll first assign the cArgs member of the structure to 1. This number reflects the number of parameters to the Bake() method:

```
DISPPARAMS myDisp;
myDisp.cArgs = 1;
```

Now, we need to assign the rgvarg structure member to the VARIANT array pMyArgArray. So, we put in this line of code:

```
myDisp.rgvarg = pMyArgArray;
```

We have one final item to set, and that is the cNamedArgs structure member. This parameter notifies Invoke() of the number of named arguments that the client specified in its call to the object method. For instance, some languages (like Visual Basic and Visual Basic for Applications) can use named arguments in their method calls. Named arguments can be used to specify parameters to a method without regard to the order in which they are listed. For example, if we have a method called MethodX(), and it took two parameters, param1 and param2, we would normally call it like this:

```
param1 = 3
param2 = 5
MethodX param1, param2
```

The call to MethodX is done by position, which means that the order in which we pass parameters is the same as the ordering defined in the IDL for the function. We can also use named arguments to call MethodX(). For example, we could say this instead:

```
MethodX param2:=5, param1:=3
```

Notice that we switched the ordering of the parameters. Since we specified what value each parameter should be assigned, ordering is not important. Calling a method using named arguments is not supported in VBScript, so the call to Invoke() would have the value 0 set for cNamedArgs:

```
myDisp.cNamedArgs = 0;
```

Note: When we have no named arguments, the rgdispidNamedArgs parameter is set to NULL.

Getting Our DISPID

We are almost to the point where we are ready to call the Invoke() method. We are, however, missing one crucial piece of information. That would be the DISPID of the Bake() method. In our VBScript, we don't speak in terms of DISPIDs when we call methods. Instead, we use a textual name (like "Bake") to refer to a method. We need a way to obtain the DISPID of a method name that we specify. The method GetIDsOfNames() of the IDispatch interface does just that:

```
HRESULT GetIDsOfNames(
REFIID riid,
OLECHAR* rgszNames,
unsigned int cNames,
LCID lcid,
DISPID* rgDispId );
```

GetIDsOfNames() works by supplying an array of names for which you wish to find the DISPIDs (parameter 2) along with the number of elements in that array (parameter 3). You can select a particular locale ID (parameter 4) for a context to interpret the names. If successful, rgDispId should contain an array of DISPIDs for each name that you supply in rgszNames. If not all names in rgszNames can be found, GetIDsOfNames() places the constant

DISP_UNKNOWN inside each element in the rgszNames array for every name that it cannot resolve. In addition, the HRESULT value DISP_E_UNKNOWNNAME is returned for every name that GetIDsOfNames() cannot resolve. S_OK is returned if all names were resolved.

Going back to our PizzaSample object (with the Bake() method), the code to find the DISPID for "Bake" can be written like this:

❶ ```
HRESULT hresult;
IDispatch* pPizza = NULL;
DISPID dispid;
OLECHAR* szMember = "Bake";
```

❷ ```
HRESULT hresult = CoCreateInstance( CLSID_PizzaSample,
                                    NULL, CLSCTX_INPROC_SERVER,
                                    IID_IDispatch,
                                    ( void **)&pPizza );
```

❸ ```
hresult = pPizza->GetIDsOfNames(
     IID_NULL,
     &szMember,
     1, LOCALE_SYSTEM_DEFAULT,
     &dispid);

if (dispid != DISPID_UNKNOWN)
{
        // do something with the object
}
pPizza->Release();
```

The preceding code begins with some variable declarations.❶ We are dealing again with an array that contains just a single element, as is the case with DISPID dispid. This variable will hold the DISPID array (with one element) returned by GetIDsOfNames(). Make sure that your code has allocated adequate memory to hold your results. After declaring our variables, we create an object instance of the PizzaSample object.❷ In our previous examples, we had CoCreateInstance() return a handle to the IID_IPizzaSample interface. We are dealing with automation now, so we obtain a handle to the IDispatch interface instead. Remember: Our object was created for automation, so we already know it supports this interface.

Now comes the call to GetIDsOfNames().❸ The szNames array is initialized with one element, the string "Bake." We pass that along to the
```

GetIDsOfNames() method along with the count, locale ID, and standard REFIID of IID_NULL. Upon success, dispid should contain the DISPID of the Bake() method.

Let's look at the complete code for creating the object, obtaining the IDispatch interface, setting up the Invoke() parameters, and calling the Bake() method:

```
VARIANTARG* pMyArgArray = new VARIANTARG[1];
VariantInit( &pMyArgArray[0] );
pMyArgArray[0].vt = VT_I2;
pMyArgArray[0].iVal = 15;

DISPPARAMS myDisp;

myDisp.rgvarg = pMyArgArray;
myDisp.cNamedArgs = 0;
myDisp.cArgs = 1;

HRESULT hresult;
IDispatch* pPizza = NULL;
DISPID dispid;
OLECHAR* szMember = "Bake";
VARIANT *pVarResult;
EXCEPINFO *pExcepInfo;
unsigned int *puArgErr;

HRESULT hresult = CoCreateInstance( CLSID_PizzaSample,
                    NULL, CLSCTX_INPROC_SERVER,
                    IID_IDispatch,
                    ( void **)&pPizza );

hresult = pPizza->GetIDsOfNames(
    IID_NULL,
    &szMember,
    1, LOCALE_SYSTEM_DEFAULT,
    &dispid);

if ( dispid != DISPID_UNKNOWN )
{
    hresult = pPizza->Invoke( dispid,
            IID_NULL,
            LOCALE_USER_DEFAULT, DISPATCH_METHOD, &myDisp,
            pVarResult, pExcepInfo, puArgErr);
}
pPizza->Release();
```

After the call to `Invoke()` is made, we need to retrieve the value returned by the method. This value is contained in the `pVarResult` parameter. In the case here, the `Bake()` method will return a string indicating the status of the baked pizza.

The `pExcepInfo` and `puArgErr` parameters are used to return exception information and the index of the argument that contains errors (if any), respectively. `pExcepInfo` essentially contains the data that would be contained in the `Err` object (in VBScript).

Midstream Summary

Here's what we've illustrated so far.

- Dynamic invocation is the method that automation clients (like VBScript) use to call COM objects.
- Automation may be the only mechanism available to us to call COM objects.
- `IDispatch` is the COM interface that enables automation.
- The `Invoke()` method of the `IDispatch` interface acts as a bridge used to call a method on another interface.
- Automation is very important since it allows us to programmatically determine more information about a COM object than does `QueryInterface()`. `IDispatch` can tell us about the interfaces that a COM object supports and the methods of those interfaces, without having to rely on a type library or supplemental definition files.

Data Types

COM and automation need to be able to work with many different types of data. The problem with working with different data types involves difficulties that we may encounter when marshaling the data. To address this problem, COM has a standard set of data types that the standard COM data marshalers understand. These data types are all part of the "super-type" `VARIANT`. We've talked about variants briefly in other chapters, but now we are going to move in for a closer look at their structure.

The VARIANT Data Type

We know that a variant can hold many different kinds of data, but if a variant describes only one "type," then how is it that different types of data can be contained in it? The answer is simple—through a structure union type (or variant record, depending on which school of programming you started in!). Here's what an abridged version of the variant definition looks like:

```
struct tagVARIANT {
        VARTYPE vt;
        WORD wReserved1;
        WORD wReserved2;
        WORD wReserved3;
union {
        long            lVal;       // VT_I4
        unsigned char   bVal;       // VT_UI1
        short           iVal;       // VT_I2
        float           fltVal;     // VT_R4
        double          dblVal;     // VT_R8
        VARIANT_BOOL    boolVal;    // VT_BOOL
        SCODE           scode;      // VT_ERROR
        CY              cyVal;      // VT_CY
        DATE            date;       // VT_DATE
        BSTR            bstrVal;    // VT_BSTR
        IUnknown        *punkVal;   // VT_UNKNOWN
        IDispatch       *pdispVal;  // VT_DISPATCH
        SAFEARRAY       *parray;    // VT_ARRAY
        // .
        // .
        // .
        VARIANT         *pvarVal;   // VT_BYREF|VT_VARIANT
        void            * byref;    // Generic ByRef
        };
};
```

If you recall, a union in C/C++ has a discriminator, and that discriminator is the variable vt. Listed in the comments for each variable declaration in the structure is the constant to use when working with vt. If, for example, we wanted to declare a new variant variable and store the number 3 in it, we could write code such as the following:

```
v.iVal = 3;
v.vt = VT_I2;          // short
```

In this code, we assign a value of 3 to the variant v. VT_I2 represents the tag for a short. It is very important to assign the type of variable to the variant.

Variants have a fixed size. The VARIANT structure is 16 bytes in length. If you look at the first four fields in the structure, you'll notice the types VARTYPE and WORD. Each of these is equivalent to an unsigned short, which is 2 bytes. In the current implementation of COM, only the first field, vt, is used. The 6 bytes of storage used for the remaining three reserved values is padding. The data portion of the VARIANT makes up for the remaining 8 bytes. This is large enough to handle any of the data types in the structure, be they pointers, integers, currency, and so on.

Variant Utility Functions

The COM API contains a set of utilities to work with variants. These functions take care of initialization, copying, and destruction of the data contained in the variant. There are also many other routines for manipulating a variant, but we will cover only the most commonly used ones.

Initializing a New Variant

```
void VariantInit(VARIANT * pv);
```

VariantInit() will initialize a new variant. Initially, when this call is made, the discriminator vt is set to VT_EMPTY. This indicates that we don't yet have a type designation for the variant. To initialize a new variant and assign it a value, you could say something like this:

```
VARIANT vMyVariant;
VariantInit(&vMyVariant);
vMyVariant.lVal = 1000;
vMyVariant.vt = VT_I4;
```

Here, we first declare a new variant variable called vMyVariant. We then pass that uninitialized variant by reference to VariantInit() for creation. We want to store the number 1000 as a long integer, so the lVal field of the structure is assigned this number. Finally, the last line sets the discriminator to VT_I4, the constant indicating that this variant is a long integer.

Destroying a Variant

```
HRESULT VariantClear(VARIANT * pv);
```

VariantClear() performs the necessary cleanup and freeing of memory held by the variant. It returns an HRESULT, which indicates the success or

failure of the call. Call this function when your routine is done using a
variant:

```
hr = VariantClear(&vMyVariant);
```

Copying a Variant

```
HRESULT VariantCopy(VARIANT * pvDst, VARIANT * pvSrc);
```

Several functions are available for copying one variant to another. Some
can also do a sort of "type conversion" by changing the discriminator.
VariantCopy() will copy pvSrc to pvDst. In order for the call to work
correctly, storage must be allocated for the destination variant with
VariantInit(). At the end of the call, both pvSrc and pvDst should be
identical. The HRESULT that is returned indicates the success or failure of
the call. This function does a "by-reference" copy of the data, meaning
that the data itself is not duplicated but that a new reference to the data
contained in pvSrc is made. Here is an example:

```
HRESULT hr;
VARIANT varDst;
VariantInit(&varDst);
hr = VariantCopy(&varDst, &varSrc);
```

Changing the Type of a Variant

```
HRESULT VariantChangeType(VARIANT * pvDst, VARIANT * pvSrc, WORD
    wFlags, VARTYPE vt);
```

Use VariantChangeType() to change the type of a variant. Normally, this
routine performs a copy of the variant variable from pvSrc to pvDst. You can
perform a conversion in place if you specify your variable as both the source
and the destination. The type that you wish to convert to is contained in the
vt parameter. The wFlags parameter would normally contain zero for any
conversion that you perform on variants that are not objects. The following
example performs an in-place conversion:

```
varSrc.lVal = 50
hr = VariantChangeType(&varSrc, &varSrc, 0, VT_I2);
```

The CComVariant Class

When working with variants, you must remember to perform many house-keeping tasks. ATL provides a wrapper class for the variant that provides utility functions for the VARIANT data type to make those housekeeping tasks easier. Another added bonus to using the CComVariant class is that the construction and destruction are handled automatically by the class. CComVariant also contains support for many overloaded operators that make tasks such as initialization a snap.

The default constructor and destructor for CComVariant remove the burden of having to call VariantInit() and VariantClear().

The CComVariant class contains many different constructors. Each one can take a different data type parameter. Table 7-1 lists the constructors and provides a description of each.

Working with Properties

One of the challenges of writing COM objects using the ATL is how to manipulate the myriad of data types available for us to use. If you come from the ANSI C/C++ camp, you'll notice that many data types don't appear to be standard ANSI C/C++ data types. This is true to an extent. When we build distributed applications where many components can be scattered across the enterprise on many different kinds of hardware, standards have to come about in order for each component piece to be able to communicate with the others. We've studied the VARIANT type and how it simplifies marshaling of data. There are also many other data types for us to explore. We will need to know how to work with each of these when we implement properties (as well as parameters to methods).

Working with Numerical Data in Properties

Adding a property to an ATL object is accomplished using the visual COM object editing tools. In Chapter 6, we worked with this when we added the Diameter property to our PizzaSample object. The process involved two steps: (1) declaring our class member variable and (2) adding the property stub code. The "Add Property" command also allowed us to specify whether or not the property was read-only or read/write through the "Function Type" settings. The stub that is generated by the Add Property command does not actually do anything; we needed to add code to save the value of the property.

Table 7-1. CComVariant Class Constructors

Constructor	Description
CComVariant( );	No initialization.
CComVariant(const CComVariant& *varSrc*);	Use another CComVariant for initialization.
CComVariant(const VARIANT& *varSrc*);	Use another VARIANT for initialization.
CComVariant(LPCOLESTR *lpsz*);	Initialize to a Unicode string.
CComVariant(LPCSTR *lpsz*);	Initialize to an ANSI string.
CComVariant(BSTR *bstrSrc*);	Initialize to a BSTR.
CComVariant(bool *bSrc*);	Initialize to a Boolean value.
CComVariant(int *nSrc*);	Initialize to an integer.
CComVariant(BYTE *nSrc*);	Intitalize to a byte.
CComVariant(short *nSrc*);	Initialize to a short.
CComVariant(long *nSrc,* VARTYPE *vtSrc* = VT_I4);	Initialize to a long integer.
CComVariant(float *fltSrc*);	Initialize to a float.
CComVariant(double *dblSrc*);	Initialize to a double.
CComVariant(CY *cySrc*);	Initalize to currency type.
CComVariant(IDispatch* *pSrc*);	Initialize to pointer to automation interface IDispatch.
CComVariant(IUnknown* *pSrc*);	Initialize to IUnknown interface pointer.

In the case of the `Diameter` property of our `PizzaSample` object, the implementation was simple enough:

```
STDMETHODIMP CPizzaSample::get_Diameter(short *pVal)
{
    // TODO: Add your implementation code here
    *pVal = m_Diameter;
    return S_OK;
}
STDMETHODIMP CPizzaSample::put_Diameter(short newVal)
{
    // TODO: Add your implementation code here
    m_Diameter = newVal;
    return S_OK;
}
```

A "put" operation for a numeric variable is straightforward to implement, as just indicated. The `put_Diameter()` function takes a single parameter, `newVal`, which contains the value to the right of the property assignment:

```
ObjPizza.Diameter = 14        ' newVal contains the value 14
```

The assignment statement simply sets the value of the `m_Diameter` class variable to the value of `newVal`. This is a minimal implementation of the `put_Diameter()` function. You may also want to add more code to do tasks such as data validation before the value gets assigned to our member variable.

In this particular sample, we use a `short` parameter. When using the `PizzaSample` object in a production environment, we need to be careful of two situations. The first is when we try to assign a number that is too large to be contained in a `short`. Runtime overflow errors may occur as a result. Second, we are counting on the user of the object to pass some sort of numeric data to the property. If the object user tried to assign a string to the property, a type mismatch error would occur. Using a `long` instead of a `short` for the property member variable could possibly solve the first problem. If we cannot be sure of the type of data that is going to be assigned to the property, we can make the property functions accept a `VARIANT` type. Once the value has been passed, we can use the discriminator to determine the type of variable that was passed. If the data is of the appropriate type (or can be converted to the correct type), we can make that conversion at that time and assign the value to the member variable.

The `get_Diameter()` function essentially performs the reverse operation of the `put_Diameter()` function. We need to retrieve the value of the member variable that corresponds to our property and return it in the `pVal` parameter. The `pVal` parameter is passed by reference to the function, and the value is what is returned on an inquiry into the property value, such as in this call:

```
nDiameter = objPizza.Diameter
```

Any of the ATL-supported data types used for numeric data (`long`, `unsigned char`, `short`, `float`, `double`) can be used in properties in the manner just described. Each one supports the standard (=) assignment operator since they are simple scalar types.

Working with Strings

Working with strings works a little differently than the scalar types we looked at so far. The process of marshaling string data is different from other variable types. For variable types such as `short` and `long`, we already know the size of the data to be marshaled. Strings, however, can be of varying lengths. Automation uses a special string ADT (abstract data type) called *BSTR* to solve this problem.

A BSTR is essentially a wide-character string. The wide-character string allows us to support Unicode, which ensures compatibility among many different languages. The BSTR also knows its own length. A DWORD value prefixes the actual character data, and this value is the length of the string. This method is advantageous because ANSI C/C++ strings are null-terminated. The length of ANSI C/C++ strings is determined by traversing the string until the null character at the end of the string is encountered. Since the BSTR does not rely on having this marker at the end of the string, the BSTR can contain null characters as part of its string.

COM provides a series of rudimentary utility functions to manage BSTRs. They handle the creation, destruction, and length-management of the string. The most common BSTR manipulation routines are described next.

Creating a New BSTR

```
BSTR SysAllocString( OLECHAR FAR* sz );
```

`SysAllocString()` will initialize a new BSTR. If sufficient memory is available, it will return a new BSTR initialized with the wide-character string in `sz`.

For example, if we wanted to create a new BSTR with the text "Pizza with Sausage," we could say something like the following:

```
BSTR myBSTR;
myBSTR = SysAllocString( OLECHAR( "Pizza with Sausage" ) );
```

We use the `OLECHAR()` macro to tell the compiler to treat our string constant as a wide-character string. This is necessary since `SysAllocString()` expects a wide-character string as its parameter.

Freeing a BSTR

```
void SysFreeString( BSTR bstr );
```

Call `SysFreeString()` to free memory occupied by a BSTR when you are done using it.

Determining the Length of a BSTR

```
UINT SysStringLen( BSTR bstr );
```

`SysStringLen()` returns the number of characters in `bstr`. This does not include any null-terminating characters, if any. (Compare this function with its counterpart `SysStringByteLen()` that counts the number of bytes, not characters, in the string.) Here is an example:

```
BSTR myBSTR;
UINT myLength;
myBSTR = SysAllocString( OLECHAR( "Pizza with Sausage" ) );
myLength = SysStringLen( myBSTR );
```

Reallocating a BSTR

```
HRESULT SysReAllocString( BSTR FAR* pbstr, OLECHAR FAR* sz );
```

`SysReAllocString()` "reuses" a previously allocated BSTR variable and assigns a new value to it. Internally, a new BSTR is allocated for the string `sz`. The `pbstr` variable is freed and then is set to point to the new BSTR created from `sz`.

The CComBSTR Class

As you may have guessed, the `CComBSTR` class is to BSTRs as `CComVariant` is to variants. `CComBSTR` contains methods for creating BSTRs, freeing BSTRs, concatenation, finding the length of the BSTR, and other miscellaneous functions.

CComBSTR has many different constructors. Most take a string literal of some kind and a length of characters to copy into the CComBSTR's one data member, m_str. Table 7-2 lists the different constructors for CComBSTR.

Let's look at a few examples of working with the CComBSTR constructor. First, let's say we had an ANSI string literal that we wanted to make into a CComBSTR. We would choose the CComBSTR(LPCSTR *pSrc*) constructor for this operation:

```
CComBSTR myCComBSTR( "This is a test string" );
```

After this operation, the data member m_str should contain the string "This is a test string." Even though our string literal was ANSI, the string will be stored as a wide-character (Unicode) string in the m_str data member.

Let's look at another example. Suppose we had a Unicode string literal, and we wanted to initialize a new CComBSTR using only the first five characters of the string. We would use the CComBSTR(int *nSize*, LPCOLESTR *sz*) constructor to accomplish this, as this example shows:

```
CComBSTR myCComBSTR( 5, OLESTR("Pizza Special" ) );
```

As shown in Table 7-3, the CComBSTR methods simplify some common string operations and provide other miscellaneous routines.

Table 7-2. CComBSTR Class Constructors

Constructor	Description
CComBSTR( );	Empty BSTR, m_str is set to null.
CComBSTR(int *nSize*, LPCOLESTR *sz*);	Initialize to Unicode string, first nSize characters.
CComBSTR(int *nSize*, LPCSTR *sz*);	Initialize to ANSI string, first nSize characters.
CComBSTR(LPCOLESTR *pSrc*);	Initialize to Unicode string.
CComBSTR(LPCSTR *pSrc*);	Initialize to ANSI string.
CComBSTR(const CComBSTR& *src*);	Initialize to another CComBSTR.

Table 7-3. CComBSTR Methods

Method Syntax	Description

Append
 	
  void Append(const CComBSTR& *bstrSrc*);
  void Append(LPCOLESTR *lpsz*);
  void Append(LPCSTR *lpsz*);
  void Append(LPCOLESTR *lpsz,* int *nLen*);
	Appends the parameter string to the m_str data member of CComBSTR.

AppendBSTR void AppendBSTR(BSTR *p*);	Appends a BSTR to the data member m_str.
Attach void Attach(BSTR *src*);	Assigns a BSTR to the CComBSTR object (m_str data member).
Copy BSTR Copy( ) const;	Returns the BSTR in m_str.
Detach BSTR Detach( );	Returns m_str from the CComBSTR object and sets CComBSTR to null.
Empty void Empty( );	Frees memory used by m_str.
Length unsigned int Length( ) const;	Returns the length of m_str.

LoadString
 	
  bool LoadString(HINSTANCE *hInst,*
  UINT *nID*);
  bool LoadString(UINT *nID*);
	Loads a string from a resource.

ReadFromStream
 	
  HRESULT ReadFromStream(IStream*
  pStream);
	Loads a BSTR object from a stream.

WriteToStream
 	
  HRESULT WriteToStream(IStream*
  pStream);
	Saves m_str to a stream.

We've seen the use of the `Copy()` method before in our `PizzaSample` object. The `Bake()` method returned a BSTR depending on the results of the "baking period":

```
STDMETHODIMP CPizzaSample::Bake(short nMinutes, BSTR *rsltMsg)
{
    // TODO: Add your implementation code here

    CComBSTR bstrReturnMsg1("Your pizza is done!" );
    CComBSTR bstrReturnMsg2( "You need to bake it longer than that!")
);

    if ( nMinutes < 10 )
    {
        *rsltMsg = bstrReturnMsg2.Copy();
    }
    else
    {
        *rsltMsg = bstrReturnMsg1.Copy();
    }
    return S_OK;
}
```

The return value from the method is the data in `rsltMsg`, and our code declared two `CComBSTR` classes. Each of these used the `CComBSTR` constructor taking an ANSI string for the initialization:

```
CComBSTR bstrReturnMsg1( "Your pizza is done!" );
CComBSTR bstrReturnMsg2( "You need to bake it longer than that!" );
```

Then, we see

```
*rsltMsg = bstrReturnMsg2.Copy();
```

The call to `Copy()` returns a copy of the `m_str` data member (which is a BSTR), and we assign it to the `rsltMsg` parameter.

CComBSTR also overloads certain C++ operators. These are very convenient for manipulation of the string data. For example, we can set the `m_str` member of the `CComBSTR` class (which contains the actual BSTR) using an overloaded assignment operator (=). So, we could write

```
CComBSTR bstrMyBSTR;
bstrMyBSTR = "I love pizza";
```

The increment operator (+=) is also overloaded. You can use it to perform string concatenations. Expanding on the preceding example, we can add the following line to concatenate another string to the base string:

```
// bstrMyBSTR now contains "I love pizza and lasagna!"
bstrMyBSTR += " and lasagna!";
```

Using the CComBSTR wrapper class for strings is convenient because the class provides built-in storage management. This means that, after code execution has ended for a particular block of code (like a function, try . . . catch block, and so on), the memory used by the CComBSTR is freed.

The "Other" BSTR Wrapper Class

In addition to the ATL-supplied CComBSTR wrapper class, Windows provides a BSTR class called _bstr_t. This class provides functionality similar to CComBSTR, but _bstr_t does not provide the automatic storage-management features that CComBSTR offers (i.e., you must explicitly free the memory occupied by the class). A brief description of _bstr_t and its member functions and operators is given in Table 7-4.

Note: You can find more information on _bstr_t from the MSDN Library. You can find the documentation for _bstr_t at http://msdn.microsoft. com/library/devprods/vs6/visualc/vclang/_pluslang__bstr_t.htm

Converting COM Data Types

COM provides a couple of ways to convert data from one type to another. If we work with variants exclusively, "converting" the data to another type is a simple affair. We need only change the VARIANT discriminator, vt, to the type we wish. COM provides two functions for performing that operation: VariantChangeType() or VariantChangeTypeEx(). Both functions are identical in functionality, but VariantChangeTypeEx() can accept a locale ID. This is useful for data types, like CURRENCY, since the standards for formatting currency values varies by country.

Like the BSTR, the CComVariant class ships with a few helper methods that wrap the lower-level type-changing functions like VariantChangeTypeEx(). The ChangeType() method provides variant type changing:

```
HRESULT ChangeType( VARTYPE vtNew, const VARIANT* pSrc = NULL );
```

Table 7-4.   The _bstr_t Member Functions and Operators

Operations	Description
Copy()	Constructs a copy of the encapsulated BSTR.
Length()	Returns the length of the encapsulated BSTR.
Operators	**Description**
Operator =	Assigns a new value to an existing **_bstr_t** object.
Operator +=	Appends characters to the end of the **_bstr_t** object.
Operator +	Concatenates two strings.
Operator !	Checks if the encapsulated BSTR is a null string.
Operator ==, !=, <, >, <=, >=	Compares two **_bstr_t** objects.
Operator **wchar_t***, **char***	Extracts the pointers to the encapsulated Unicode or multibyte BSTR object.

vtNew contains the type to which to convert. pSrc contains the variant to convert. If this value is NULL, then the variant of the CComVariant will be used. This would be an in-place conversion.

As an example, let's convert a BSTR value that holds the string "345." We want to convert it to a long so that we can perform, for instance, mathematical functions on the value. We could write the following:

```
CComVariant myVariant( "345" );
myVariant.ChangeType( VT_I4, NULL );
myVariant.lVal += 10;
myVariant.ChangeType( VT_BSTR, NULL );
```

This code first initializes a new CComVariant, myVariant, using an ANSI string literal in the constructor. The next statement performs an in-place conversion of myVariant to VT_I4 (long integer). The following statement refers to the lVal member of the variant, which should contain the value 345. We add 10 to that value. The final statement converts the variant back to a BSTR, the original form.

Working with Methods

COM methods have the ability to accept parameters as part of their definition. When we added a method to an ATL object using the "Add Method" command, the dialog box contained an option for entering the definition for the parameters (the "Parameters" dialog). The text entered in this box is the IDL for the method. In our `PizzaSample` object, the `Bake()` method was defined as follows:

```
[in] short nMinutes, [out, retval] BSTR *rsltMsg
```

This IDL definition means that the function takes a single parameter of type `short` that is passed by value to the method. The `[in]` clause indicates this. It means that its value is used as input, and it cannot be changed.

Recall that the `Bake()` method returns a string with a status message. In our IDL string, we designate this by specifying `[out, retval]`. In IDL, `[out]` means that the parameter's value can be changed by the function. This is similar to functions that are called by reference, like the C/C++ STDIO function `scanf()`. To obtain the data from `scanf()`'s read operation, we needed to supply the address of some preallocated block of memory or variable. `[out]` parameters work in much the same manner. The additional `retval` clause means that the parameter is to be returned as the value of the function. That is, the expression:

```
ObjPizza.Bake( 30 )
```

would evaluate to the string "Your pizza is done!" Notice that the string is returned by the function and is not included in the parameter list.

Handling Other Data Types

So far, all of the data types we have been working with return simple data types, like strings and numbers. There are still some data types that we have not investigated yet. For example, how would we implement a property or method parameter that was an array of strings? Suppose, we wanted to pass around an object reference or return an object reference from a method call.

So far, we haven't dealt with these types of situations. In the next sections, we'll address these implementation issues.

Returning an Object Reference

In the course of the many COM objects that you will write, the need may arise to return an object reference to the user as the result of a method call. An example of this may be a business object that returned an ADO recordset that contained the results of a query. This may be convenient over other methods (such as returning all the data to the user through a property or method parameter as a string or other data type). If we returned a reference to an ADO Recordset object that contained the results of our query, it could provide the user of the object the ability to perform further queries against the returned data. That's a very flexible solution.

To illustrate this, let's imagine that we have a COM object with a method that returns an ADO Recordset. Returning a reference to an object requires a little trick with the `QueryInterface()` method. Here's a code snippet that illustrates the idea. This code shows how a COM method would return an ADO Recordset object.

```
STDMETHODIMP CSomeObject::ReturnRecSet(IDispatch **rstMyRecSet)
{
    _ConnectionPtr pMyCN;
    _RecordsetPtr pMyRS;
    _variant_t vtEmpty;          // used for an empty VARIANT

    pMyCN.CreateInstance(__uuidof(Connection));
    pMyCN->Open("DSN=Megabytes", "", "", -1);
    pMyRS = pMyCN->Execute("Select * From Users",
                        &vtEmpty, adCmdUnknown);

    pMyRS->QueryInterface(IID_IDispatch,
                (void**)rstMyRecSet);


return S_OK;
}
```

The IDL that corresponds to this method is this:

```
[out, retval] IDispatch **rstMyRecSet
```

The first part of this code creates an ADO Connection object. An SQL statement that retrieves all the fields from the "Users" table is executed. The Execute method of the ADO Connection object returns a Recordset object, which we hold in the pMyRS variable.

Now we return the object interface. Remember that all COM interfaces inherit from the IUnknown interface, so the QueryInterface() method is available to us through the Recordset interface smart pointer.

Since VBScript deals with automation interfaces, we need to return a reference to the IDispatch interface. The recordset object reference returned will be the retval of the method. So, if we used this COM object in VBScript, calling it would look something like this:

```
Dim rstSomeRecSet
Set rstSomeRecSet = ObjMyObj.ReturnRecSet
```

Handling Arrays

In our discussions about properties and methods, we have mentioned only scalar data types. In some cases, you may want to return an array of items, like strings or some other automation data type. ATL and COM provide a set of functions and data types to handle manipulation of arrays.

Most languages have a capability to create and manipulate arrays. In most languages (C/C++ is a good example), we think of arrays as pointers. In actuality, they are very much the same. An array represents a contiguous block of memory with elements of the same size. A pointer to the first element references the array. There is a problem with this implementation of an array. Since COM is a language-neutral standard, we need to be able to access COM arrays in a generic way. Remember that languages like VB and Java do not have any concept of a pointer. In addition, languages have differences in syntax in how arrays are accessed.

The COM SAFEARRAY

A SAFEARRAY structure is used for containing an array of one or more dimensions. ATL provides a set of wrapper classes and functions for the SAFEARRAY structure, which includes functions for initialization and access of the array elements. The layout of the SAFEARRAY structure is as follows:

```
typedef struct tagSAFEARRAY
{
    USHORT cDims;
```

```
        USHORT fFeatures;
        ULONG cbElements;
        ULONG cLocks;
        PVOID pvData;
        SAFEARRAYBOUND rgsbound[ 1 ];
} SAFEARRAY;
```

The first parameter, cDims, indicates the number of dimensions that the array contains. In our examples, we will use single-dimension arrays for simplicity. The second parameter, fFeatures, contains flags that describe the contents of the array and that are for advanced use. cbElements identifies how many bytes of storage each element takes up. cLocks is used to track memory usage (for advanced use). The pvData is where the guts of the array are (i.e., the actual data elements). PVOID is typedefed to void *. The last parameter, SAFEARRAYBOUND, is actually another structure that describes the dimensional structure of the array, and we'll look at that structure next.

The SAFEARRAYBOUND Structure

The SAFEARRAY structure's general function is to give some indication about the kind of data contained in it. The last member of this structure, SAFEARRAYBOUND, describes the dimensions of the array:

```
typedef struct tagSAFEARRAYBOUND
{
    ULONG cElements;
    LONG lLbound;
} SAFEARRAYBOUND;
```

The rgsbound member of the SAFEARRAY structure is an array of SAFEARRAYBOUND structures, one for each dimension in the array. cElements is the maximum number of elements in the array. The lLbound (lower bound) variable indicates what index to use as the lower bound of the array. For example, C/C++ typically uses zero-based arrays, while other languages (like VB or Delphi) may use an array based on, say, an index of 1. Think about what development environment your component will be used in, and make your lower array bound based on the corresponding number. Also remember that lLbound can be any number, positive or negative.

Creating a New SAFEARRAY

Use the `SafeArrayCreate()` function to initialize a new SAFEARRAY. This takes the work out of setting the structure members manually:

```
SAFEARRAY* SafeArrayCreate( VARTYPE vt, UINT cDims, SAFEARRAYBOUND*
                            rgsabound );
```

VARTYPE is an enumerated constant that tells `SafeArrayCreate()` what type of elements the array contains. Table 7-5 lists the different constants with a description of each.

Table 7-5. Constants for the VARTYPE Parameter

Constant	Description
VT_BOOL	Boolean
VT_BSTR	BSTR
VT_CY	Currency
VT_DATE	Date
VT_DISPATCH	Pointer to the **IDispatch** automation interface
VT_ERROR	SCODE
VT_I2	Signed short integer
VT_I4	Signed long integer
VT_R4	Float
VT_R8	Double
VT_UI1	Unsigned char
VT_UNKNOWN	Pointer to the **IUnknown** interface
VT_VARIANT	A variant

Armed with this information, we now can construct an array using the `SafeArrayCreate()` function. As an example, let's create an array of ten Boolean values. The first step is to make a SAFEARRAYBOUND structure and fill it in with the data we need to indicate a single-dimension array with ten elements. We can code the following:

```
SAFEARRAYBOUND aBoolArrayBound;
aBoolArrayBound.cElements = 10;
aBoolArrayBound.lLbound = 1;
```

We first declare a SAFEARRAYBOUND structure, `aBoolArrayBound`. We set the `cElements` and `lLbound` elements to indicate a single-dimension array with ten elements. We then declare a SAFEARRAY pointer to hold the pointer returned by `SafeArrayCreate()`:

```
SAFEARRAY* pBoolArray;
```

We now call the `SafeArrayCreate()` function and initialize the array with the parameters that we just provided:

```
pBoolArray = SafeArrayCreate ( VT_BOOL, 1, &aBoolArrayBound );
```

A SAFEARRAY Component Example

We are now going to demonstrate how to use a SAFEARRAY in a COM object. In particular, we need to know how to pass an array as a parameter and perhaps use a SAFEARRAY as a property. After we create the component, we'll show how easy it is to use it from VBScript.

The ArraySamp Component

We'll demonstrate using a SAFEARRAY as a property in a rudimentary component called `ArraySamp`. This is a component with no methods and a single property, `VarArray`, which can hold an array of variants. Follow these steps to create the component:

1. Begin by starting a new project using the ATL COM Wizard, and call it "ArraySamp." Select DLL as the component type.
2. Insert a new ATL object. Give the component a short name of "Array," and leave the defaults for the rest of the text boxes.

3. Right-click on the "CArray" class, and select "Add Member Variable." For the variable type, enter "SAFEARRAY*." For the variable name, enter "m_VarArray." Make the variable private. (See Figure 7-2.)

4. Add the "VarArray" property. Right-click on the "IArray" interface, and select "Add Property." Enter "VARIANT" for the property type, and make sure the get and put functions are selected in the function type area, as shown in Figure 7-3.

We now have the skeleton for our array component. We next need implementation code to populate and retrieve the contents of the m_VarArray SAFEARRAY.

Setting the VarArray Property

Let's begin with the put_VarArray() function:

```
STDMETHODIMP CArray::put_VarArray(VARIANT newVal)
{
        // Check to see if user is putting an array into our property
❶       if ( ( newVal.vt & VT_ARRAY ) == 0 )
        {
                return E_INVALIDARG;
        }
        // Is the property being set an array of variants?
❷       if ( ( newVal.vt & VT_VARIANT ) == 0 )
        {
                return E_INVALIDARG;
        }
```

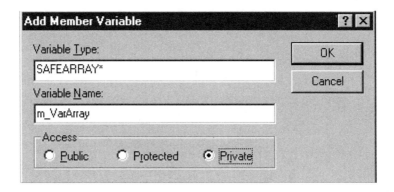

Figure 7-2. Making the variable private.

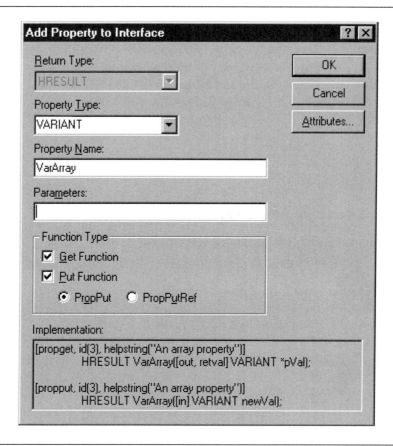

Figure 7-3.   Selecting the get and put functions.

```
                // Check to see if the variable was passed by reference
❸              if (newVal.vt & VT_BYREF)
                {
                        SafeArrayCopy( *( newVal.pparray ), &m_VarArray );
                }
                else
                {
                        SafeArrayCopy( newVal.parray, &m_VarArray );
                }
                return S_OK;
        }
```

The first part of the code checks the incoming variable type—❶that is, the type of data contained in the newVal parameter:

```
if ( ( newVal.vt & VT_ARRAY ) == 0 )
{
        return E_INVALIDARG;
}
```

newVal is a variant, so we can check the value of vt to see whether the variant has a subtype of VT_ARRAY. In our code, we perform a logical AND operation to do this. If we find that the variable passed in is not an array, then we return the HRESULT, E_INVALIDARG, which will trigger a runtime error in VBScript. The runtime error will indicate that the property is of the wrong data type:

```
Microsoft VBScript runtime error:
Invalid procedure call or argument
```

We also check newVal to see if it is an array of variants.❷ The next part of our code checks to see whether the value being passed is passed by reference instead of by value.❸ Just as before, a logical AND is performed between the constant VT_BYREF and vt:

```
// Check to see if the variable was passed by reference
if (newVal.vt & VT_BYREF)
{
        SafeArrayCopy( *( newVal.pparray ), &m_VarArray );
}
else
{
        SafeArrayCopy( newVal.parray, &m_VarArray );
}
return S_OK;
```

SafeArrayCopy() will take an entire SAFEARRAY structure and copy it to another. The first parameter is the source, and the second is the destination. In this case, the destination is our class member variable, m_VarArray. If we pass the array by reference, getting at the base address of the array requires an indirection operator on the array, as the preceding code shows. Notice that we reference the pparray tag instead of parray when using this type of indirection. Incidentally, our VarArray property will always pass its parameter by value. Passing values by reference really applies only to parameters to methods. After copying the array to the class member variable, we return from the function with the HRESULT, S_OK.

Returning the VarArray Property

The code for get_VarArray() is slightly more complicated than the code for setting the property. The main difference is that a new variant must be initialized and configured for the output parameter pVal. Here's the complete code for the get operation:

```
STDMETHODIMP CArray::get_VarArray(VARIANT *pVal)
{
    // Create a temporary SAFEARRAY and copy the contents of our
    // class member SAFEARRAY to the temporary SAFEARRAY
    SAFEARRAY* saTmp;
    SafeArrayCopy( m_VarArray, &saTmp);

    // Perform a variant initialization on the pVal parameter and set
    // the type to an array of variants
    VariantInit( pVal );
    pVal->vt = VT_ARRAY | VT_VARIANT;

    // Set the array
    pVal->parray = saTmp;

    return S_OK;
}
```

First, we need to make a copy of our member variable m_VarArray. We do this using the familiar SafeArrayCopy() function. The following code copies the contents of m_VarArray to saTmp:

```
SAFEARRAY* saTmp;
SafeArrayCopy( m_VarArray, &saTmp);
```

Now that we have a temporary working copy of our array, we shift our attention to pVal, our output parameter. We allocate space for it by calling VariantInit(). We also designate the variant as an array of variants. We do this by applying a logical OR to the VT_ARRAY and VT_VARIANT constants:

```
VariantInit( pVal );
pVal->vt = VT_ARRAY | VT_VARIANT;
```

In the final step, we set the `parray` member of the `pVal` union to the temporary SAFEARRAY that we created:

```
pVal->parray = saTmp;
```

Initializing Class Member Variables

When a COM object is instantiated, the class member variables will normally not be initialized to any values. It is very likely (especially in C++) that they will contain "garbage." It would be convenient to be able, upon class construction, to initialize class variables to useful values. How do we invoke such code, and how does the object know when to run it?

The answer lies in a special function called `FinalConstruct()`. You add this function to your COM object class when you want to perform preliminary initialization on the class members of your object. Using Visual C++, this process is easy. Simply right-click on the "CArray" class object, and select "Add Member Function." Figure 7-4 shows the syntax to enter in the dialog box.

In our `FinalConstruct()` function, we initialize the class member variable `m_VarArray`. We start be creating a new SAFEARRAYBOUND structure and

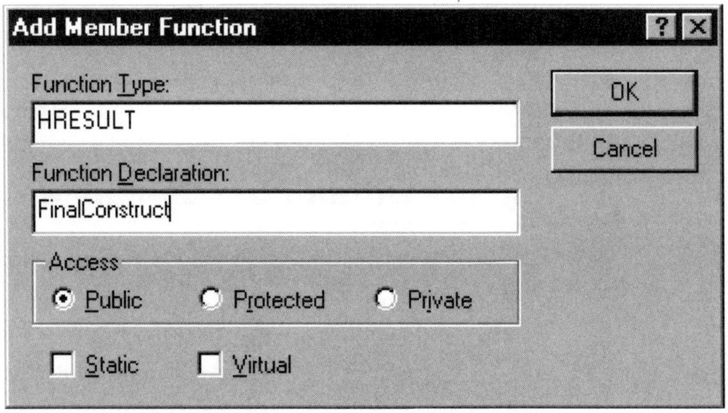

Figure 7-4. The Add Member Function dialog.

setting it up to specify a zero-length array with one dimension. Then, the array is created using the `SafeArrayCreate()` function:

```
SAFEARRAY* SafeArrayCreate( VARTYPE vt, UINT cDims, SAFEARRAYBOUND* ↵
rgsabound );
```

The first parameter, `vt`, specifies the type of array to create (i.e., the data type of the individual elements). `cDims` is the number of dimensions in the array. `rgsabound` is a pointer to a SAFEARRAYBOUND structure. Our array is a single-dimensional array of variants. So, we call `SafeArrayCreate()` like this:

```
// Make a new SAFEARRAYBOUND with zero length
SAFEARRAYBOUND sab[] = {0, 0};
// Create the array
m_VarArray = SafeArrayCreate( VT_VARIANT, 1, sab );
```

Here's the complete function implementation:

```
HRESULT CArray::FinalConstruct()
{
    // Initialize the new array

    // Make a new SAFEARRAYBOUND with zero length
    SAFEARRAYBOUND sab[] = {0, 0};

    // Create the array
    m_VarArray = SafeArrayCreate( VT_VARIANT, 1, sab );

    return S_OK;
}
```

Accessing ASP Objects within COM Components

Occasionally, you may want your component to interact with the ASP environment. It would be convenient if we could do tasks like requesting information about what was sent in the query string, asking what session or application variables have values, or retrieving HTTP environment variables. We know how to do this already; the ASP intrinsic objects support this functionality. But what happens if you are inside a C++ component? It is not directly obvious how to access these facilities.

Adding an ActiveX Server Component

When you are working with an ATL COM project, you have the option to add a special type of ATL object called "ActiveX Server Component." When you select "New ATL Object" from the Insert menu, you will see the option in the dialog box, as Figure 7-5 shows.

Adding an ActiveX Server component to your project works in the same way as adding a "Simple Object." A new property sheet is added to the dialog called "ASP." This is where we configure options for the new ASP object, as Figure 7-6 shows.

The option labeled "OnStartPage/OnEndPage" adds two methods called `OnStartPage` and `OnEndPage` to the new object. These methods are called when the ASP page starts to be parsed and when processing of the ASP script terminates. It is in these two events that the method requests an interface called `IScriptingContext`.

IScriptingContext

The Intrinsic Objects section instructs the wizard to incorporate use of these objects in our component. By default, all of them are selected, giving us complete access to the entire ASP object model.

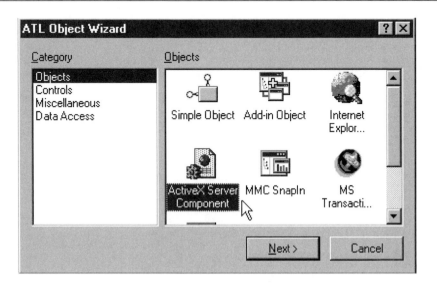

Figure 7-5. Adding an ActiveX Server component.

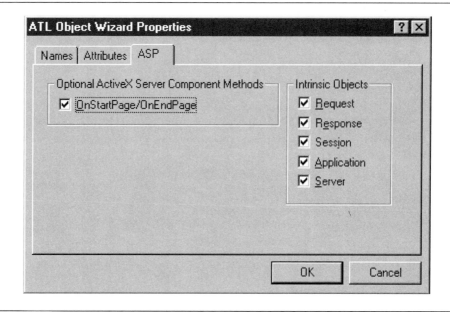

Figure 7-6. Configuring options for the new ASP object.

When we look at the ASP "plumbing" code that the wizard generated, we see the following:

```
STDMETHODIMP CAsp::OnStartPage (IUnknown* pUnk)
{
        if(!pUnk)
                return E_POINTER;

        CComPtr<IScriptingContext> spContext;
        HRESULT hr;

        // Get the IScriptingContext Interface
        hr = pUnk->QueryInterface(IID_IScriptingContext, ⌐
(void **)&spContext);
        if(FAILED(hr))
                return hr;

        // Get Request Object Pointer
        hr = spContext->get_Request(&m_piRequest);
        if(FAILED(hr))
        {
```

```
                              spContext.Release();
                              return hr;
               }


               // Get Response Object Pointer
               hr = spContext->get_Response(&m_piResponse);
               if(FAILED(hr))
               {
                       m_piRequest.Release();
                       return hr;
               }


               // Get Server Object Pointer
               hr = spContext->get_Server(&m_piServer);
               if(FAILED(hr))
               {
                       m_piRequest.Release();
                       m_piResponse.Release();
                       return hr;
               }


               // Get Session Object Pointer
               hr = spContext->get_Session(&m_piSession);
               if(FAILED(hr))
               {
                       m_piRequest.Release();
                       m_piResponse.Release();
                       _piServer.Release();
                       return hr;
               }


               // Get Application Object Pointer
               hr = spContext->get_Application(&m_piApplication);
               if(FAILED(hr))
               {
                       m_piRequest.Release();
                       m_piResponse.Release();
                       m_piServer.Release();
                       m_piSession.Release();
                       return hr;
               }
               m_bOnStartPageCalled = TRUE;
               return S_OK;
       }
```

```
STDMETHODIMP CAsp::OnEndPage ()
{
        m_bOnStartPageCalled = FALSE;
        // Release all interfaces
        m_piRequest.Release();
        m_piResponse.Release();
        m_piServer.Release();
        m_piSession.Release();
        m_piApplication.Release();
        return S_OK;
}
```

The IScriptingContext interface contains methods that return handles to the ASP intrinsic objects. OnStartPage() begins by querying for the IScriptingContext interface. If that succeeds, we then proceed by calling methods to retrieve interface pointers to the ASP intrinsic objects. The interface pointers are stored in class member variables. When OnEndPage() is called, all of the interfaces that we retrieved are released.

An Example of Retrieving a Variable from the Query String

Now that we have interface pointers to the ASP objects, let's look at an example of what can be done with them. Add a new method to the component, called EchoQueryString(), with no parameters. Add this code to the method:

```
STDMETHODIMP CAsp::EchoQueryString()
{
        // The IRequestDictionary interface
        IRequestDictionary *pRequest;
        // Some variants
        CComVariant                     varText;
        CComVariant                     vVar, vName( "var" );
        varText = "This is the 'var' variable: ";

        // Get a handle to the QueryString collection
        m_piRequest->get_QueryString( ( IRequestDictionary **)&pRequest );

        // Get the value QueryString variable named "var" and store it
in vVar
        pRequest->get_Item( vName, &vVar );
```

```
                    // Write out the text to the browser
                    m_piResponse->Write( varText );
                    m_piResponse->Write( vVar );

                    return S_OK;
            }
```

This is a simple method that will retrieve a variable called "var" from the `Request.QueryString` collection. We obtain the query string by retrieving it using the `get_QueryString()` method. This returns a pointer to an `IRequestDictionary` interface. With this interface, we can access the "var" key in the collection by calling the `get_Item()` method of the `IRequestDictionary`:

```
pRequest->get_Item( vName, &vVar );
```

To write output to the browser, let's perform the C++ equivalent of `Response.Write` in VBScript:

```
// Write out the text to the browser
m_piResponse->Write( varText );
m_piResponse->Write( vVar );
```

That's all there is to it! Of course, you can do many more things with the ASP intrinsic objects. The Visual C++ documentation provides an excellent reference on how to use the ASP object interfaces. Consult it for more details.

Note: A good place to find reference material on the ASP intrinsic interfaces is at `http://msdn.microsoft.com/library/sdkdoc/iisref/buil1foz.htm`

Error Handling

In the course of writing ASP applications, you may have come across an error, such as the following one, that was returned to your browser:

```
Microsoft VBScript runtime error '800a0009'
Subscript out of range: '[number: 4]'
/dict.asp, line 43
```

This error is known as an *automation error.* In this case, the VBScript runtime environment generated the automation error due to some code that attempted to set a value past the bounds of an array. Our COM components can return errors like this as well. Normally, you would want to return an error such as this when your code has encountered an unusual circumstance, such as a violation of business logic rules due to invalid input.

An error like this is returned whenever a COM method returns an HRESULT in the failure category (i.e., such as E_FAIL, E_OUTOFMEMORY, etc.) as opposed to S_OK. Simply returning this on an error in your component will raise the type of error shown in the preceding code, but it would not provide any useful information to the user of the component as to what went wrong.

ISupportErrorInfo

There is a special COM interface, called ISupportErrorInfo, that contains a method to assist in handling automation errors. It should look familiar to you because when we built our COM object from the Visual C++ wizards, we were asked whether we wanted to support this interface (checkbox). If we checked the checkbox, the following code was added to the project:

```
STDMETHODIMP CPizzaSample::InterfaceSupportsErrorInfo(REFIID riid)
{
    static const IID* arr[] =
    {
        &IID_IPizzaSample
    };
    for (int i=0; i < sizeof(arr) / sizeof(arr[0]); i++)
    {
        if (InlineIsEqualGUID(*arr[i],riid))
            return S_OK;
    }
    return S_FALSE;
}
```

This code was taken from the PizzaSample COM object. InterfaceSupportsErrorInfo() is the single method of the ISupportErrorInfo interface. Its job is to determine whether the interface specified by riid supports error handling. It returns S_OK if error handling is supported; S_FALSE, if it is not.

The function starts by declaring an array of interface IDs that we know support error handling. This code is generated by the ATL COM Wizard, and it states that our one interface, the IPizzaSample interface, supports error handling:

```
static const IID* arr[] =
{
        &IID_IPizzaSample
};
```

The next part of the code uses a `for` loop to do a linear search of the interface array for the interface `riid`. The `InlineIsEqualGUID()` function returns a true/false value if the two GUIDs passed as parameters match. If we find our match, we exit out of the loop by returning `S_OK`.

When constructing COM objects, if you did not check the `ISupportErrorInfo` checkbox in the ATL COM Wizard, don't worry. You can simply copy and paste the code given here into your object class implementation file (in our example, this would be `PizzaSample.cpp`). The only changes you need to make are the name of the class in the function definition and the name(s) of the interfaces you wish to support error handling.

Raising an Error with Error()

We are now ready to discuss how to actually raise an automation error in our code. It's an easy two-step process, and our `PizzaSample` COM object includes an example of how to do this:

```
STDMETHODIMP CPizzaSample::RollDough(short nDiameter)
{
    // TODO: Add your implementation code here
    m_Diameter = nDiameter;
    if ( m_DoughRolled != 1 )
    {
        m_DoughRolled = 1;
    }
    else
    {
        Error("The dough is already rolled",IID_IPizzaSample, 0);
        Return E_FAIL;
    }
    return S_OK;
}
```

This is the code for the `RollDough()` method with automation error handling in place. It is almost entirely self-explanatory. We check our m_DoughRolled flag to see whether the dough has been rolled already. If it has, we return an error through the Error() method. The Error() method is an inherited one; it comes from the CComCoClass class. CComCoClass is a class used internally by ATL that defines the class factory model for the COM object (it uses the IClassFactory interface, which contains the familiar CreateInstance() method). The Error() method has many different overloaded forms, and we'll concentrate on the form just used in the PizzaSample object. This form allows us to send back a textual description of the error message. So, if we call the RollDough() method more than once, we get an error returned to us that looks something like this:

```
Pizza.PizzaSample.1 error '80004005'
The dough is already rolled
/piz.asp, line 12
```

The ATL Error() method is tied into the VBScript Err object. When Error() is called, the VBScript Err object properties are filled in with the values given in the Error() method. In our code, we call the Error() method in this fashion:

```
Error("The dough is already rolled",IID_IPizzaSample, 0);
```

The first parameter is the description of the error. This is the error that will be placed in the Description property of the Err object. The second parameter is the interface ID of the IPizzaSample interface. This translates to the Source property of the Err object.

In addition to calling the Error() method, we need to return an HRESULT value from our method. You've seen that most of our COM methods have returned the HRESULT, S_OK. When an error occurs in your method class function, you'll need to return an HRESULT in the *E* category (like E_FAIL, E_UNEXPECTED, E_INVALIDARG). This signals, through the COM channels, that the method did not execute correctly and that the VBScript engine should check the Err object for additional information about the error (since some HRESULTs, such as E_FAIL or E_UNEXPECTED, are very unspecific).

Running an Example of Error Handling

A short demonstration in ASP will show how automation error handling works for the RollDough() method. Consider this VBScript fragment:

```
On Error Resume Next

Set pizza = Server.CreateObject( "Pizza.PizzaSample" )

pizza.RollDough 12
pizza.RollDough    13 ' this will cause an error!
Response.Write "<B>Number:</B> " & Err.Number & "<BR>"
Response.Write "<B>Description:</B> " & Err.Description & "<BR>"
Response.Write "<B>Source:</B> " & Err.Source & "<BR>"
Set pizza = Nothing
```

This example will deliberately cause the second call to the `RollDough()`
method to fail. We then want to inspect all of the individual fields of the `Err`
object. In order to prevent the standard-error VBScript runtime error handling from halting script execution, we place an `On Error Resume Next` at the
top of our code. When we run this script, we get the following output:

```
Number: -2147467259
Description: The dough is already rolled
Source: Pizza.PizzaSample.1
```

Chapter Review

Let's review what we've learned about automation.

- Automation, the successor to older technologies like OLE Automation
  and DDE, allows us to call the methods of a COM object dynamically.
  This is called *dynamic invocation.*

- Automation allows us to call methods of an object without any prior
  knowledge of what methods are available. Automation allows us to
  query the methods supported, the parameters to those methods, and
  any types the object uses.

- The Universal Marshaler is the software that sends data across
  processes that COM objects use. The Universal Marshaler supports the
  `VARIANT` data type, which, as you recall from Chapter 2, is the only type
  supported in VBScript.

- Automation happens through an interface called `IDispatch`. A COM
  interface that inherits from `IDispatch` is called a *dispinterface.* The
  `IDispatch` method contains methods used for getting information

about an automation object's properties, methods, and interfaces. It also contains the `Invoke()` method, which does the real work of calling a method on an interface.

- The `VARIANT` data type is a discriminated union made up of several automation-compatible data types. The discriminator is the `vt` variable. The `vt` variable contains a constant that indicates the type of the variable.

- COM provides a series of utility functions to manipulate variants. `VariantInit()` initializes new variants, and `VariantClear()` disposes of the variant. There are also functions that copy variants, change the underlying type of a variant, and perform miscellaneous functions on the variant.

- ATL provides a wrapper class for the `VARIANT` data type called `CComVariant`. The advantages to using the `CComVariant` class are many. The class handles calling of the lower-level variant utility functions like `VariantInit()` and `VariantClear()`. There are many different constructors for a variant, which enables the class's variant value to be initialized to any COM-supported data type or object.

- Scalar data types are relatively easy to implement in properties and methods. You can assign the member variables of your class (which hold properties data) directly using the assignment operator (=) in most cases.

- Strings are handled in automation using the `BSTR` data type. BSTRs are null-terminated, wide-character strings with a prefixing length value (like a Pascal string). This tells the marshaler how much data to transmit and also allows the string to contain null characters. Wide-character strings are for Unicode compatibility.

- COM provides some utility functions to use for working with BSTRs. Some common ones are `SysAllocString()`, which initializes a string; `SysFreeString()`, which frees the memory occupied by a BSTR; and `SysStringLen()`, which returns the length of the string.

- The `CComBSTR` class is another ATL wrapper class. It provides much of the same advantages of other wrapper classes like `CComVariant`. It contains many constructors. The constructors can take different data types as parameters, including Unicode strings, ANSI strings, and other BSTRs.

- You can convert data types contained in a `CComVariant` to other types by using the `ChangeType()` method.

■ COM methods need to have an IDL definition for them. When a new COM method is generated for an interface using Visual C++, it prompts for the parameters to the method. Along with the parameter names and types, we supply IDL keywords to indicate how the parameter is used. [in] states that the parameter is input-only. [out] states that the parameter can be modified by the method. [out, retval] states that the parameter is to be used as the returned value of the method in the calling program.

■ It is possible to return an object reference as a return value from a method or as a property. This involves querying the interface pointer for the IDispatch interface.

■ Passing arrays between component processes is handled by the SAFEARRAY. The SAFEARRAY does not rely on explicit pointers like arrays in conventional languages. SAFEARRAYs contain their own functions for array management.

■ The ATL facilitates rich error-handling capabilities. Using a combination of HRESULTs and the Error() function, you can return custom error messages from your component that can be accessed using the VBScript Err object.

■ Using On Error Resume Next in your code can enable you to check the Err object manually.

■ You can access the ASP intrinsic objects by having Visual C++ generate an ActiveX Server component ATL object. This wizard-generated code exposes special interfaces to the familiar Response, Request, Application, Session, and Server objects.

What's Next

We'll explore new technologies like Active Directory Services Interface (ADSI), Microsoft Transaction Server (MTS), Microsoft Message Queuing (MSMQ), and Collaborative Data Objects (CDO). Some of these technologies are relatively new and show great promise as tools for implementing advanced Web application features.

The coming chapters will also introduce you to the practices of securing your Web application. Important security concepts that will be covered include the Windows NT file system and its implementation of security. How IIS leverages off of NT security will also be discussed. We'll also talk about general cryptography concepts and how cryptography is used to implement digital signatures and facilitate secure socket communications.

■ Further Reading

■ *ATL Internals* by Brent Rector and Chris Sells, Addison-Wesley, 1999—This book does a good job of explaining all the ins-and-outs of the Active Template Library (ATL). It's very good reference material.

A Primer on Microsoft Transaction Server, Active Directory, and Microsoft Message Queuing

Introduction

We have seen some powerful technologies that are a part of our Web application arsenal. ASP provides the presentation-layer glue that binds the client's interface (the Web browser) to the middle and lower tiers of the application (data and components). Also, ADO provides a very useful interface for accessing data stores of various sources. Business objects, constructed using COM and ADO, are the heart of the Web application. However, using these elements together is not enough. Although these elements by themselves can make for a powerful solution, the solution is vulnerable to scalability problems.

There is also a stability issue when applications are deployed over the Internet. You know from experience the unreliability that the Internet can sometimes exhibit. You may have encountered this when you try to make an online purchase. Although making an online purchase may seem simple on the surface, the logic behind the scenes probably incorporates many components and interacts with many different systems. These systems may also span many networks and computers. The chances of failure increase when communications between these systems are interrupted. Interruptions could cause our online transaction to fail, leaving behind a corrupted data set and a frustrated customer.

Then there is the problem with the heterogeneous nature of all of these systems. Each has its own way of storing information, be it in databases, directory services, or other sources of data. From a development standpoint, this presents a challenge since many of these storage systems contain proprietary APIs. The coding process becomes exceedingly complex, and not all systems are guaranteed to communicate nicely with one another.

Microsoft Transaction Server (MTS)

The problem with using COM components and ActiveX Data Objects in ASP is the overhead involved with managing the creation and destruction of these objects and maintaining data integrity. This process is, unfortunately, fairly resource-intensive. The underlying COM class factory must allocate memory for the component and perform other housekeeping tasks in order to deliver you a handle to an interface. Occasionally, a script might take a while to execute, and a component instance might be in use for just a fraction of the lifetime of that script. Meanwhile, another user requests a script that calls the same COM component. Since the first user's script that created an instance of the component may not be using it at a given moment in time, it would be desirable to make the component available for use to the second user rather than creating a whole new instance. In effect, we can "pool" component instances, just as we pool ODBC database connections.

Microsoft Transaction Server (MTS) is the software that manages these pools of COM object instances. Here's how it works: MTS acts as a runtime environment for components. That is, they execute inside the MTS *object context,* instead of being created by the Web server software. Without MTS, COM components are created as new entities, without regard to the load on the server. For high-traffic Web sites that utilize many COM components, this would mean that scores of COM component instances might be active on the server, each using a portion of the system resources. We can instruct MTS, via special commands, to create an instance of the same component under the MTS runtime environment. When we instantiate a COM object in this manner, we get an object context handle returned. To the programmer, creating an object normally and creating the object under MTS are very similar. We call the properties and methods in the same manner as we have always done. Since we are dealing with the component's object context and not the component instance itself, MTS is free to do what it pleases with the resources used by the actual component instance. This includes letting another process use the preinstantiated component via a new object context reference. The programmer thinks that he/she still has an instance to the object, but, in reality, the programmer has only a "ghost" instance to it. This greatly increases scalability since many users can use the same instance of the COM component.

We can send a signal to MTS when we are finished using a COM component instance in a number of ways. When we run components under MTS, we never actually destroy an object—we "deactivate" it. This recycles the resources used to hold a reference to the object back into the MTS pool. Setting the object equal to `Nothing` will deactivate the component instance. If the ASP script finishes, ASP also deactivates the component. Two MTS API functions called `SetAbort` and `SetComplete` will also deactivate a component. These functions handle the transactional processing of MTSs as well, which we will cover next.

Transaction Server manages transactions (as you can probably guess from its name). Transactions are groupings of small tasks (called *atomic* tasks) that collectively succeed or fail as a whole. Transactions are either all or nothing. That is, if one of the atomic tasks fails, the entire transaction fails. Transactions must also "undo" any atomic changes made prior to the execution of the failing atomic task. If all the tasks succeed, we must ensure that all of these changes are applied. These processes are called *rollback* and *commit,* respectively. The `SetComplete` function will signal MTS that the transaction should be committed, and `SetAbort` informs MTS to roll back the changes made to data.

The "changes" that we refer to here are changes that are made to permanent storage (typically, a database or file system). Here's a classic example of a transaction. It involves the transfer of monies from one account to another. This transaction is made up of the following steps:

1. Get the amount to be transferred, and check the source account for sufficient funds.
2. Deduct the transfer amount from the source account.
3. Get the balance of the destination account, and add the amount to be transferred to the balance.
4. Update the destination account with the new balance.

Suppose a system failure occurs at step 4. This means that the source account had the transfer amount deducted but that the amount was not added to the destination account. Therefore, we just lost that money from the source account. Clearly, this is not good because the integrity of our database has been damaged.

Each of the account transfer's steps can be checked for success or failure. If a failure occurs before all values have been updated, we need to "undo" the deduction that was made to the source account. This is called a *rollback*. If every step succeeded, we need to apply all of the changes we made to the database. That is called a *commit*.

Many DBMS software packages support transactions as a standard feature, either through their own API or through OLE-DB/ODBC. MTS can instruct the DBMS to commit and roll back transactions using the native methodologies of the DBMS when a commit or rollback command has been issued by the object context of the component. It's very convenient since we don't need to concern ourselves with writing the transaction processing code ourselves. MTS supports transaction processing for a DBMS through a *resource manager.* At the time of this writing, MTS Resource Managers are available for Microsoft SQL Server and Oracle.

To utilize MTS, you must inform MTS that you have components that you would like to run under the MTS context. The components that you develop for your application should each perform one of the atomic tasks that make up your transaction. The next step is to collectively group these components into a logical group called a *package.* All objects in a package are related to a single task. Packages are created using the MTS Explorer, which is part of the Microsoft Management Console under Windows NT and as a separate application on Windows 9x.

The Megabytes Ordering Component

The best way to illustrate how to utilize MTS is to create a component that utilizes MTS functions. The component we are about to build is the PizzaOrder component. It can create new customer orders, add items to the order, and also cancel (delete) the order from the database.

Preparing to Use the PizzaOrder Component

Up until this point, we have been using a Microsoft Access database to keep track of our data. The main problem with this type of setup is the limited scalability. The Jet database engine, which powers Microsoft Access, was designed to accommodate a limited number of concurrent users. Using a Jet-based database is fine for workgroup or department-level access on an Intranet, but an Internet site will need to support many hundreds, perhaps thousands, of users. So, as our user base grows, so do our DBMS requirements. Another reason for upgrading our DBMS is to gain MTS support. The transaction management features of MTS are not supported for Jet databases.

Upsizing to SQL Server 7.0

We are going to upgrade our database to use Microsoft SQL Server 7.0. Fortunately, this is not terribly difficult. We just need to follow some simple step-by-step instructions to get up and running:

1. The first step is to launch SQL Server 7.0 from the Windows Start menu. Once the Management Console is loaded, select "Create Database Wizard."

2. The first screen of the wizard asks you to specify the name of the database. Call the database "Megabytes." Pick a directory in which to store the SQL Server database file. Type the directory name, or select one using the browse button. You will also need to select a location for the SQL transaction log. This is the internal log used by SQL Server to record actions taken against the database. Click Next to continue. (See Figure 8-1.)

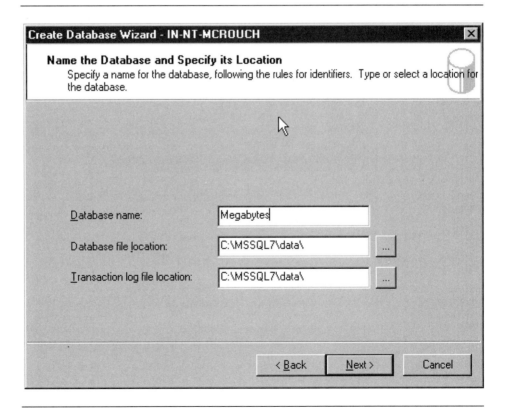

Figure 8-1. Specifying name and location of database.

3. The wizard then asks you to specify names for the database files. By default, the names will be filled in for you based on the name of the database that you selected in step 2. You are free to override these defaults with your own names. You will also need to specify an initial size for the files. Pick an appropriate value based on your disk space and storage needs. (See Figure 8-2.)

4. SQL Server has the ability to automatically manage the storage used by the database data. When the storage for a particular database is used up, SQL Server can automatically allocate more space. In the next screen of the wizard, you can choose to invoke the automatic-sizing feature, or you may specify that database size management be controlled manually. If you elect to automatically size the database, you can define the growth increments (in megabytes or percentage of total database size). Click Next to continue. (See Figure 8-3.)

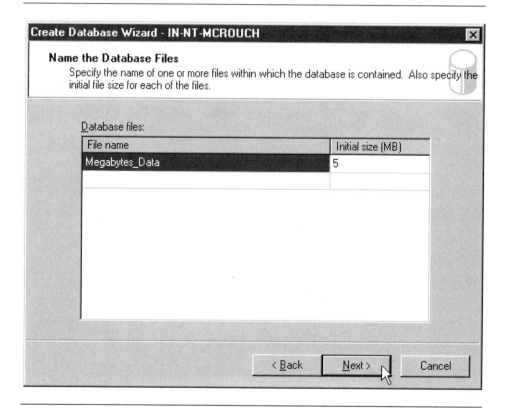

Figure 8-2. Specifying names and initial sizes of database files.

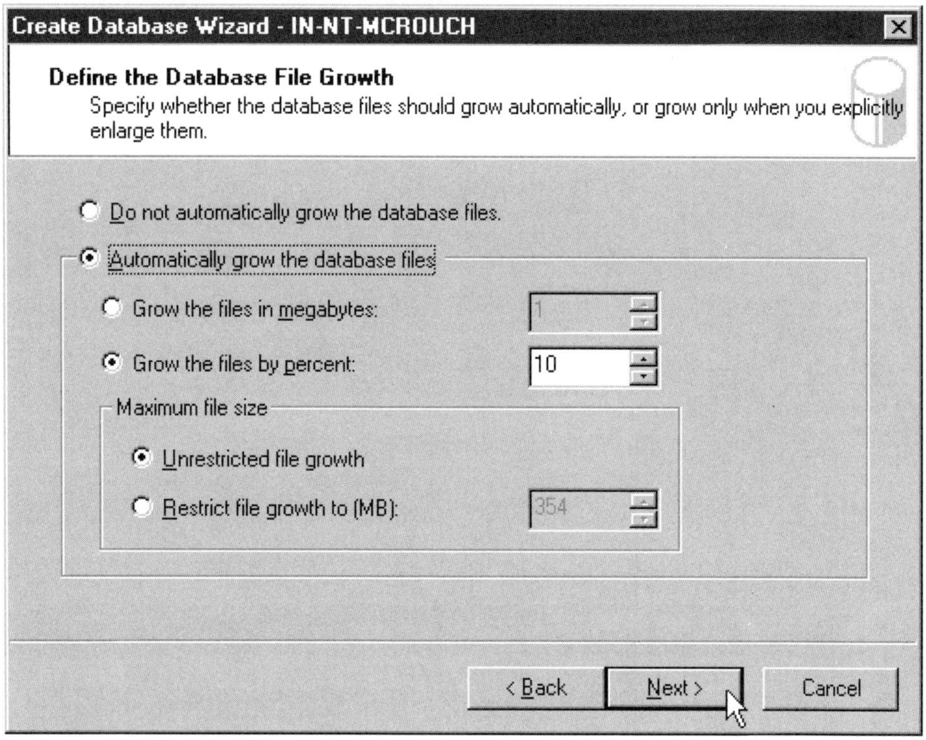

Figure 8-3. Defining database file growth.

5. In this step, we define the name and size of the transaction log. Follow the same general procedure as you did in step 3. Click Next to continue. (See Figure 8-4.)

6. Repeat the procedure in step 4 for the transaction log. Click Next to continue. (See Figure 8-5.)

7. You have now completed the process of creating the SQL 7.0 Megabytes database! Figure 8-6 shows a summary of the options and parameters that you selected. If you need to change any of them, click the Back button to navigate back to the screen of your choice.

You have created a blank database in SQL Server. The next step is to define the tables in this new database from the table in the original database. Returning to the Management Console, expand the hierarchy, beginning with the Server node. Expand the hierarchy further until the Megabytes database is reached, as shown in Figure 8-7.

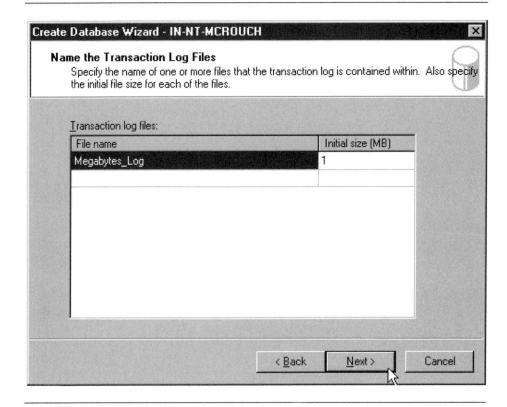

Figure 8-4.   Specifying names and initial sizes of transaction logs.

Follow these steps to create tables for our database:

1. Right-click on the Tables node and select "New Table" from the menu.

2. Enter the name for the new table. We will create the MenuItems table first, so enter that name as shown in Figure 8-8. Click OK to continue.

3. A new window will appear where we enter the column data for the table. Enter the column names and types as they appear in Figure 8-9. We also need to set a primary key for the table. You can do this by highlighting a column (the primary key of the MenuItems table is item_name) and clicking the primary key button. The item_name column must be non-null since primary key fields are not allowed to contain any null values. Unhighlight the Allow Nulls checkbox for the item_name column.

4. Click the Save button in the toolbar to save your changes.

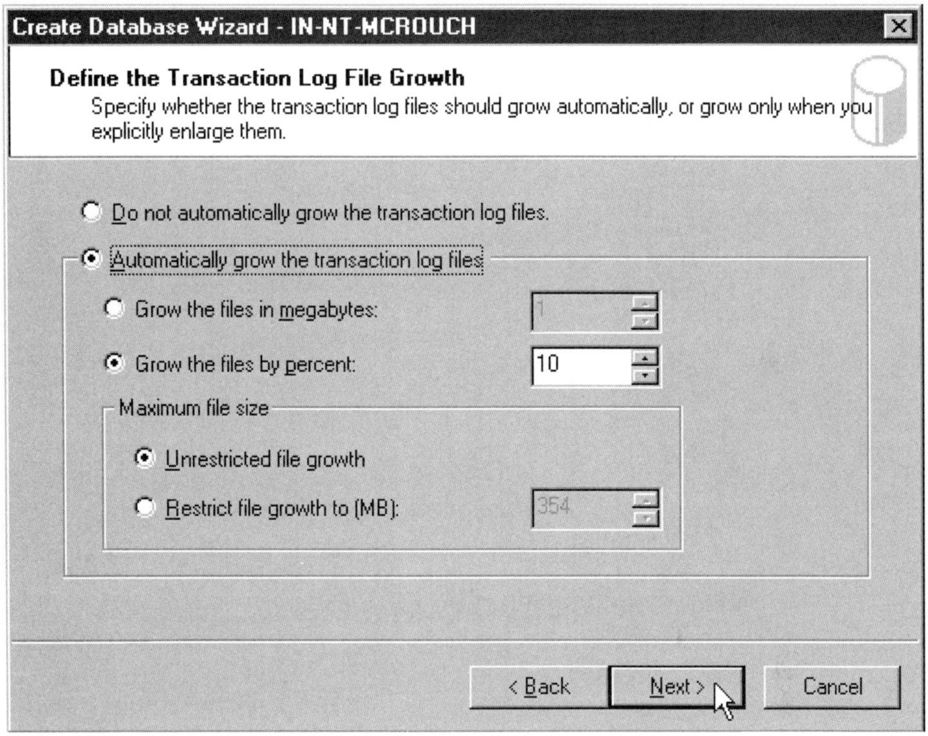

Figure 8-5. Defining transaction log growth.

You have just created a table in SQL Server. We need to continue the preceding steps for each table in our database. Those tables are Orders, OrderDetail, and Users.

The next step is to import the data from the Access database into our new tables in SQL Server. SQL Server includes a wizard for importing data called the *Data Transformation Services Import Wizard.* Follow these steps to get it up and running:

1. Start the DTS Import Wizard. The start screen will appear. (See Figure 8-10.)

2. The first screen asks where the source data is coming from. Select "Microsoft Access" from the drop-down list as the source. Next, select the .mdb file for our database for the file name. Click Next to continue. (See Figure 8-11.)

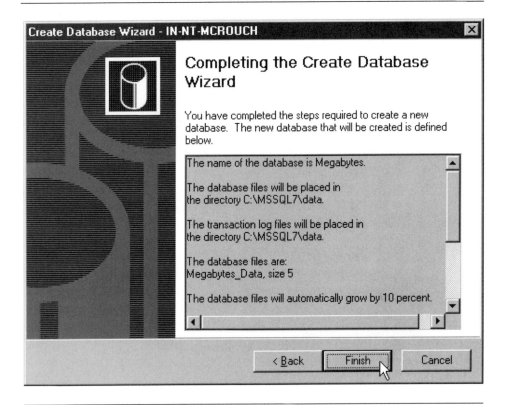

Figure 8-6.   Summary of options and parameters selected.

3. We now need to choose a destination for our data. This will be the database that we created in the earlier set of steps. Select "Microsoft OLE DB Provider for SQL Server" from the drop-down list as the destination. For the server, select the machine on which the database is housed. In this example, we select "local." You may set security settings for the import wizard to use if your database requires a special login. Finally, select the database that we want the imported data to go to. We select "Megabytes." Click Next to continue. (See Figure 8-12.)

4. Select the default option on the next screen. This states that we want to copy data directly from tables in the source database rather than use a special SQL query. Click Next to continue. (See Figure 8-13.)

5. Select the tables you wish to copy by checking the box next to the table name. Click Next to continue. Our example shows the selection of one

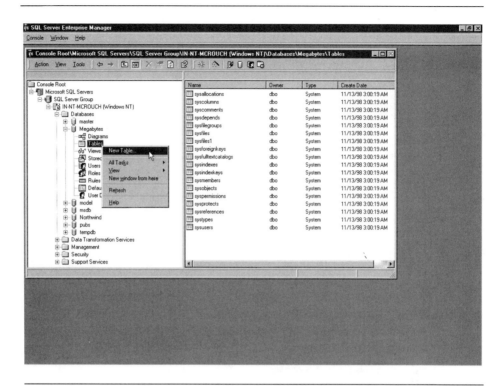

Figure 8-7. Selecting the new table.

table, `MenuItems`. You can select multiple tables to convert. We will need the `Orders` and `OrderDetail` tables as well. (See Figure 8-14.)

6. Next, select the "Run immediately" option so that importing begins right away. (See Figure 8-15.)

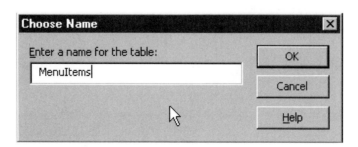

Figure 8-8. Naming the new table.

2:New Table in 'Megabytes' on 'IN-NT-MCROUCH'

Column Name	Datatype	Length	Precision	Scale	Allow Nulls	Default Value	Identity	Identity Seed	Identity Increment	Is RowGuid
▶ item_name	char	Set primary key	0	0						
item_desc	char	255	0	0	✓					
price	money	8	19	4	✓					
food_type	char	50	0	0	✓					

Figure 8-9. Entering column data for the new table.

7. The import process will begin, and a summary screen will be displayed. (See Figure 8-16.)

You can check the data that was imported by right-clicking on the table name in the tree view and selecting "Return All Rows" from the tasks. If

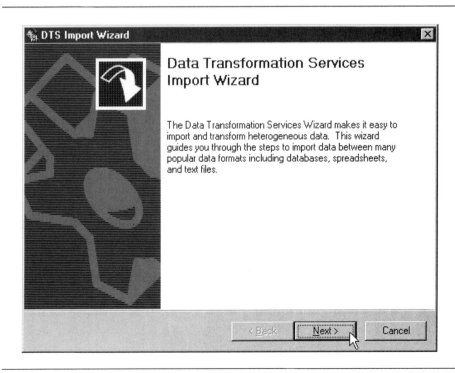

Data Transformation Services Import Wizard

The Data Transformation Services Wizard makes it easy to import and transform heterogeneous data. This wizard guides you through the steps to import data between many popular data formats including databases, spreadsheets, and text files.

< Back   Next >   Cancel

Figure 8-10. The DTS Import Wizard start screen.

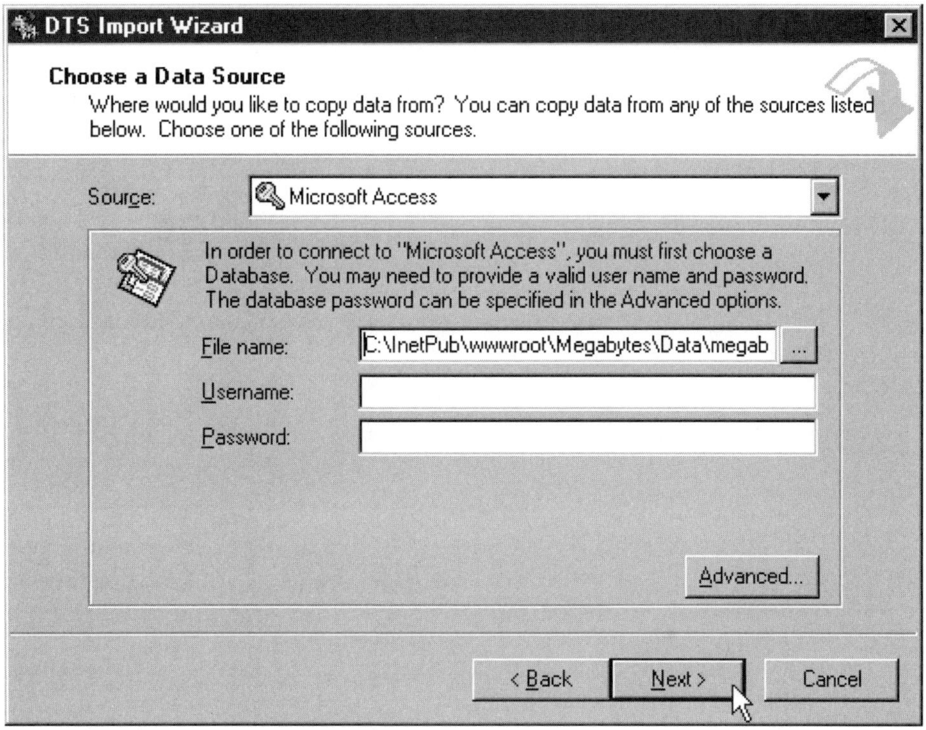

Figure 8-11. Choosing a data source.

everything progressed as planned, you should see something like the screen shown in Figure 8-17.

Configuring an ODBC Data Source for the Database

Before we use our new database with ADO/ASP, we need to create an ODBC data source for it, as follows:

1. Open the Windows Control Panel, and double-click the ODBC icon. Click on the "System" tab to open the system-level ODBC sources. Click the Add button. Select "SQL Server" for the driver of the new data source.

2. As shown in Figure 8-18, fill in the name of the data source, an optional description, and the database server. Click Next to continue.

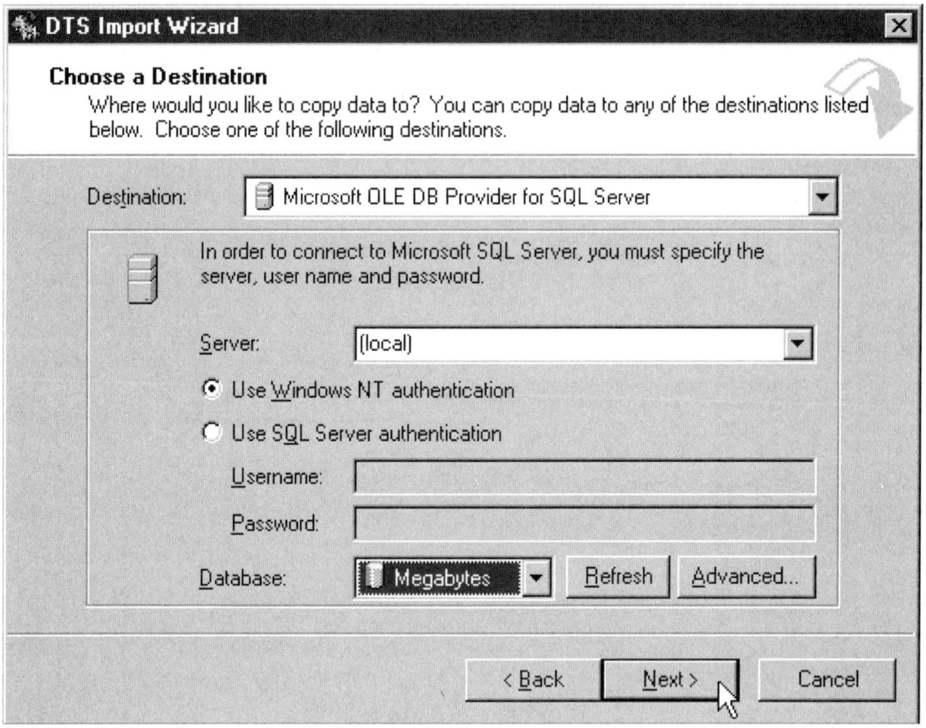

Figure 8-12.   Choosing a destination.

3. As shown in Figure 8-19, check the "Change the default database to" checkbox, and select "Megabytes" from the drop-down list. Leave the default options as they appear. Click Next to continue.

4. The final screen of the ODBC setup, as shown in Figure 8-20, contains more options to configure, such as log file locations, regional settings, and character translations. You may leave the defaults as they exist.

5. Click Finish to complete the ODBC setup process. Your ODBC data source is now ready for use.

Note: SQL Server is a database management system that contains its own integrated security system. When you step up your ODBC data source to the SQL Server Megabytes database, you'll need to specify security settings, like a user ID and a password. The ODBC Setup gives you two options for security and user authentication: using integrated NT security or using SQL Server

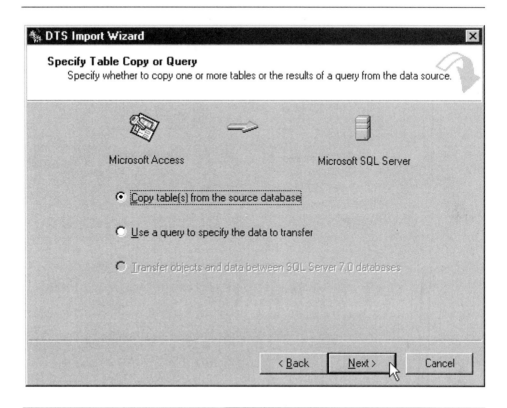

Figure 8-13. Specifying table copy.

security. Since we are accessing our SQL Server database from IIS/ASP, it is usually easier to select the SQL Server authentication. Selecting NT security will cause a security check to be performed against the database using the current security context, which is typically an anonymous guest account for Web access. This NT guest account usually does not have permissions to access the SQL Server database directly, which is why SQL Server security is often used in these situations. For more information on security, see Chapter 9.

Creating the PizzaOrder Component

So far, all of the business logic for the Megabyte's application is implemented using VBScript and ADO inside ASP. We discussed before the advantages of

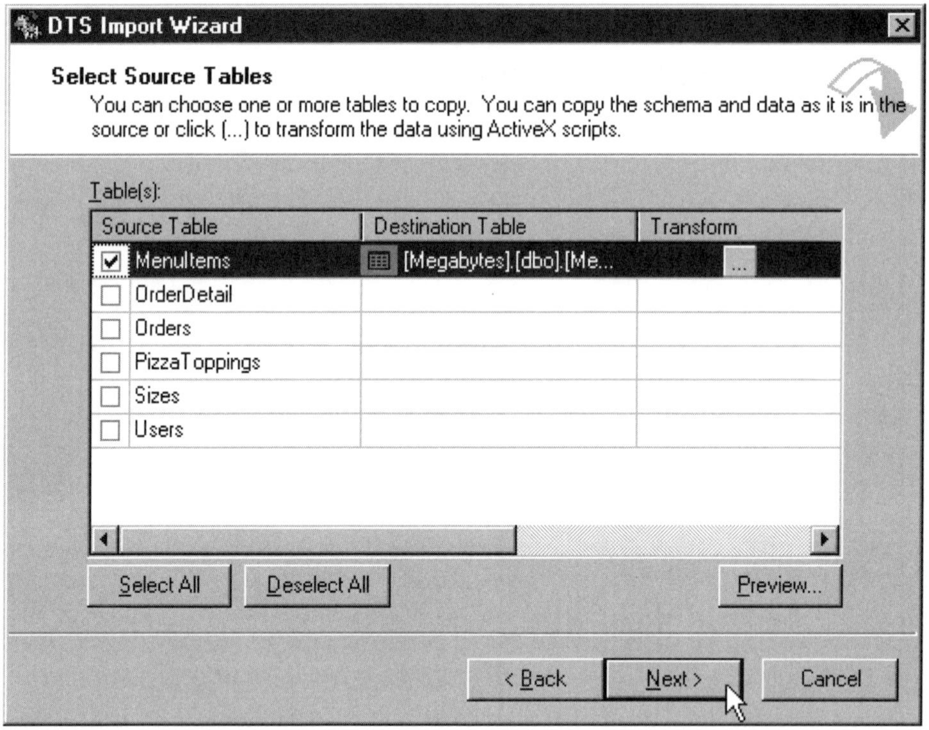

Figure 8-14.   Selecting source tables.

encapsulating business logic into a COM component. Making a COM component that is "MTS-ready" is almost just as easy as creating a regular one (i.e., a simple COM object, like the PizzaSample component). Visual C++ provides a wizard to create an MTS-compatible component, which puts in some MTS "plumbing" code. We then fill in the functionality.

The PizzaOrder component handles the logic behind placing an order in the Megabytes database. It involves using two different tables: the Orders table and the OrderDetail table. The Orders table holds information about a customer order, like the order number, delivery address, and so on. The OrderDetail table contains information about the various line items of the customer order. Table 8-1 lists the properties and methods of the order component and describes their functionality.

Let's begin by constructing the component, as follows. After we've built the object, we'll incorporate it into the Megabyte's application:

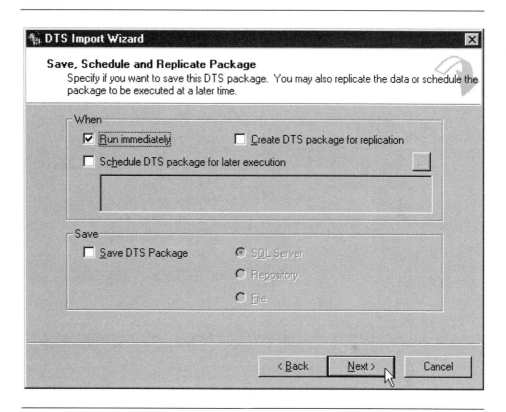

Figure 8-15. Scheduling the import process to run immediately.

1. Start Visual C++. From the File menu, choose New.

2. The ATL COM AppWizard appears. Select "Dynamic Link Library" for the server type. Check the box that says "Support MTS." (See Figure 8-21.)

3. From the Insert menu, select "New ATL Object." The ATL Object Wizard appears. Highlight the object that says "MS Transaction Server Component." Click Next to continue. (See Figure 8-22.)

4. The Names screen appears. Enter "Order" for the short name of the component and "Pizza.Order" in the Prog ID box. (See Figure 8-23.)

5. Click the MTS tab. The default option for "Interface" is dual, which is the option we want (since the COM object must support automation).

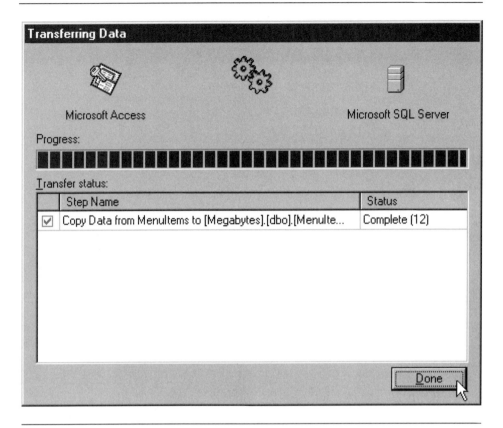

Figure 8-16.   Import process summary progress screen.

Click the option marked "Support IObjectControl." Click OK to add the code for the object. (See Figure 8-24.)

The Order.cpp File

Let's investigate the code that the wizard produced. Of particular interest is the Order.cpp file. Besides the normal COM wizard code, other functions have been added to the class. We also want to support automation error handling. Recall that, in order for our object to support this, we need to add support for the ISupportsErrorInfo interface. To do this, we simply add the

2:Data in Table 'MenuItems'			
item_name	item_desc	price	food
Meat Lasagna	A savory layering of pasta, marinara, three ch	7.59	EntrT
Wave a Dead Chicken Parmesan	Skinless, boneless chicken fillets breaded in her	8.75	EntrT
Pizza	Our luscious thin-crust pizza, baked in our spec	<NULL>	Pizza
Italian Baked Cod	Fresh baked cod fillets crusted with spicy brea	10.35	EntrT
Baked Ravioli	Ricotta filled pasta rounds topped with our spe	7.99	EntrT
Fried GUI Mozzarella	Mozzarella cheese, crispy on the outside, hot a	4.99	Appe
BitBread	Our toasted garlic-laden toast. Strong enough	2.99	Appe
Minestrone Soup	Lots of good-for-you vegatables cooked in our	2.95	Soup
Prosciutto-wrapped Chicken	Half chicken wrapped in Italian Parma ham with	9.75	Speci
Baked Sea Bass	Market fresh whole bass baked with lemon and	13.25	Speci
Risotto-stuffed Bell Peppers	Roasted red and yellow peppers stuffed with s	8.99	Speci
Penne with roasted red pepper cream sa	Just incredible. Watch your arteries; lots of bu	7.99	Speci

Figure 8-17. Checking the imported data.

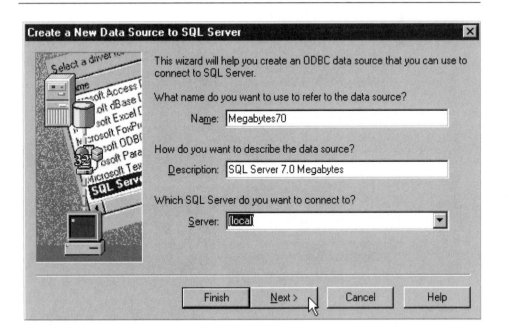

Figure 8-18. Step 2 for configuring an ODBC data source.

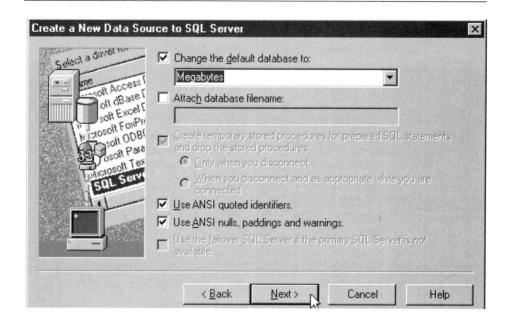

Figure 8-19.   Step 3 for configuring an ODBC data source.

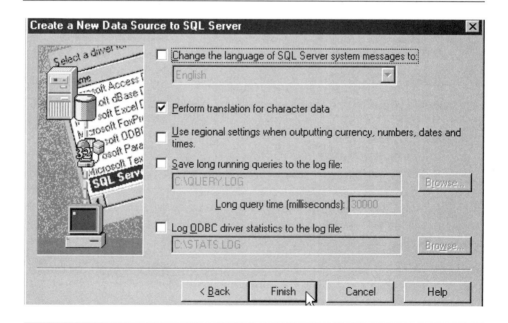

Figure 8-20.   Step 4 for configuring an ODBC data source.

Table 8-1.   Order Component Properties and Methods

Property	Description
ConnectionStr	The ODBC connection string. Set this to a valid ODBC connection string for the component to use. (e.g., "DSN=Megabytes"). Read/write.
OrderDateFulfilled	The date that the order was completed and delivered to the customer. Read/write.
OrderDatePlaced	The date that the customer placed the order. Read/write.
OrderDeliveryAddress	The customer delivery address. The order gets delivered here. Read/write.
OrderNumber	The customer order number. Read/write.
OrderStatus	The status of the customer order. Read/write.
Username	The customer username. Read/write.
Method	**Description**
OrderNew	Create a new customer order.
OrderDelete	Delete the current customer order.
OrderAddItem(ItemName, Quantity)	Add the quantity specified of a food item to the current customer order.
OrderSave	Save the customer order with all the items added to it.

supporting code to the `Order.cpp` file. Combined, the wizard-generated code and the automation error-handling plumbing look something like this:

```
// Order.cpp : Implementation of COrder
#include "stdafx.h"
#include "Orders.h"
```

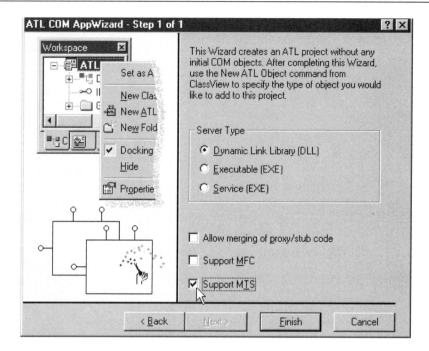

Figure 8-21. The ATL COM AppWizard dialog.

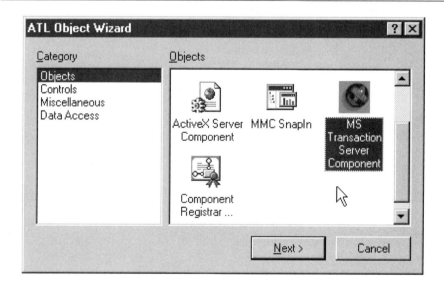

Figure 8-22. The ATL Object Wizard dialog.

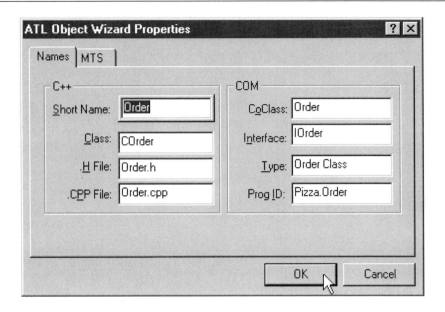

Figure 8-23. The Names dialog.

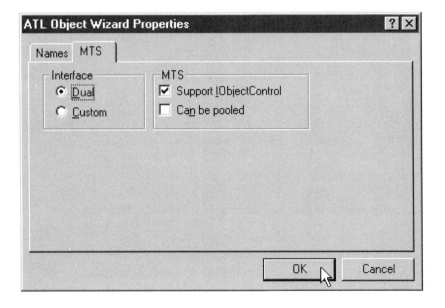

Figure 8-24. The MTS dialog.

```
#include "Order.h"
#include <stdio.h>


/////////////////////////////////////////////////////////////////////////
/////
// COrder


STDMETHODIMP COrder::InterfaceSupportsErrorInfo(REFIID riid)
{
    static const IID* arr[] =
    {
        &IID_IOrder,
    };

    for (int i=0;i<sizeof(arr)/sizeof(arr[0]);i++)
    {
        if (InlineIsEqualGUID(*arr[i],riid))
            return S_OK;
    }
    return S_FALSE;
}
HRESULT COrder::Activate()
{
    HRESULT hr = GetObjectContext(&m_spObjectContext);
    if (SUCCEEDED(hr))
        return S_OK;
    return hr;
}


void COrder::Deactivate()
{
    m_spObjectContext.Release();
}
```

Transaction Server: Activate() and Deactivate()

When we selected "MS Transaction Server Component" as our ATL object, the wizard added two member functions to the class: Activate() and Deactivate(). These functions are invoked on object creation and deactivation. They are responsible for retrieving the object context and releasing it when we are finished with the component.

GetObjectContext()

The `GetObjectContext()` function returns an interface to us that allows us to create instances of other COM objects within our main COM object under the MTS context and perform transactional processing. The `IObjectContext` interface, which is returned by `GetObjectContext()`, contains two methods of interest: `SetAbort()` and `SetComplete()`. If any of the components should fail, we need to call the `SetAbort()` method. Likewise, if the component performs its function successfully, calling `SetComplete()` will inform Transaction Server that this step completed successfully. After component execution, the handle to the object context is returned to the MTS pool. Every component in the package must complete its execution successfully for the whole transaction to succeed.

Commits and Rollbacks with SetComplete() and SetAbort()

What happens if we call `SetComplete()` inside our object? This tells MTS that we have succeeded with an atomic step in the transaction process. We also are telling MTS that we are done using the component and that resources used by the component can be used by another request for the object. The internal state of the component is lost as well. It also sends an instruction to the MTS Resource Manager for the data source to commit the transaction if the rest of the components in the package have executed successfully.

Similarly, when we call `SetAbort()`, we are also telling MTS that the component is no longer needed and that the state can be disposed of. The main idea to remember about calling `SetAbort()` is that it sends a signal to the MTS Resource Manager to roll back any and all changes made to the data source.

Adding the PizzaOrder Properties and Methods

The `PizzaOrder` component will make copious use of ADO, and the calling conventions of the ADO methods are somewhat different from those in VBScript. One of the objectives of this section is to familiarize you with MTS and gain a better understanding of the C++ calling conventions of the ADO objects. Throughout this section, you'll be introduced to key concepts that will help you use ADO from C++.

Initialization of the Class

The `PizzaOrder` object performs some initializations upon object creation. We add an implementation of `FinalConstruct()` to do this:

```
HRESULT COrder::FinalConstruct()
{
    m_OrderNumber = 0;
    m_MaxLineNumber = -1;
    m_OrderDeliveryAddress.Attach( L"");
    m_OrderDatePlaced = ( DATE )0;
    m_OrderDateFulfilled = ( DATE )0;
    m_OrderStatus.Attach( L"" );
    m_Username.Attach( L"" );
    return S_OK;
}
```

The code is fairly straightforward. We use an order number of zero to indicate that there is no current order set for the object. The other order properties are set to blank values. The `Attach()` member function of the BSTR class is used to initialize (attach) the `m_str` member of the class with a string constant.

The OrderNumber Property

Setting the `OrderNumber` property is a typical start to using the `PizzaOrder` component. When we set the `OrderNumber` property, we assign the class member variable `m_OrderNumber` the value contained in the `newVal` parameter. This is the first step in the process. The code is straightforward:

```
// Set the order number for the class
m_OrderNumber = newVal;
```

A customer order has several items associated with it, like the customer's address, the order status, and so on. We want to retrieve that information for the customer order and populate the properties of the class. So, we need to build an appropriate SQL statement to do that:

```
// Format the string for our SQL statement
sprintf( sSQLStmt,
    "SELECT order_status, order_number, delivery_address, ⏎
datetime_ordered, datetime_fulfilled, username FROM Orders WHERE ⏎
order_number = %ld",
    m_OrderNumber );
```

In this example, we use the `stdio.h` library function `sprintf()` to format the SQL statement string. You may find it convenient to use this method of string formatting if you are used to working with C-standard I/O routines. But, in order for us to use the SQL statement string in ADO, it needs to exist as an automation-compatible data type, like BSTR. The next statement constructs a new CComBSTR using the ANSI string constructor from our ANSI string:

```
// Convert the SQL ANSI string to BSTR
bstrSQLStmt = sSQLStmt;
```

We are now ready to instantiate a Recordset object. Previously, we declared pOrderRec to be a smart pointer to a Recordset object _Recordset. We will use the CreateInstance() method to create the object. Incidentally, this code and all the ADO code following it will be placed inside a C++ try block, which enables us to easily catch any COM-related errors that may occur:

```
// Create a Recordset object for retrieving the order data
pOrderRec.CreateInstance( __uuidof( Recordset ) );
```

Next, we open the Recordset object with our query. We use a keyset cursor with optimistic locking:

```
// Open the Recordset object
pOrderRec->Open( bstrSQLStmt.m_str, m_ConnectionStr.m_str,
adOpenKeyset, adLockOptimistic, 0 );
```

Next, we check for the existence of the order by checking the RecordCount property for a value greater than zero:

```
// If no rows, then order does not exist
if ( ( nRecordCount = pOrderRec->RecordCount ) == 0 )
{
     m_OrderNumber = 0;
     pOrderRec->Release();
     Error( "That customer order does not exist", IID_IOrder, 0 );
     return E_FAIL;
}
```

If the RecordCount is zero, then we know that our SQL query returned no rows; hence, the order does not exist. We indicate this by returning an automation error stating that the order does not exist.

If the query returned a row, then we start to retrieve the fields from the query. We begin with the OrderStatus. All of the character fields in the query (order_status and delivery_address) use almost the exact same code. The order status is the first field in the SQL statement, so that makes it field #0. Here's the code:

```
// Retrieve the order status. Field #0. Then
// convert the variant into a BSTR and assign it to the OrderStatus
property

fldOrderStatus = pOrderRec->Fields->GetItem( ( _variant_t )0L );
vTmp = fldOrderStatus->Value;
if ( vTmp.vt != VT_NULL )
{
    bstrTmp2 = vTmp.bstrVal ;
    bstrTmp2.CopyTo( &m_OrderStatus.m_str );
}
```

We defined fldOrderStatus as a FieldPtr, which is an ADO Field object. The first line calls the GetItem method of the Fields collection to return a Field object for the first item (item #0). vTmp is a CComVariant that receives the value of the fldOrderStatus object (from the Value property).

The next part of the code

```
if ( vTmp.vt != VT_NULL )
{
    bstrTmp2 = vTmp.bstrVal ;
    bstrTmp2.CopyTo( &m_OrderStatus.m_str );
}
```

does a check of the vTmp variant to see whether it is null. This situation would occur if the database field order_status contained a null value. If it is null, we must not attempt to perform the BSTR copying routines that follow because they would cause a runtime error.

Previously, we declared a temporary CComBSTR bstrTmp2 to hold the BSTR part of the variant. We need to copy the CComBSTR to the class member variable m_OrderStatus to complete the process of setting that property.

The query also contains two date/time fields. Let's explore how to retrieve the date the order was placed from the recordset:

```
// Retrieve the date order placed. Field #3
fldOrderDatePlaced = pOrderRec->Fields->GetItem( ( _variant_t )3L );
vTmp = fldOrderDatePlaced->Value;
if ( vTmp.vt != VT_NULL )
{
    m_OrderDatePlaced = vTmp.date;
}
```

We begin this section of the code just like the others, but this time we are referencing field #3 in the `Fields` collection. We copy the value to the temporary `CComVariant vTmp`. If the variant does not contain a null, we simply assign the date portion of the variant to the `m_OrderDatePlaced` class variable using the normal assignment operator (=).

Implementation of the Other PizzaOrder Properties

The other `PizzaOrder` properties—namely, `OrderStatus`, `OrderDeliveryAddress`, `OrderDatePlaced`, and `OrderDateFulfilled`—are all implemented in a similar manner. Each property has a corresponding class member variable, and the get and put functions reference this class variable. `OrderStatus` and `OrderDeliveryAddress` both return and set BSTR values. Let's look at the code for `get_OrderStatus()` and `put_OrderStatus()`.

Here's the code for the get function (`get_OrderStatus`):

```
STDMETHODIMP COrder::get_OrderStatus(BSTR *pVal)
{
    // Retrieve the order status
    if (!IsOrderNumberSet() )
    {
        DoError( "You must set the OrderNumber property or call ⏎
OrderNew to access this function" );
        return E_FAIL;
    }

    *pVal = m_OrderStatus.Copy();
    return S_OK;
}
```

The business rules of the component state that the `OrderNumber` property must contain a value before retrieving the value of any other property. So, the function first calls `IsOrderNumberSet()` to see whether the `OrderNumber` property (i.e., the m_OrderStatus variable) is nonzero. If it is zero, we return an automation error stating that the OrderNumber property must be set (either directly or by calling OrderNew). Then, returning the string is just a matter of copying the BSTR inside the m_OrderStatus to the pVal parameter using the Copy() method of the CComBSTR class.

Setting the property (put_OrderStatus) is a bit simpler:

```
STDMETHODIMP COrder::put_OrderStatus(BSTR newVal)
{
    // Set the order status
    if (!IsOrderNumberSet() )
    {
        DoError( "You must set the OrderNumber property or call ↵
OrderNew to access this function" );
        return E_FAIL;
    }

    m_OrderStatus = newVal;
    return S_OK;
}
```

Again, the same business rules apply for the OrderNumber property. The m_OrderStatus assignment operator (=) is used to set the CComBSTR to the BSTR newVal.

Implementing the get_OrderDatePlaced and put_OrderDatePlaced functions are easier since the variant is treated as a scalar type. We need only use the assignment operator (=) to get and set the class member variables for the property. The following code is straightforward:

```
STDMETHODIMP COrder::get_OrderDatePlaced(DATE *pVal)
{
    if (!IsOrderNumberSet() )
    {
        DoError( "You must set the OrderNumber property or call ↵
OrderNew to access this function" );
        return E_FAIL;
    }

    *pVal = m_OrderDatePlaced;
    return S_OK;
}
```

```
STDMETHODIMP COrder::put_OrderDatePlaced(DATE newVal)
{
     if (!IsOrderNumberSet() )
     {
          DoError( "You must set the OrderNumber property or call
OrderNew to access this function" );
          return E_FAIL;
     }
     m_OrderDatePlaced = newVal;
     return S_OK;
}
```

OrderNew() for Creating a New Order

When using the PizzaOrder component, the programmer has the option to
call up an existing order or to create a new order using the OrderNew()
method. The OrderNew() method simply adds a new row to the Orders table
by selecting the greatest order number, adding 1, and inserting the value in
the table. Once the row is inserted, we set the OrderNumber property to the
order number of the newly created customer order. Here's the code:

```
STDMETHODIMP COrder::OrderNew()
{
     _ConnectionPtr      cnn;                    // ADO Connection
     _variant_t          vtEmpty;
     long nMaxOrderNum;
     CComVariant vTmp;
     _RecordsetPtr rstMax;
     char sSQLStmt[ 255 ];

     try
     {
          // Create a new order by inserting a new row in the Orders
table
          cnn.CreateInstance( __uuidof( Connection ) );
          cnn->Open( m_ConnectionStr.m_str, "", "", 0 );

          rstMax = cnn->Execute( "SELECT MAX(order_number) FROM
Orders", &vtEmpty, 0 );
          vTmp = rstMax->Fields->Item[ (_variant_t)0L ]->Value;
          if ( vTmp.vt == VT_NULL )
          {
               nMaxOrderNum = m_OrderNumber = 1;
```

```
            }
            else
            {
                 nMaxOrderNum = vTmp.lVal;
                 m_OrderNumber = ++nMaxOrderNum;
            }
            sprintf( sSQLStmt, "INSERT INTO Orders ( order_number ) ↵
VALUES ( %ld ) ",
                              nMaxOrderNum );
            cnn->Execute( sSQLStmt, &vtEmpty, 0L );
            cnn->Close();
      }
      catch ( _com_error e )
      {
            Error( "OrderNew failed to create a new order", IID_IOrder, 0
);
            return E_FAIL;
      }
      return S_OK;
}
```

We start by creating a new instance of the ADO Connection object and opening it using the connection string contained in the ConnectionStr property. The first SQL command that we execute selects the maximum order number from the Orders table. If there are no orders in the table, a null will be returned as a result of the query, and we test for this by checking the value of vTmp.vt for null (VT_NULL). In this case, we designate the first order as order #1. If an order exists, the order's number is extracted from the lVal (long) value of the variant vTmp. We then assign the m_OrderNumber member variable (which maps to the OrderNumber property) to the long value incremented by 1.

Using the new order number, we then proceed to create the new order in the Orders table. We build our SQL INSERT statement in the same fashion as the other. We call Execute(), and, if no errors occurred, then the order is created.

OrderAddItem() for Adding Items to the Order

The purpose of the OrderAddItem method is to add a new food item to the customer order. With the OrderNumber property set (through either a previous call to OrderNew or an assignment of the OrderNumber property), we can begin to add items to the order. The OrderDetail table holds the individual items of the order, and the OrderAddItem procedure adds rows to this table.

The method begins with the normal check of the m_OrderNumber variable, as the other methods do. We then begin a try . . . catch in which we select the highest line item of the current order and set it to a private class member variable called m_MaxLineNumber. In an effort to save the overhead incurred by querying the database unnecessarily, we check the m_MaxLineNumber variable for a valid value before attempting to retrieve it from the database. If the m_MaxLineNumber is not set (it contains –1), we need to start preparing an appropriate SQL statement to retrieve the value. In the previous examples, we've used stdio functions to create our strings. To get some practice using BSTRs, we'll construct a BSTR to be used for the SQL statement:

```
// Check in m_MaxLineNumber for the highest line number for the order
if ( m_MaxLineNumber == -1 )
{
    // Cached max line number not set, calculate it from the db and
    // set m_MaxLineNumber to it
    bstrSQL = "SELECT MAX( line_item ) FROM OrderDetail WHERE ⏎
order_number = ";
```

In the following steps, we are going to format the rest of the SQL statement string. This means that the long integer values need to be converted to string data. ATL provides a series of conversion functions for this purpose. One of these functions is the VarBstrFromI4() function. It converts a variant long (VT_I4) to a BSTR. The converted BSTR value is passed back in the last parameter, bstrOrdNum. The number string is then concatenated to the main SQL statement using the CComBSTR overloaded += operator:

```
VarBstrFromI4( m_OrderNumber, NULL, NULL, &bstrOrdNum );
bstrSQL += bstrOrdNum;
```

Our SQL statement is now ready for execution. We call the Open() method of the Recordset object:

```
rstMax->Open( bstrSQL.m_str, m_ConnectionStr.m_str,
         adOpenKeyset,
         adLockOptimistic,
         0 );
vTmp = rstMax->Fields->Item[ ( _variant_t )0L ]->Value;
```

Even though the preceding query retrieves the results from an aggregate function and not a database field, it is still designated as item #0 by ADO. We

reference it as such when we retrieve that value into our temporary
CComVariant variable.

   If there are no line items for the current order, the SQL query will return
a null value. We check for this, and, if it is null, we set the m_MaxLineNumber to
1, making it the first line item in the order. If there is already a line item for
the order (as the value of the SQL query would indicate), we increment the
value and assign it to m_MaxLineNumber:

```
rstMax->Open( bstrSQL.m_str, m_ConnectionStr.m_str,
                    adOpenKeyset,
                    adLockOptimistic,
                    0 );
vTmp = rstMax->Fields->Item[ ( _variant_t )0L ]->Value;


if ( vTmp.vt = VT_NULL )
{
     m_MaxLineNumber = 1;
}
else
{
vTmp.lVal += 1;
     m_MaxLineNumber = vTmp.lVal;
}
```

   Now that we have the line item number for the new food item, we create
a new Connection object and use it to execute an SQL INSERT statement that
will add a row to the OrderDetail table. We start to concatenate a string for
the SQL statement. We use the ATL variant conversion functions again but
this time we convert the Quantity and m_MaxLineNumber values to strings:

```
// open db connection
cnnAddItem.CreateInstance( __uuidof( Connection ) );
          cnnAddItem->Open( m_ConnectionStr.m_str, "", "", 0 );


// construct SQL statement
bstrSQL = "INSERT INTO OrderDetail ( order_number, item_name, quantity, ⏎
line_item ) VALUES ( ";
VarBstrFromI4( m_OrderNumber, NULL, NULL, &bstrTmp );
bstrSQL += bstrTmp;
bstrSQL += ", '";
bstrSQL += ItemName;
bstrSQL += "', ";
```

```
VarBstrFromI4( Quantity, NULL, NULL, &bstrTmp );
bstrSQL += bstrTmp;
bstrSQL += ", ";
VarBstrFromI4( m_MaxLineNumber, NULL, NULL, &bstrTmp );
bstrSQL += bstrTmp;
bstrSQL += ")";

// Add the row
cnnAddItem->Execute( bstrSQL.m_str, &vtEmpty, 0 );
```

OrderSave and OrderDelete

These two methods are in charge of saving the properties of a customer order in the database and deleting the customer order, respectively. The functionality of building an SQL statement is similar to the other methods we've constructed thus far. One item of particular interest is the OrderSave() method. We deal with converting some variants that contain dates to BSTRs. The conversion functions are similar to the ones we've already used. This code fragment from the OrderSave() method shows how the m_OrderDateFulfilled value is converted:

```
if ( m_OrderDateFulfilled > 0 )
{
    VarBstrFromDate( m_OrderDateFulfilled, NULL, NULL, ↵
&bstrDateFulfilled );
    szSQLStmt += "datetime_fulfilled = '";
    szSQLStmt += bstrDateFulfilled;
    szSQLStmt += "', ";
}
else
{
    szSQLStmt += "datetime_fulfilled = NULL, ";
}
```

The ACID Test: Design Considerations for COM Components

Let's talk for a few moments about some design considerations for transaction-enabled components. When designing components for MTS, you need to keep a set of rules in mind. These rules are based on a general set of guidelines that were formed as a result of many programmers' experiences with MTS. They are known as the *ACID test*. ACID is an acronym for *Atomicity, Consistency, Isolation,* and *Durability*.

- *Atomicity* means that either the operation that the component performs is completely successful or the data that the component operates on does not change at all. This is important because if the transaction has to update multiple data items, we do not want to leave it with erroneous values. If a failure occurs at any step that could compromise the integrity of the system, the changes are "undone" or rolled back.

- *Consistency* deals with preserving the system state in the event that a transaction would fail. This operation is called a *rollback*.

- *Isolation* means that a transaction acts as though it has complete control of the system. In effect, this means that transactions are executed serially, one at a time. This process keeps the system state consistent since two components executed at the same time that operate on the same data can compromise the integrity of the system.

- *Durability* is the ability of a system to return to any state that was present before the execution of a transaction. For example, if a hard drive crash occurs in the middle of a transaction, we can restore the original state from a transaction log that is stored on another disk that the system recorded to.

By following these rules in the design phase of your COM objects, you can ensure that your data integrity is intact and that your system will have high levels of reliability for your users.

Adding the Component to the Transaction Server Environment

In order for a component to be used by Transaction Server, you must perform a special type of registration for the object. This involves creating a new package. The package will then house our `PizzaOrder` component. Let's walk through this process:

1. Start Microsoft Transaction Server.

2. The main Transaction Server window appears. Figure 8-25 shows the main screen in large-icon view. Each icon represents a package that is installed in the MTS runtime environment. To add a new package, click the "New" icon in the toolbar.

3. As Figure 8-26 shows, the next screen gives you the option to select either to install a prebuilt package or to create a new, empty one. Click the button labeled "Create an empty package."

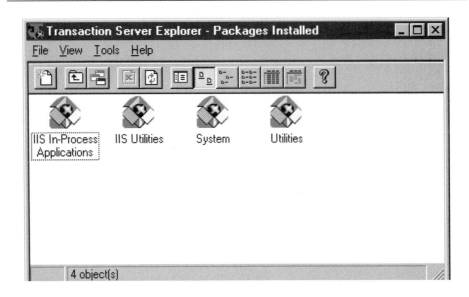

Figure 8-25. The main MTS window before new package creation.

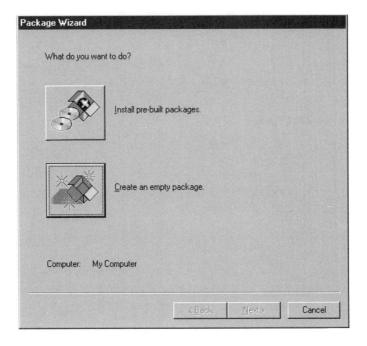

Figure 8-26. Selecting new, empty package.

4. Type the name of the new package. Call it "Pizza." (See Figure 8-27.)

5. As Figure 8-28 shows, the Transaction Server window now shows the `Pizza` package we just created. Double-click to open/expand the package. Open the Components folder. Click the "New" button in the toolbar to add a new component.

6. Two options appear in the window. You may add a component to the package that is already registered using the `regsvr32` utility, or you may add another component by browsing for it on your drive. When we performed a build of the `Orders.dll` file, Visual C++ registered the component for us. So, we select the "Import component(s) that are already registered" option. (See Figure 8-29.)

7. As Figure 8-30 shows, the next screen shows all of the registered COM objects that are in-process. Scroll down until you locate our DLL (`Pizza.Order.1`). Highlight it, and click Finish. You have now added the component to the package.

8. Back in the Transaction Server window, right-click on the `Pizza.Order` component, and select "Properties." Click on the Transaction tab. (See

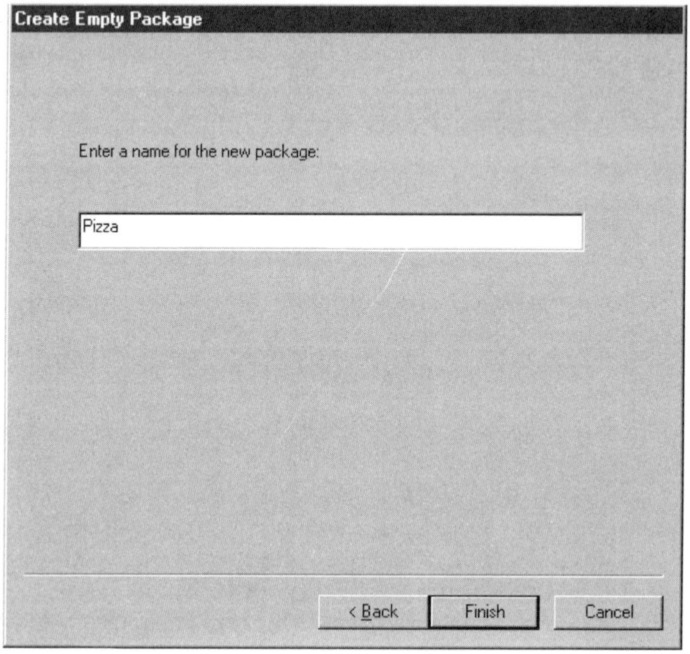

Figure 8-27. Entering new package name.

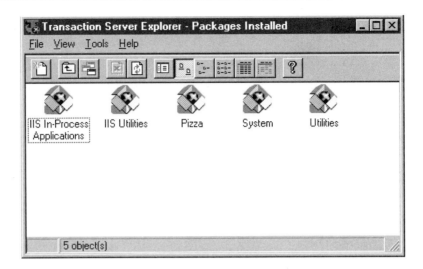

Figure 8-28.   The main MTS window after new package creation.

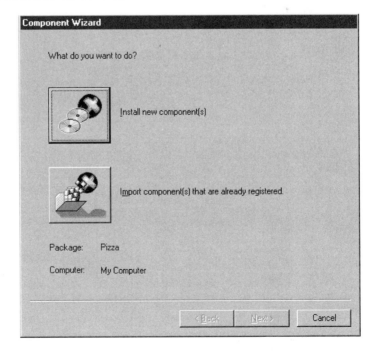

Figure 8-29.   Importing already registered component.

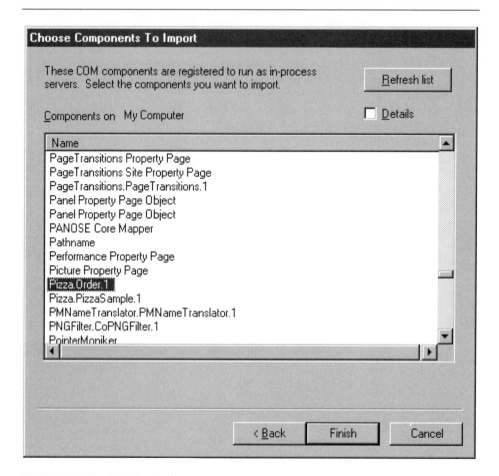

Figure 8-30.   Choosing component to import.

Figure 8-31.) Transaction Server allows you to configure the transaction-level support for a component. Here are the four different levels of support and their functions:

■ Requires a transaction—The component must run inside a transaction.

■ Requires a new transaction—The component needs its own transaction in which to run. If the component is not called from within a transaction, a new transaction is automatically created.

■ Supports transactions—You may run the component inside or outside a transaction without any ill effects.

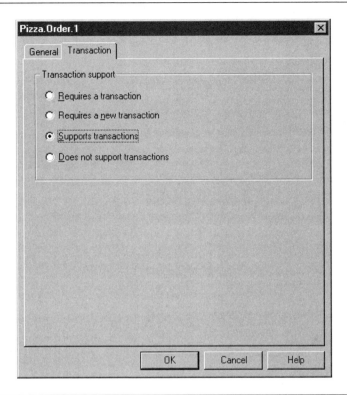

Figure 8-31.   Selecting transaction-level support.

■ Does not support transactions—This is the default setting for new
MTS components. Execution of the component is always outside a
transaction regardless of whether or not a transaction has been initiated for the component.

Select the "Supports transactions" option. This would allow our
component to execute inside or outside a transaction. We'll see next
how to call the component inside a transaction.

Transactional ASP: Using the Component inside ASP

With the introduction of IIS 4.0 and the latest version of PWS came support
for transaction-enabled ASP. Using a special identifier at the beginning of an
.asp file, you can have the ASP page and the components it uses run inside a

transaction. This is important because a transaction-enabled ASP page will call the MTS-enabled components and catch the notification of success or failure of the transaction. The ASP page also will call SetComplete() or SetAbort() for the final time, thereby completing the transaction.

To enable transactions in your .asp file, add the following line before any other code:

```
<%@ Transaction=required %>
```

Continue with your ASP after this line. To create components, you can still use the Server.CreateObject() function to instantiate objects. To access the object context interface, simply call the methods of ObjectContext, which is an intrinsic object in transaction-enabled .asp files. So, if you wanted to abort a transaction, you would write

```
If ATerribleFailureOccurred() Then
      ObjectContext.SetAbort()
Else
      ObjectContext.SetComplete()
End If
```

Another feature in transaction-enabled Web pages is the use of two script-level events: OnTransactionCommit and OnTransactionAbort. Declare them in your script like this:

```
Sub OnTransactionCommit()
      ' TODO: Add code to execute upon commit of the transaction
End Sub

Sub OnTransactionAbort()
      ' TODO: Add code to execute upon aborting the transaction
End Sub
```

Whenever the SetAbort() or SetComplete() functions are called (either inside the .asp file or in the component), their corresponding event subroutines are called. Note that script execution stops after one of these subroutines is executed. Also, changes to data made in the ASP script itself (outside of the data source) are not automatically rolled back by a call to SetAbort(), so OnTransactionAbort() should contain whatever code is necessary to "undo" those changes to the data.

Integrating the PizzaOrder Component into the Megabyte's Application

We are now going to create a special transaction-enabled ASP page to run the `PizzaOrder` component in the Megabyte's application. We will modify the `menu.asp` file to incorporate use of the `PizzaOrder` component.

The first step is to enable transactions for the page. The first line of code currently states the default language to use for the server-side script. It is currently VBScript:

```
<%@ Language=VBScript %>
```

Change that line to say

```
<%@ Transaction=required Language=VBScript %>
```

The page is now transaction-enabled. Next, add the event handlers toward the bottom of the file:

```
Sub OnTransactionCommit()
End Sub

Sub OnTransactionAbort()
End Sub
```

Here's how the ordering process works. The following code performs the order-taking process:

```
If Request.Form( "submit1" ) = "Add Items" Then
    Set objOrder = Server.CreateObject( "Pizza.Order" )
    objOrder.ConnectionStr = "DSN=Megabytes"
    objOrder.OrderNew
    objOrder.OrderDatePlaced = Now
    objOrder.OrderSave
gOrderNum = objOrder.OrderNumber
    For Each sVar in Request.Form
        If Left( sVar, 4 ) = "QUAN" Then
            objOrder.OrderAddItem Replace( Mid( sVar, 6 ), "_", " "
), _
            CInt( Request.Form( sVar ) )
            End If
    Next
End If
```

We first check the value of the `submit1` form variable to see whether the form was submitted. If the form was submitted, we continue with the processing of the order.

We start by creating the `Pizza.Order` object. The `Pizza.Order` object needs to have the `ConnectionStr` parameter set to a valid ODBC connection string to our data source. Next, we call the `OrderNew()` method to create a new customer order. Placing a date/time stamp on the customer order will help us track the order later, so we do that by setting the `OrderDatePlaced` property to the current date/time using the VBScript `Now()` function. Calling `OrderSave` will save the changes to the modified order properties (i.e., `rderDatePlaced`) to the database. Our script will use the new customer order at a later point in the script, possibly after the object's state is lost. To preserve it, we assign it to a temporary variable:

```
objOrder.OrderNew
objOrder.OrderDatePlaced = Now
objOrder.OrderSave
gOrderNum = objOrder.OrderNumber
```

Retrieving the values that the user entered in the form is a simple matter of iterating through the `Forms` collection. We use a `For Each` loop for this purpose. Keep in mind that the `Forms` collection will contain form values not only for the food quantities but also for other form elements (like the submit button used to send the form data to the server). When we initially generated the form, we used a naming convention for the food quantity fields. The names were prefixed with "QUAN_" to differentiate them from other HTML input fields. Using this knowledge, we use the VBScript `Left()` function to "filter" them:

```
For Each sVar in Request.Form
    If Left( sVar, 4 ) = "QUAN" Then
        nQuan = CInt( Request.Form( sVar ) )
        If nQuan > 0 Then ' skip zero quantities
            objOrder.OrderAddItem Replace( Mid( sVar, 6 ), "_", ↵
" " ),_
            CInt( Request.Form( sVar ) )
        End If
    End If
Next
```

With each food item quantity in the `Forms` collection, we call the `OrderAddItem` method. We use the name of the HTML form variable as the name of the food item. Since we replaced the spaces in the variable name with underscores, we substitute backspaces for the underscores, hence restoring the original text. The quantity to add is retrieved from the value of iterator sVar.

After we complete the For Each loop, we want to commit the transaction to save all changes we made to the customer order. We need to call SetComplete() within the ASP page:

```
ObjectContext.SetComplete
```

This will trigger the OnTransactionCommit event for the page. In the OnTransactionCommit subroutine, we send a message back to the browser indicating the new order number that was assigned to the order. We also include a link back to the menu.asp page so that the customer can enter a new order or return to the Megabyte's homepage:

```
Sub OnTransactionCommit()
        Response.Write "Your order number is: " & gOrderNum & _
            "<BR><A href="menu.asp"">Return</A>"
End Sub
```

Microsoft Message Queuing (MSMQ)

We've talked about distributed systems that can span multiple networks. This creates many problems for the designers and programmers of these systems. Some of these problems we have addressed already, but others still need some resolution.

1. Data sources can be spread out over many different servers and data-bases that are connected over (sometimes) unreliable networks. For example, an online ordering system may interface with many different types of systems, such as accounting, purchasing, supply, and ware-house inventory. When an order is placed, many of these systems can be updated. Data integrity is mission-critical here. If a failure occurs along the way, it could cause many cascading problems. These prob-lems are solved using transactions—specifically, MTS when we are dealing with Windows.

2. Even though transactions play a large part in keeping database integrity interact, slow networks or unreliable networks (such as analog modem connections) can be interrupted for a number of

different reasons. This could also cause a chain of updates (a transaction) to fail. The failure may not be the fault of the server-side processing, but it will be a failure nonetheless. It would be more robust if we were able to retry a particular transaction(s) if some failed for this reason.

3. We live in a world of many tongues. More specifically, the systems that encompass a large distributed network are very likely to be heterogeneous. Many different software packages, languages, and operating systems will be involved. Some may support COM; some may not. Maybe some of these data sources will be ODBC-compatible, but your chances of this may not be great. Having every piece agree on a common language would be a giant leap toward a more elegantly designed system.

Problems 2 and 3 are new to us thus far, and they are addressed with a technology called *message queuing* (MQ). Message queuing works by using a *store-and-forward* technique for communication between systems across the enterprise. To understand how message queuing works, it helps to look at a classic example of an implementation of MQ. Consider your e-mail system. It is a method of communication between two parties, but, unlike "live" forms of communication, like a telephone conversation that relies on the fact that both parties are actively connected, e-mail does not require you to be present to receive a message. An e-mail message to you is received by the mail server and is *stored* there until you retrieve it (i.e., it is *forwarded* to your e-mail reader program)—hence, the name *store-and-forward.*

How does this relate to MQ in enterprise applications? Generally speaking, the concept is exactly the same, although the messages are typically not e-mail-style messages, but commands in that universal language mentioned earlier. Messages are sent to *message queues,* a first-in, first-out storage area where another application, called a *listener application,* retrieves them. To add robustness to the message queuing process, there is a provision in the message queuing system to ensure that the message is delivered only once. Again, this works like our e-mail example. When we attempt to retrieve the messages from the server, we send a message back to the server for each message indicating that we successfully retrieved it and that it can be removed from the server (queue). Like e-mail systems, the MQ system has the ability to prioritize messages. Messages that are marked as urgent make their way through the queue much faster than those messages of lower priority. MQ also provides the ability to digitally sign messages and to perform user authentication.

The MSMQ Explorer

Once *Microsoft Message Queuing* (MSMQ) is installed, you will see that it consists of many different parts, which center on the MSMQ Explorer. The *MSMQ Explorer* is an application used to manage MSMQ elements interactively. The data is in a hierarchical format.

At the top the hierarchy is the *Primary Enterprise Controller* (PEC). This is where information about all MSMQ servers and queues is stored for the entire enterprise. The enterprise is comprised of *sites,* which are servers that include *routing servers* and *site controllers* (primary and backup). Routing servers can provide the actual queuing of messages and can facilitate their delivery. Primary and backup site controllers hold copies of the information about their site from the information contained in the PEC.

The MSMQ Explorer can manage message queues. It handles creating and destroying them. We can also send test messages to other message queues across the enterprise.

MSMQ is part of the Windows NT 4.0 Option Pack and must have SQL Server installed in order for it to run. MSMQ utilizes SQL Server to manage the queues.

Elementary Setup of MSMQ

Before we start using MSMQ to send messages to a queue, we need to set up that queue. Our sample computer has MSMQ installed and is configured as a Primary Enterprise Controller. This means that other machines in the enterprise look at the PEC for queue information on all machines in that enterprise. The enterprise contains one site called "Matt." The Matt site houses the computer known as "in-nt-mcrouch." For demonstration purposes, these entities are all on a local server. When you launch MSMQ Explorer and expand the tree all the way out, you will see something like what appears in Figure 8-32.

Here are the steps for setting up a queue:

1. To set up a queue and send test messages to it, highlight the computer name in the tree view (in our example, `in-nt-mcrouch`).

2. Select "Send Test Messages" from the Tools menu. A dialog box opens up asking you to select a queue. If we do not have any queues defined already, the Destination drop-down will not contain any entries. At this time, we can create a new queue by clicking the New Queue button. (See Figure 8-33.)

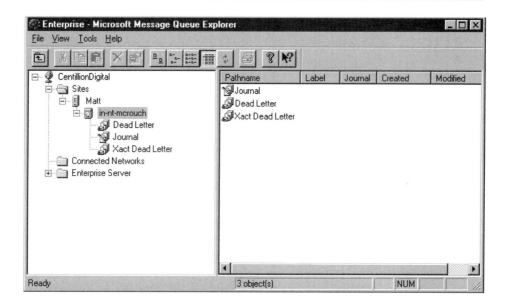

Figure 8-32. Expanded view of the enterprise.

3. Another dialog box appears asking for the pathname to the new queue. Enter the pathname in the format `computer\queue` (e.g., `in-nt-mcrouch\mattqueue`). Click OK to create the queue.

4. To send a test message, simply select the queue you wish to send a message to from the drop-down list, and click the Send button. The text at the top of the dialog should show that a message has been sent.

5. To view the message that was sent to the queue, highlight the queue in the tree view. The right windowpane will show the messages currently

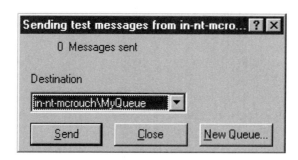

Figure 8-33. Selecting a queue.

in the queue. You might need to click the "Refresh" button in the toolbar if your messages don't appear immediately in the list. You can also view the details of a particular message by double-clicking on it. (See Figure 8-34.)

6. One final step: When a queue is created using the preceding steps, you may want to change the label property of the queue to a meaningful name. You can do this by right-clicking on the queue in the tree view and selecting "Properties" from the menu. Change the "Label" field to some other meaningful name that describes the data that will go into this queue. (See Figure 8-35.)

Sending a Message

Take a look at Listing 8-1, which shows a brief example in ASP of sending a message to our newly created queue. Notice that the code makes use of several different objects, which we will examine shortly.

Listing 8-1. Sending a Message (example8-1.asp)

```
<!-METADATA TYPE="TypeLib" NAME="Microsoft Message Queue Object Library"
UUID="{D7D6E071-DCCD-11D0-AA4B-0060970DEBAE}" VERSION="1.0"->
```

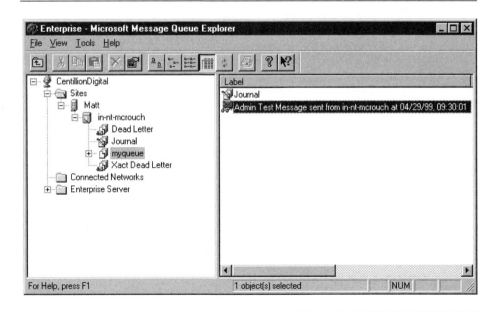

Figure 8-34.   Viewing the message sent.

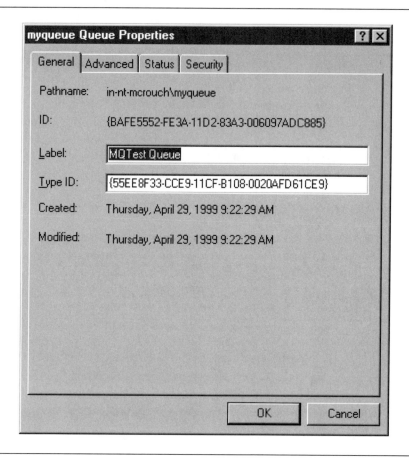

Figure 8-35.   Changing the label property.

```
<%
Dim mqQuery
Dim mqQInfos
Dim mqQInfo
Set mqQuery = Server.CreateObject("MSMQ.MSMQQuery")
Set mqQInfos = Server.CreateObject("MSMQ.MSMQQueueInfos")

Set mqQInfos = mqQuery.LookupQueue(,,"MQTest Queue" )
mqQInfos.Reset

Set mqQInfo = mqQInfos.Next
If mqQInfo Is Nothing Then
```

```
        Response.Write "Cannot open queue"
        Response.End
End If

Set mqTXQueue = mqQInfo.Open(MQ_SEND_ACCESS, MQ_DENY_NONE)

Set mqTXmsg = Server.CreateObject("MSMQ.MSMQMessage")

mqTXmsg.Body = "This is a test message from ASP"
mqTXMsg.Label = "Test from Active Server Pages"
mqTXMsg.Send mqTXQueue

Response.Write "done"
%>
```

Before we begin looking at the code for sending a message to a message queue, also notice in Listing 8-1 the METADATA HTML tag at the top of the file. This is a special directive in ASP that tells the script engine to bring in the type library information for the type library with the given UUID. Our code brings in type library information for Microsoft Message Queuing. We do this so that we can use predefined constants from the library in our code without having to declare Consts manually.

The MSMQ Objects

Our sample MSMQ code utilizes the following objects.

MSMQ.MSMQQuery

The MSMQ.MSMQQuery object is used to locate information about public queues in the enterprise. It has one method called LookupQueue(), which we use in our code. The job of LookupQueue() is to return a collection of queues that meet the criteria that we specify. All of the parameters to LookupQueue() are optional. Here's the syntax:

```
object.LookupQueue ([QueueGuid] [, ServiceTypeGuid] [, Label] [,
CreateTime] [, ModifyTime] [, RelServiceType] [, RelLabel] [,
RelCreateTime] [, RelModifyTime])
```

where QueueGuid is a GUID that uniquely identifies a queue; ServiceTypeGuid is the type of queue service; Label is the queue's label;

`CreateTime` is the time the queue was created; and `ModifyTime` is the time when queue properties were last modified. `RelServiceType`, `RelLabel`, `RelCreateTime`, and `RelModifyTime` are used for filtering the queues returned.

The code looking up our code is done by querying for the label property of the queue. We skip the first two parameters:

```
Set mqQInfos = mqQuery.LookupQueue(,,"MQTest Queue" )
```

`LookupQueue()` returns an object reference to an `MSMQ.MSMQQueueInfos` object (explained next).

MSMQ.MSMQQueueInfos

The `MSMQ.MSMQQueueInfos` object holds a collection of queue objects—specifically, a series of `MSMQ.MSMQQueueInfo` objects. This is the object that is returned by the `LookupQueue()` function. It is not a collection like the collection objects we've been dealing with thus far. It is a special one with different methods.

In our code, we call `LookupQueue()`, and then we call the `Reset()` method on the returned `mqQInfos` object. The `Reset()` method takes no parameters. `Reset()` will point the "cursor" to the first record in the collection. Starting at the beginning of the queue, we call `Next()` to retrieve the first item in the collection:

```
mqQInfos.Reset

Set mqQInfo = mqQInfos.Next
If mqQInfo Is Nothing Then
      Response.Write "Cannot open queue"
      Response.End
End If
```

We then need to check to see whether `Next()` actually returned something. If the object handle evaluates to `Nothing`, then we know that we've reached the end of the collection. In our MSMQ Explorer example, we set up a single queue with a label of `MQTest Queue`. On our particular PEC, this is a unique name, so it should be the only queue in the collection. If we did not find anything, we display a message back to the user and terminate script processing with a call to `Response.End`.

We've successfully located our queue, so now we need to open the queue so that we can send messages to it. The `Open()` method of the `MSMQ.MSMQQueueInfo` object performs this action:

```
Set mqTXQueue = mqQInfo.Open(MQ_SEND_ACCESS, MQ_DENY_NONE)
```

The parameters of the `Open()` method describe the mode in which to open the queue and who can access the queue messages, respectively. Possible parameters for the access mode (first parameter) are as follows:

- `MQ_PEEK_ACCESS`—We are only allowed to "peek" at the messages. Peeking at a message does not remove it from the queue, unlike `MQ_RECEIVE_ACCESS`.
- `MQ_SEND_ACCESS`—This mode allows messages to be sent only. This access mode is analogous to a write-only "drop box."
- `MQ_RECEIVE_ACCESS`—Messages can be read from the queue and deleted once successfully read. We can also peek at messages.

The `Open()` method returns an `MSMQ.MSMQQueue` object. We will use this queue object in the upcoming `Send()` method.

MSMQ.MSMQMessage

The `MSMQ.MSMQMessage` object is used to package up a message to be sent to a queue. Our code sets two properties: `Body` and `Label`. `Body` is what you would expect it to be—the main content of the message. `Label` is the short description of the message.

When we are ready to send our message to the queue, we simply call the `Send` method. It takes one argument, the object that references our open queue (`mqTXQueue`):

```
mqTXMsg.Send mqTXQueue
```

Reading from the Message Queue

The other part of an MSMQ application is the listener. The listener's job is to receive messages from the queue and do any appropriate processing with the message. The code for looking up our queue and setting it up for receiving is very similar to the code in the example given in Listing 8-1 earlier.

Listing 8-2. Reading from the Message Queue (example8-2.asp)

```
<!—METADATA TYPE="TypeLib" NAME="Microsoft Message Queue Object Library"
UUID="{D7D6E071-DCCD-11D0-AA4B-0060970DEBAE}" VERSION="1.0"—>
<%
Dim mqQuery
```

```
Dim mqQInfos
Dim mqQInfo
Set mqQuery = Server.CreateObject("MSMQ.MSMQQuery")
Set mqQInfos = Server.CreateObject("MSMQ.MSMQQueueInfos")
Set mqQInfos = mqQuery.LookupQueue(,,"MQTest Queue" )
mqQInfos.Reset

Set mqQInfo = mqQInfos.Next
If mqQInfo Is Nothing Then
        Response.Write "Cannot open queue"
        Response.End
End If

Set mqTXQueue = mqQInfo.Open(MQ_RECEIVE_ACCESS, MQ_DENY_NONE)
Set mqMyMsg = mqTXQueue.Receive(,,,1000)

If mqMyMsg Is Nothing Then
        Response.Write "queue is empty"
Else
        Response.Write "Received: " & mqMyMsg.Label & " - " & mqMyMsg.Body
End If
%>
```

Notice, in Listing 8-2, that the code for querying for the `MQTest Queue` is the same as the code in Listing 8-1. We call the `Open()` method on our `mqQInfo` object just as before. The parameters have changed a bit to open the queue for receive access:

```
Set mqTXQueue = mqQInfo.Open(MQ_RECEIVE_ACCESS, MQ_DENY_NONE)
```

We now call the `Receive()` method. All of the parameters are optional. Here's the syntax:

```
Set object2 = object1.Receive ([pTransaction] [, WantDestinationQueue]
[, WantBody] [, ReceiveTimeout])
```

The last parameter is of particular interest. The `ReceiveTimeout` value, expressed in milliseconds, is the maximum amount of time that the method call will wait for a message to arrive on the queue. It is very important to explicitly define a timeout value here. This is especially true if you are reading messages synchronously, as we are in our example. Script execution stops if no

message is received within the timeout period. The default is to wait indefi-
nitely. Here's the code to call `Receive()`:

```
Set mqMyMsg = mqTXQueue.Receive(,,,1000)
```

When we call `Receive()`, the method will return an `MSMQ.MSMQMessage`
object. We can then reference the `Label`, `Body`, and other properties to get to
the "guts" of the message. Our code displays the `Label` and `Body` in the page.
To be sure that we are not trying to read an empty queue, we check the
`mqMyMsg` object to see whether it is set to `Nothing`:

```
If mqMyMsg Is Nothing Then
      Response.Write "queue is empty"
Else
      Response.Write "Received: " & mqMyMsg.Label & " - " & mqMyMsg.Body
End If
```

Active Directory Services Interface (ADSI)

In previous chapters, you were introduced to the problem of trying to manage
multiple data sources with a common API. The ODBC technology, along with
its evolutionary pieces (OLE-DB and ADO), sought to unify the way we
access general data sources, be they relational databases or some other data
store. Microsoft carried over the idea of this layered abstraction approach to
other systems, such as Messaging API (MAPI). The concept is the same:
Instead of having a common code-base talking to multiple database engines as
with ODBC, MAPI allows us to write one piece of code to interact with many
different messaging and e-mail systems. With all of this newfound application
power that allows us to access many different data stores, we are still left with
many more data areas to access—specifically, directories.

The term *directory,* as it relates to the *Active Directory Services Interface*
(ADSI), is a general one. It does not specifically refer to directories on your
file systems (folders), but to any data that is stored in a hierarchical manner.
Examples of directories include a name/address book, an employee roster, or a
store of account information on a multiuser computer system. We refer to
each of these "directories" as a *namespace.* Specifically, a namespace is a root
node in the directory service. The children of these nodes are called *container
objects.* Container objects can contain other container objects and also *leaf
objects* (these have no children). As an example, imagine that we have a hypothetical software company that we have made into a directory service. We can

represent the structure of the company in a hierarchical manner, as shown in Figure 8-36.

At the top of our hierarchy is our namespace, which we have called "SoftwareCorp." The namespace contains container objects, the first one being a container object called "Divisions" that holds the different divisions of the company. Each company division (BusinessApps, SystemUtilities, and VideoGames) is a container object as well. Each of these contains leaf objects that represent the departments in each division.

Note: The samples for ADSI in this chapter require Windows NT 4.0.

The ADS Namespace Container

Since each of the items in our namespace is organized hierarchically, we can easily obtain information about the structure of the namespace simply by navigating the hierarchy. ADSI provides a sort of "master" namespace called the *ADS namespace.* This namespace contains all of the namespaces available on your computer for the providers installed. Once we browse the available namespaces, we can select the one we want and drill-down to the desired container object that holds the data we wish to access.

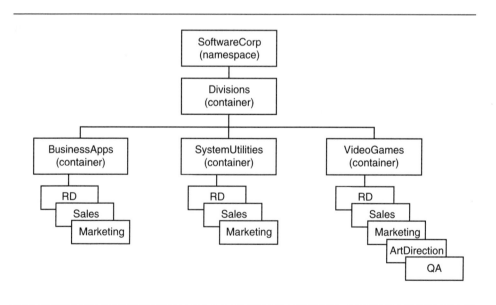

Figure 8-36. Diagrammatic representation of a sample directory service.

In automation-supported languages, like VBScript, each namespace and container is treated as a separate COM object. This is unlike the C/C++ version of ADSI, which provides alternative COM interfaces to the objects. In this book, we will concentrate only on the automation interface to ADSI.

Retrieving a handle to an object follows this general syntax (in this example, we are retrieving a handle to the ADS namespace):

```
Set ComputerObj = GetObject("ADS://")
```

Notice that we do not use `Server.CreateObject` to get an object as we normally do. Instead, VBScript provides the `GetObject()` as an intrinsic method, which is globally available to your scripts. `GetObject()` takes one parameter, the pathname to the namespace or container object. The syntax of the pathname follows that of URLs. In a URL, the text preceding the "`://`" is the protocol used for the request. In ADSI, that value represents the namespace.

ADSI ships with many different providers, and each one has a different purpose. The current version of ADSI (v2.5) contains the following providers, all grouped under the ADS namespace:

1. *Windows NT 4.0 Directory Services*—This is the most widely used directory service. In short, Windows NT 4.0 Directory Services allows us to completely administer a Windows NT server or domain. We can perform all kinds of user and group management (including creation, modification, and deletion of users and groups, plus group membership). We can control Windows NT services, including starting, stopping, and setting the start-up status. Management of print queues and print jobs is also supported. We may also manage file shares on an NT server.

2. *Lightweight Directory Access Protocol (LDAP), Exchange Server*— LDAP is an Internet standard protocol for communicating with a wide variety of directory services. One application for LDAP is to provide access to data on Microsoft Exchange Server. ADSI will allow access to items such as message stores and recipient (user) data.

3. *Internet Information Server 4.0*—With the Internet Information Server 4.0 provider, we can perform many administrative tasks. For example, we can manage virtual directories in the Web server filespace, set up other Internet services like FTP, manage log files, and configure settings for the servers.

4. *Novell NetWare 3.1*—ADSI supports access to Novell NetWare 3.1.

5. *Novell Directory Services (NDS)*—ADSI also allows access to NDS.

This text concentrates on the first three services listed here. If you are curious abut the Novell services, you can find additional information at the sites listed under "Further Reading" at the end of this chapter.

In the following sections, we will look at some examples of using ADSI. We will start here with the Windows NT 4.0 provider. Listing 8-3 shows a sort of "Hello World" application that echoes back properties about our server.

Listing 8-3. Displaying Server Properties (example8-3.asp)

```
<%
     ' Declare a variable for our Windows NT 4.0 object
Dim objMyComputer


' Get a reference to an object that represents the computer
' called "Matt". "Matt" is not a member of any domain, so
' we omit the domain.
Set objMyComputer = GetObject("WinNT://Matt")


' Display the properties of the computer.
Response.Write "The name of my computer is : " & _
objMyComputer.Name & "<BR>"
Response.Write "The ADS Path of my computer is : " & _
objMyComputer.ADSPath & "<BR>"
Response.Write "The class name of my computer is : " & _
objMyComputer.Class & "<BR>"
Response.Write "The GUID of my computer is : " & _
objMyComputer.GUID & "<BR>"
Response.Write "The parent object of my computer is : " & _
objMyComputer.Parent & "<BR>"
Response.Write "The schema path of my computer is : " & _
objMyComputer.Schema & "<BR>"
%>
```

Standard ADSI Object Properties and Methods

Each ADSI object implements a series of standard properties and methods. Table 8-2 shows the default properties for the ADSI object. These properties

Table 8-2. Default ADSI Object Properties and Methods

Property	Description
Name	Name of the object.
ADSPath	Full pathname to the object.
Class	Class of the object (e.g., User, Group, Service, etc.).
GUID	Unique identifier for the object (as given by the ADSI provider).
Parent	Parent object.
Schema	Full pathname to the schema.
Method	**Description**
GetInfo	Get the properties of the object and return them in the ADSI object properties.
SetInfo	Write changes made to the object back to the directory service.
Get	Get the value of an object property.
Put	Save the value of an object property.

and methods comprise the IADs interface. Every ADSI object is required to implement this interface in order to be ADSI-compliant.

The ADSPath property is of particular interest to us. This is how we specify a unique path to an object in a namespace. The structure of the pathname is very similar to a URL. To illustrate, suppose we want to obtain information on the Windows NT group "Administrators" on the computer "Matt." We can get a handle to the ADSI object for this item by writing the following code:

```
Set objGroup = GetObject( "WinNT://Matt/Administrators" )
```

At the "top" level, we select the "WinNT" namespace. This is contained under the master (ADS) namespace. The computer "Matt" is not a member of a Windows NT domain, so we omit the domain name and specify the computer name directly. This leaves us at the computer level of the hierarchy. The computer object is a container, with one of its children being a group object. For the group, we specify "Administrators." Now, the `objGroup` variable is a group container object.

Standard Container Object Properties and Methods

As mentioned, all ADSI objects implement the `IADs` interface. Container objects implement the same interface, but they also have another interface, called `IADsContainer`. This interface contains properties and methods used for manipulating the members of a container object. Members of a container object can include things like the users in a particular group, the installed Windows NT services on a machine, the jobs in a print queue, or the virtual directories on a Web site. We have the ability to create, delete, copy, and move these object members with the properties and methods of the `IADsContainer` interface.

The process of retrieving the members of an ADSI object is called *enumeration.* An ADSI container object contains a method called `Members`. This returns a list of member objects in the container object. We can use a `For Each` loop to traverse through each one. We can also specify a `Filter` on the container object so that the `Members` method returns only object members that are of interest to us. The `Filter` contains class names, in an array, like "Computer," "User," "Group," or "Service." The `Filter` property is very useful since enumeration on a high-level object (such as a domain) can return very large numbers of items. To illustrate, suppose we want to list the Windows NT services installed on the computer "Matt." Listing 8-4 shows how we construct the script.

Listing 8-4. Retrieving Members of an Object (example8-4.asp)

```
<%
    Dim objMattComp
    Dim objService

    Set objMattComp = GetObject( "WinNT://Matt" )
    objMattComp.Filter = "Service"

    For Each objService In ObjMattComp.Members
        Response.Write objService.Name & "<BR>"
    Next

    Set objMattComp = Nothing
%>
```

Using ADSI for User and Group Management

ADSI can be used to manage Windows NT users and groups. With ADSI, you can create, edit, and delete users and groups from Windows NT. The users and groups can be local or can belong to a domain controller.

Creating a New User

To create a new user involves a couple of steps. The first step is to retrieve a handle to the machine name on which we will create the new account. We get this handle just as we did in preceding examples. See Listing 8-5 for the code.

Listing 8-5. Creating a New User (example8-5.asp)

```
<%
Dim objMachine, objUser
Set objMachine = GetObject( "WinNT://myserver" )

Set objUser = objMachine.Create( "User", "joe" )
ObjUser.SetInfo
%>
```

Here's what transpires in the code of Listing 8-5: After we retrieve a handle to the machine name object, we call the standard IADsContainer method Create(), which creates a new object. Since we are creating a new user, the first parameter is "User," which signifies an object of the "user" class. The username is given in the second parameter ("joe"). The new user object is returned in the object objUser.

Now that we have a handle to the objUser object, we can set the properties of the new object. Let's set the full name of the user account and assign a new password. Setting the full name for the user is a matter of simply setting the FullName property of the objUser object:

```
ObjUser.FullName = "Joe Smith"
```

The IADSUser interface includes two methods for modifying the account password: SetPassword() and ChangePassword(). Use SetPassword() when the account does not yet have a password assigned. This is the case when you just created the account using Create(). ChangePassword() will also assign a password, but it requires you to supply the existing password. Next we call SetPassword() for the objUser object:

```
ObjUser.SetPassword( "mysecret" )
```

Note: It's important not to forget to call `SetInfo()` to commit the changes made to the object properties. If you don't, changes will be lost.

Creating a New Group

Groups are created in much the same way as users. The first step of obtaining an object reference to the machine object is the same for the users. That call is followed up with another call to the `Create()` method. See Listing 8-6 for the code.

Listing 8-6. Creating a New Group (example8-6.asp)

```
<%
Dim objGroup, objMachine
Set objMachine = GetObject( "WinNT://mymachine" )
Set objGroup = objMachine.Create( "group", "Pizza Lovers" )
ObjGroup.SetInfo
%>
```

The Future of ADSI

Microsoft is heavily investing in the ADSI technology. It will be an integral part of Windows 2000 when it is released. The secret to ADSI's long-term success is due in part to its open architecture. We are able to write an ADSI provider for many different types of directory services. The current providers that we discussed in this chapter are just the beginning. With the release of Windows 2000, different directory services such as the Windows Registry and the Control Panel could be replaced with Active Directory. An even more powerful future feature of ADSI will be the ability to create new objects within a schema. The properties of these objects can be manipulated at will. For instance, we could add more attributes to user accounts that are not included among the default ones.

Collaborative Data Objects (CDO)

Collaborative Data Objects (CDO) is the newest technology from Microsoft that unifies the way in which we access messaging systems such as e-mail, scheduling, and calendar services. The CDO technology actually has its origins in the older technology of Messaging API (MAPI). The idea behind MAPI is similar to that of ODBC. If we are working with an application that supports ODBC and we want to be able to access a particular database, we use a compatible ODBC driver for that database. We then execute queries against that database via the ODBC driver. The same concept applies to MAPI. If our MAPI-compliant application wishes to send an e-mail message to an e-mail system with which we wish to interface, we talk to that e-mail system through a MAPI driver.

CDO improved upon MAPI. It is a lighter-weight API, and it is better suited to Internet applications. The objects support automation, so they can be used from any script environment. CDO also ships with a "lite" version called *CDONTS*, which we will check out next. This version is designed to interface with the Windows NT 4.0 Option Pack and its accompanying SMTP server. With CDONTS, you can send e-mail messages using SMTP without having to resort to using the complete CDO interface.

Sending an e-mail message using CDONTS could not be easier. Before you run this code, you need to make sure that the STMP Service is installed and running on your server. Sending the messages takes just a small amount of code, as shown in Listing 8-7. The properties of the `NewMail` object should be self-explanatory. When we are ready to send the message, we simply call the `Send()` method.

Listing 8-7. Sending Messages Using CDONTS (example8-7.asp)

```
<%
Dim objMail
Set objMail = Server.CreateObject("CDONTS.NewMail")

objMail.From = "Matt"
objMail.To = "user@host.net"
objMail.Subject = "Test of CDONTS"
objMail.Body = "This is a test of the CDONTS mail object"

objMail.Send
Response.Write "mail sent"
Set objMail = Nothing
%>
```

Chapter Review

We've covered a lot of material and seen many exciting technologies at work. Here are the key points of this chapter relating to Microsoft Transaction Server (MTS).

- Microsoft Transaction Server acts as a broker of COM objects and manages database transaction processing. By caching COM component instances and database connections, speed and scalability are greatly increased.

- The Transaction Server API provides functions to inform the system when a transaction should be completed or aborted.

- Transaction Server can automatically *roll back* and *commit* changes made to a data source through its own API. This frees the programmer from ever having to write transactional processing code in the native language of the DBMS.

- Components that participate in a transaction are grouped together in a logical unit called a *package*. The package represents all the steps in the transaction. Every component piece must succeed in order for the transaction to be successful. Packages are configured using the Microsoft Management Console, the integrated environment for administrating the Windows NT 4.0 Option Pack server software pieces.

- Transactional database processing requires the use of a *resource manager,* a special piece of software that communicates directly with the DBMS and issues transaction processing calls. MTS ships with two resource managers, one for SQL Server and another for Oracle. The Access database used for the Megabyte's application needs to be converted to SQL Server to take advantage of transactional processing. Many of the SQL Server 7.0 wizards simplify this task.

- The `PizzaOrder` component is an example of a business object. A *business object* is a COM component that wraps up middle-tier business rules. The `PizzaOrder` component uses ADO to update database tables.

- MTS components can be built in Visual C++ 6.0 using the supplied ATL COM Wizard. The wizard gives the option to generate an ATL object with MTS "boilerplate" code already inserted. The COM object also supports OLE Automation error reporting.

- MTS components always retrieve the object context. The *object context* allows us to run the component inside a transaction and to instantiate other components inside the MTS environment. The `IObjectContext` interface is also responsible for committing and aborting a transaction, using the `SetComplete()` and `SetAbort()` methods, respectively.

- The `FinalConstruct()` function allows us to perform initialization of our object's properties and methods upon creation of an object instance. `FinalConstruct()` is implemented as a private member function of the class.

■ ACID, an acronym for *A*tomicity, *C*onsistency, *I*solation, *D*urability, is a set of guidelines to follow when developing components for use inside a transaction. Components should be *atomic,* meaning that they need to perform only the most basic of operations, such as adding a single row to a database table. Components should be *consistent,* preserving system state even if they fail. Components should run in *isolation,* meaning that they act as though they have complete control of the data on which the component operates. This prevents another instance of the component from modifying the data while the first component instance is changing it. Components should be *durable,* meaning that a system utilizing components can restore back to a given system state using information that the component logged while running.

■ Components have varying levels of transaction support, and this can be configured using the MTS Explorer. The "Requires a transaction" option states that the component must run inside an existing transaction. "Requires a new transaction" designates that the component needs to run in a transaction by itself. "Supports transactions" means that the component can participate in a transaction if it chooses to do so, but it is not required. "Does not support transactions" is the default setting. Components always run outside of a transaction.

■ In addition to being able to call the `SetAbort()` and `SetComplete()` methods from the `IObjectContext` interface, ASP has the ability to call these methods using the intrinsic object `ObjectContext`. We can also define two subroutines in a transaction-enabled page: `OnTransactionAbort()` and `OnTransactionCommit()`. Program flow is automatically directed to these functions when a transaction is aborted or committed, respectively. A transaction-enabled page contains a `Transaction=required` clause at the top of the file.

Here are the key points relating to Microsoft Message Queuing (MSMQ).

■ Microsoft Message Queuing addresses reliability issues that come about with having a distributed application. The main problem is that certain systems in the distributed application may not be available or the data flow between them may be extremely slow. By using a *store-and-forward* technique for storing system messages, applications can retrieve messages as needed without having to rely on a live connection between systems.

- MSMQ conforms to industry standards for message queues. This means that other non-Microsoft systems can use MSMQ message queues.

- MSMQ defines a hierarchy of an enterprise, which is a collection of servers that interact with MSMQ. At the top of the hierarchy is the Primary Enterprise Controller (PEC). Under the PEC are routing servers, which provide queuing capabilities, and site controllers, which hold copies of the information about their site from the information contained in the PEC.

- The MSMQ Explorer can be used to manage message queues. This includes creating queues, editing properties, and deleting queues. The MSMQ Explorer can also send test messages to the queue to ensure that queues are configured correctly.

- MSMQ uses a variety of objects. The `MSMQ.MSMQQuery` object is used to locate information about public queues in the enterprise. The `MSMQ.MSMQQueueInfos` object holds a collection of queue `MSMQ.MSMQQueueInfo` objects. This is the object returned from a queue lookup using `LookupQueue()`. The `MSMQ.MSMQMessage` object is used to package up a message to be sent to a queue.

Here are the key points relating to Active Directory Services Interface (ADSI).

- Active Directory Services Interface is a common programming API used to access many different types of directory services. Examples of directory services are the file system, the Windows Registry, print queues, the Internet Information Server Metabase, and the Windows NT User and Group database.

- ADSI is organized into *namespaces,* which contain objects called *containers.* The container objects can contain other container objects as well as *leaf objects,* which have no children.

- ADSI ships with providers for Windows NT 4.0 Directory Services, Novell NetWare 3.1, Novell Directory Services (NDS), Lightweight Directory Access Protocol (LDAP), Exchange Server, and Internet Information Server 4.0.

- ADSI will be an integral part of Windows 2000 when it is released. Future versions of ADSI/ActiveDirectory will include the ability to modify namespaces and object properties.

Finally, here are the key points relating to Collaborative Data Objects (CDO).

■ Collaborative Data Objects provides a uniform programming interface to access many different kinds of messaging services. It is the successor to the Messaging API (MAPI), which sought to unify the way we access e-mail, scheduling, and calendar applications.

■ A subset of CDO called *CDONTS* can be used to send e-mail from Web pages with relative ease. It utilizes the STMP server that is included in the Windows NT 4.0 Option Pack.

What's Next

In the following chapters, we will discuss the different methods that you can use to secure your site. Topics range from good design practices to restricting user access and securing the data communications between a browser and a Web server. The basic principles of cryptography will be discussed, as will how you can use commercially available products and services to implement various types of secure communications.

■ Further Reading

■ *Windows NT Server Web Site*—http://www.microsoft.com/ntserver.

■ *ADSI*—http://msdn.microsoft.com/library/sdkdoc/adsi/adsistartpage_7wrp.htm.

■ *CDO* for NTS—http://msdn.microsoft.com/library/sdkdoc/cdo/amsmtp_9k15.htm.

■ MSMQ—http://msdn.microsoft.com/library/sdkdoc/msmg/msmg_examples_com_0rub.htm.

■ *MTS*—http://msdn.microsoft.com/library/sdkdoc/mts20sp1/partiivb_28c2.htm.

Securing Your ASP Application

Introduction

Keeping out unwanted visitors from your site is essential, and there are a number of ways to ensure that unwanted visitors stay clear of your site. If your site is used for a commercial purpose and if financial transactions are taking place, security is paramount. Protecting the privacy of the user and preventing access to sensitive system resources are equally important. Protecting the site comes down to two tasks that you need to accomplish as the site administrator:

1. Providing a means to restrict access to your site based on users.
2. Making sure that the data transmitted between the Web user and the Web server cannot be intercepted by a third party.

Robust security is achieved by taking appropriate measures at many different levels. The first step involves how files are organized in the site directory. An ASP application contains many different types of files. HTML files, ASP files, CGI scripts, and multimedia files could all be a part of your site's content. It makes sense, for the sake of code maintainability, to place the Web files in a hierarchical structure according to their type. This not only makes finding files easier but also enables us to set up certain permissions for each of the directories in the hierarchy. For example, we can set up a separate directory that contains just ASP files. "Scripts" permissions can be configured for this directory only. Other files, like the multimedia files, can have "Read" access assigned to the directory in which they reside. Still other files, such as CGI executables, can be set with "Execute" permissions in their own directory. The exact site tree and the types of directories that you set up are a matter of preference, and the application requirements may dictate a particular site structure. Above all, it should be easy to understand and be able to facilitate security control for different classes of files in directories.

ASP/HTML Design

Most secure or "members-only" sites have a mechanism for entering a username and password. The username and password of the site member are often entered into an HTML form. This data is sent to an ASP or CGI script for validation.

1. The form should not show the password as it is typed in but should use an HTML "password" field for password entry, like this:

   ```
   Password: <INPUT TYPE=password NAME=usrPasswd>
   ```

2. The form that contains the password field should use only the "post" method of sending data. This will prevent the password data from being passed along in the query string where it runs the risk of being seen by prying eyes.

3. At the top of every HTML page or ASP script, we need to ensure that the password validation occurs every time before any content is sent to the browser. This involves calling a function or COM component that performs the validation. If the validation fails, then the validation routine can perform a browser redirect to another page.

Windows NT Security

The Windows NT operating system is designed in such a way that any action that you perform on the computer involves a security check. It follows that, whenever you are working inside the Windows NT environment, you (the user) should have an identity. This is your user account (or username). These usernames are stored in a user accounts database. The user accounts database can exist in two different areas. The first is on the server itself. When a user attempts to gain access to this server, the security check is performed against the database residing on the server. The accounts in this database are referred to as *local user accounts*. The other area in which the user accounts database may live is on a machine called the *Primary Domain Controller* (PDC). The job of the PDC is to authenticate users on a local area network. This local area network may contain several servers. Collectively, these servers are logically grouped into a domain. The job of the PDC is to provide a centralized area for authentication to occur for machines in the domain. If a user wishes to gain access to a particular server's resources within the domain, the user need only log into the PDC. Windows NT determines what type of authentication to perform (local or on a domain) by determining whether the user elected to log into a domain or not.

Windows NT can secure many different types of resources. These include, but are not limited to, files, directories, and services. Any object on the Windows NT system, be it a file, service, or registry key, contains privileges associated with it in *access control lists* (ACLs). The ACL contains a list of unique identifiers (SIDs) that correspond to a user account. When a request for a resource is made, the currently logged-in user is matched against the user SIDs in the ACL for the resource.

File Systems

It is important to note that Windows NT can be hosted on two types of file systems. These file systems are known as the *NT File System* (NTFS) and the *File Allocation Table* (FAT). The FAT file system is the filing system used by DOS and 16-bit Windows. Windows NT supports only the security features we have discussed if Windows NT is installed on a hard drive that has been formatted with the NTFS file system. Since DOS and 16-bit Windows did not directly support file-level security, the new file system was required to facilitate this type of security.

User Rights, Groups, and Policies

Windows NT identifies users by account names and groups. A user is identified by a unique username. Users can be clustered into groups. Users in a group share common characteristics and access capabilities. Groups enable system administrators to assign security rights on a group level instead of assigning security rights to each individual user.

A *user right* is a permission granted by the security system to perform a specific task. There are several different types of security rights. For instance, you can assign the user right "Log on locally" to a user or group. The "Log on locally" user right grants a user or group the ability to access the server from another computer on the network. You can see all of the different types of user rights from the Windows NT User Manager. (See Figure 9-1.)

User rights are associated with a particular resource on a particular Windows NT system. For example, a file in the NTFS file system contains

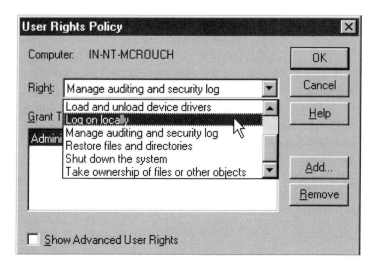

Figure 9-1.   The User Rights Policy dialog.

information regarding access permissions for every group and user on the server/domain. This system allows us to just associate the user credentials with a user account. The resource permissions and privileges associated with Windows NT resources can then be traced back to a user account.

Types of User Authentication in Internet Information Server

Internet Information Server provides a layer of security that utilizes the built-in security of Windows NT. As mentioned, security permissions are set for each object in Windows NT. The IIS Web Service, therefore, must follow the security procedures of any other Windows NT resource. On the Internet, we typically do not know the identity of anyone who might happen across our site. They certainly are not going to have a valid account to log into our server to retrieve a file. We need a mechanism that allows access to our Web site to the general population while still maintaining strict security control.

Anonymous Access

IIS provides the ability for an anonymous user to access files on the Web server without having the user supply user credentials. By default, IIS enables this type of access. Were it not enabled, the user's Web browser would pop up a dialog box asking for a username and password. With "Anonymous Access" enabled, IIS performs retrieval of files by using a special Windows NT user account (sometimes referred to as the Web "guest" account) that is set up to have guest privileges to the Web files. This account is created upon installation of IIS. It is named IUSR_*MachineName*, where *MachineName* is the name of the Windows NT server. The password is also configured automatically, making the entire authentication process transparent to the user.

Anonymous access to system resources on your server may give you a bit of pause. With so much media focus on "crackers" obtaining access to sensitive corporate information, it is no surprise that securing anonymous access is at the top of the Webmaster's list of priorities. Theoretically, the very fact that a Windows NT account is used to gain access to any file on the Windows NT system could be a problem. Could that same account used for anonymous access be used to gain control of other files or services critical to the server? It is possible, but, in short, the answer is generally no. Here's why:

1. The IUSR_*MachineName* account is assigned "Guests" permissions only. This means that the anonymous access account is a member of the default Windows NT group called "Guests." The Guests account has very limited permissions. In a typical installation, users in the Guests group just have read-only permission (or execute permission, if the account needs to run a CGI executable) to files that are visible in the Web server filespace (i.e., files in virtual directories or the Web root directory).

2. IIS allows only an incoming Web user to view files in the virtual directory spaces. A Web user cannot specify a URL that points to a directory outside of this virtual directory space to gain access to a file.

3. If, for some reason, through covert cracking techniques or otherwise, the unauthorized user does know the path of a protected file, the permissions set on the file will not include accounts in the Guests group. Thus, the system will deny access.

Using a Username/Password Database

Some Web sites require you to enter a username and password in order to be granted access. In some Web sites, this type of security is performed by a server-side validation of account information that the user sends via an HTML form. The validation involves querying a database for the account name that is entered and checking to see whether the supplied password matches for the account name. The user is then sent, sometimes through a redirection header, to the protected pages. This method of protection requires coding by you, but remember that IIS provides integrated security, which may suit the needs of your implementation very well.

Using Windows NT Challenge/Response Authentication

NT Challenge/Response Authentication provides strong security. The name of this type of security stems from how authentication is performed. In a nutshell, the user is "challenged" for permission to access a protected resource when a previous attempt to access the protected file failed due to the user's current credentials not being adequate enough to access the resource. The user then sends back a "response" to the server with credentials that are expected to allow access to the resource. Using this method, passwords are not transmitted over the network in any form. Since this is true, the user's Web browser will not prompt for a username and password. Instead, the Web browser uses the username and password that the user logged in with to the local workstation. If an account with the same username exists on the Web server and this account has permission to access the file requested, the file is delivered. This security authorization happens using a network connection separate from the HTTP network stream.

Using Challenge/Response Authentication is not the best choice in all situations. This method has two requirements to make it successful, as follows:

1. Internet Explorer is the only browser that supports Challenge/ Response Authentication. If your target audience may be using different types of Web browsers, you should not use Challenge/ Response.

2. Many Internet users may have Internet access only through a proxy/ firewall. This may create a problem with the network connection that is used for the authentication.

In light of these two facts, Challenge/Response Authentication is useful only in an Intranet setting where persistent connections are more reliable.

Basic Authentication

The most common type of authentication for Web servers to perform is Basic Authentication. This is the "security" that is implemented in the HTTP protocol. Basic Authentication uses the HTTP response headers to signal that a username and password are required to access the Web page. To see how this works, let's investigate the HTTP exchange that transpires during Basic Authentication.

First, a request is made for a document, so an HTTP GET command is issued by the browser that looks something like this (simplified for clarity):

```
GET /passwd.asp HTTP/1.0
```

IIS sees that the file, `passwd.asp`, is protected from guest access, so it returns a 401 status code in the HTTP response. The 401 status code indicates that password authorization is required to access the file:

```
HTTP/1.1 401 Authorization Required
Server: Microsoft IIS/4.0
Date: Thu, 08 Apr 1999 03:46:51 GMT
Content-Type: text/html
Cache-control: private
```

The 401 HTTP status code will trigger a password dialog box to appear in the user's browser. Now, the user needs to send the username and password information. When this information is entered, the username and password are concatenated into a single string separated by a colon (:). This string is then encoded using the base64 encoding algorithm. The encoded string is placed inside the HTTP header with the request:

```
GET /passwd.asp HTTP/1.0
Authorization: BASIC base64encodedstring
```

The header shows what is appended to the HTTP request. *base64encodedstring* contains the base64 encoded version of the username and password string to which we just referred. If the user is granted access, which means that the username and password supplied match a user with credentials to access the file, a normal 200 status code is returned along with the contents of the request:

```
HTTP/1.1 200 OK
Server: Microsoft IIS/4.0
Date: Thu, 08 Apr 1999 03:46:51 GMT
Content-Type: text/html
Cache-control: private

[Contents of request go here]
```

It is important to understand that using Basic Authentication transmits the username/password data over the network, which makes it vulnerable to interception. Crackers have several network-monitoring tools that can "sniff" network packets as they are transmitted. These packets can contain the password information. Even though the password is encoded using base64, this format can very easily be decoded programmatically using the cracking tool. You can change the type of authentication that is used by the Web server by using the IIS configuration tools.

If Challenge/Response Authentication is selected, an attempt to use that authentication protocol is used. As stated, only Internet Explorer supports this. If another browser is detected, Basic Authentication is used instead. This switch is transparent to the user. If transmitting the password over the network is a concern, you may want to consider other security solutions if some user might be using a non-Microsoft browser.

Coding and Setting Up Security on Your Site

You can set up protected files on your site by using a couple of methods. The first involves programmatic security using the ASP `Response` object. The second is setting permissions for the file using Windows Explorer.

The first method involves sending a 401 status code with the server response. We can say the following in our VBScript:

```
<%
        Response.Status = "401 No way Jose"
        Response.AddHeader "WWW-Authenticate", "NTLM"
        Response.End
%>
```

`Response.Status` will send the 401 status code. The `WWW-Authenticate` header tells the browser what type of authentication method to use. In our example, `NTLM` will attempt to do Challenge/Response Authentication. Another choice would be this header:

```
Response.AddHeader "WWW-Authenticate", "Basic"
```

This would attempt Basic Authentication.

The second method involves no coding to implement the security. You can set the permissions of the files in the Web directory space using Windows Explorer, as follows:

1. Right-click on the file you wish to protect.
2. Select "Properties" from the menu.
3. Click the "Security" tab, and click the "Permissions" button.
4. At this point, the system will show what users and groups have access to the file. You can change these by selecting "Add . . ." and "Remove." Clicking Add will display a screen showing all the available users and groups.
5. You can then select users and groups that can access the file. The drop-down list box labeled "Type of Access" lets you assign the access privilege you want for the users and groups that you highlighted.

Secure Connections

So far, we've discussed how to protect access to resources (files) on the Web server. This provides us with the ability to protect the contents of a file from any unwanted users. But, interactive Web sites are not just making requests for files. They are also transmitting supplemental data. For instance, the values that are filled in an HTML form are subject to the same type of network surveillance used to grab passwords from the network stream. Sometimes, sensitive information is sent in these HTML forms. Securing this information is especially important when the transactions are financial in nature, such as is the case with e-commerce sites. The user does not want to compromise the security of his/her credit card and/or bank account information.

Securing the request data from the browser (and the subsequent Web server response) is the job of a technology called *Secure Sockets Layer* (SSL). Netscape Communications introduced SSL, and Microsoft released a competing technology known as *Private Communications Technology* (PCT). Each of these is compatible with the other. In fact, both are built on an Internet standard called the *X.509 certificate format* (discussed in just a bit). The SSL and PCT technologies are made possible by using a layer of software on the TCP/IP stack called *Secure Software Services* (SCS). SCS provides functions to protect the privacy of the packets. It also makes sure that the packets are not tampered with. The lower-level software used for authentication is also included in the SCS software.

A Crash Course in Cryptography

Secure communications work on the principle of *cryptography*, which is the process of applying a mathematical formula to a message in order to scramble it. This makes it unreadable to anyone who does not have the decryption key. A *key* is a piece of data that the mathematical encryption formula uses to encrypt the data. Keys vary in length. The longer the length of the key, the more secure the message is. Commercial-grade encryption uses a key that is 128 bits in length. Software that uses cryptography that is bound for sale in international markets (outside the United States and Canada) can use up to 40-bit encryption only. The 40-bit standard of encryption has been in use for a number of years. But with the advent of new computer technology and faster processors, cracking a message by "brute force" (i.e., trying every possible key) becomes frighteningly simple. Even garden-variety PCs equipped with fast Pentium processors can break a 40-bit key in a matter of hours. The U.S. government's concern with national security has now resulted in the switch to 128-bit encryption. Even the most powerful computers on the planet cannot crack this key within any reasonable time. Having more powerful encryption is important domestically as well. Currently, this is the only method that can be used to ensure that credit card and bank account information is kept private.

Single-Key Cryptography

In general, there are two methods for encrypting a message. The first method involves using a single key to encrypt and decrypt a message. The sender and receiver of the message have the encryption/decryption key. The method for information exchange is straightforward:

1. The sender composes a message and encrypts the data using the key.
2. The message is sent to the receiver, who uses the same key to decrypt the message.

However, this simple method of exchanging messages has a major flaw in terms of the logistics used in distributing the key. Since the key itself cannot be encrypted, it is vulnerable to interception—at which point, the system breaks down.

Double-Key Cryptography

The problem with using single-key cryptography is solved by using two keys. One key is used for encrypting the message, and the other is used for decrypting the message. The keys are referred to as the *public* key and the *private* key, respectively. Here's how the system works:

1. The public and private keys are generated using an algorithm that relates the two with a factoring formula. Using this formula, it is possible (however, very, very unlikely) to determine the private key from the public key. As the length of the key increases from, say, 40 bits to 128 bits, the likelihood of discovering the private key diminishes to impossibility.

2. The public key is distributed to anyone who wants it. The recipients of the public key are now ready to send messages to the holder of the private key.

3. The sender encrypts a message using the public key and sends it to the holder of the private key. Using the decryption algorithm, the sender uses the private key to decrypt the message.

It is interesting to point out that the level of security that an encryption scheme offers relies on two factors. The first is keeping the private key secret. The second is the length of the keys. Some weaker encryption schemes rely on a secret algorithm. These are never good encryption schemes because the program used to implement the secret algorithm is subject to reverse engineering. This would expose the process used for encryption and decryption. The most popular public/private key encryption scheme used is the RSA (from RSA Data Security, Inc., named after its creators, *Rivest, Shamir,* and *Adleman*). The RSA algorithm is common knowledge (in the IT world), but its strength comes from the use of large keys that are impossible to crack using current hardware in a reasonable amount of time.

Digital Signatures

Digital signatures are the electronic counterpart to handwritten signatures. They work by reversing the normal roles of the public and private keys. To "sign" a message, the sender takes the private key and the message and generates a "digest" of the message. This message digest is created using what is known as a *one-way hash* algorithm. The one-way hash ensures that the complete message cannot be derived from the message digest alone. The message digest is then appended to the original message.

At the receiving end, the recipient uses the sender's public key to decrypt the message. If this is successful, we know that the message actually came from the expected sender. Digital signatures also provide us with a method to see whether the message has been tampered with. Since the message digest was created from a message that the sender originally composed, an altered message would produce a digital signature that is different from the first one. The recipient's encryption software can verify this using the sender's public key.

Certificates

Certificates are an application of digital signatures. The first step in configuring IIS to use secure connections is to obtain a certificate from a *Certificate Authority.* One of the jobs of a Certificate Authority is to verify the legitimacy of the company or person applying for a certificate. The third party is necessary because, without one, anyone can create a forged certificate that falsifies the identity of the person creating the certificate. Receiving certificates from a third party is great, but how do we trust the third party? We can trust them because the Certificate Authority attaches a digital signature to the certificate. When we receive our certificate from the Certificate Authority, we also need to retrieve the public key of the Certificate Authority. In this way, we can verify that the certificate is valid.

Your Web browser can store these certificate public keys. For example, Internet Explorer stores them in the "Internet Options" area. Figure 9-2 shows some Certificate Authorities, people, and Web sites that can be trusted to issue valid certificates.

Once we have our certificate, we can then configure IIS to support SSL. This feature is supported in IIS only (no support in PWS is provided). Many certifying-authority Web sites offer instructions for configuring your Web server to support secure communications. This involves installing your certificate. Here are some sites to get you started:

Verisign, Inc.—`http://www.verisign.com`.

Entrust—`http://www.entrust.com`.

Custom Authentication Schemes

Sometimes, your system may require a different type of password authentication system that is beyond the capabilities of SSL, Basic Authentication, or Challenge/Response Authentication. By using an ISAPI filter, you can implement a custom security scheme. Recall that the ISAPI filter can intercept the

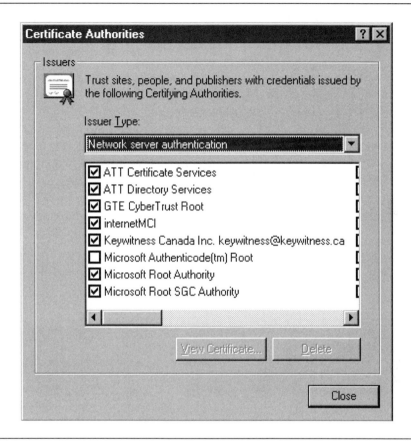

Figure 9-2. Trusted issuers of valid certificates.

user's request before the Web server processes it. We can examine all of the headers that the Web browser appended to the request and also retrieve other information passed along, such as the query string or data contained in an HTTP POST. For example, we can retrieve the values that users enter in a login request form and use these values to authenticate them using accounts on, say, a mainframe or UNIX server. If the user passes the authentication process, the ISAPI filter can redirect the user's request to the actual content on the Web server. This type of authentication is not possible with the stock features of IIS. ISAPI filters are a powerful feature and are commonly used to implement security validations such as this.

   Note: A commercial COM object used for Web security and authentication called *AuthentiX* (http://www.flicks.com) is a good example of an ISAPI filter used to implement an authentication scheme.

Chapter Review

In this chapter, we covered how to secure your ASP application. We restrict access to our Web site in two ways:

1. Restricting users
2. Securing data transmissions

Here are the key points to remember from this chapter.

■ Files in the Web server space can be assigned file permissions called *Read, Scripts,* and *Execute.* Read permissions should be assigned to static content (HTML, multimedia files). ASP files should be assigned Scripts access so that the server-side script can be executed. Execute permissions should be set for files that don't fall into the category of ASP files, such as CGI executables. These files should be grouped into folders according to their type. The IIS permissions should then be set for the directory. Organizing them in this way makes for easy site maintenance since fast file location by the Webmaster is facilitated.

■ A secure Web site starts with good HTML design. It starts with simple things like using "password" input fields instead of normal text fields. When designing HTML forms, it's a good idea to use POST instead of GET so that the form contents are not exposed in the query string (which is often displayed in the user's Web browser). We can also call a COM object at the beginning of our page that performs a security validation.

■ IIS leverages off Windows NT security. Every request of a resource on a Windows NT system involves a security check. Access control lists (ACLs) are appended to every Windows NT resource, and these ACLs contain unique identifiers that map to a user account. With Anonymous Access enabled, IIS uses a system-created account that contains guest privileges. IIS impersonates the user connecting to the Web site by using the IUSR_*MachineName* account for nonprotected content. For protected content, the user information that was supplied with the authentication is used for impersonation.

■ File security using ACLs is a feature of the NTFS file system. The disk that the secure content resides on needs to be formatted with this option.

■ Windows NT identifies users by account names and groups. User rights, which can be assigned to users and groups, are permissions granted to the holder of the right to be able to carry out a specific action on the system. Certain user rights are required for the account that IIS impersonates so that the account can access the files that it needs.

■ Authentication comes in two flavors on IIS: Basic and NT Challenge/Response. Most Web browsers support Basic Authentication. Upon receiving an HTTP 401 response code, the Web browser prompts the user for a username and password. The username and password are sent as a base64-encoded string. NT Challenge/Response, an authentication supported only by Internet Explorer, "challenges" a user for permission to access the protected resource. The user sends back credentials, on a separate network stream, to the server that are expected to allow the user access. No password is transmitted in this sequence.

■ ASP can provide programmatic control of security by sending custom responses, like 401, to the browser.

■ Security can also be implemented by setting user and group permissions in Windows Explorer. The user needs to provide user credentials that have access to the resource.

■ Secure Sockets Layer (SSL) encrypts the data coming to and from the Web server. This protects the data from being monitored by unauthorized parties. Security such as this is important in e-commerce and financial applications.

■ SSL uses cryptography and certificates. Cryptography is the process of mathematically transforming data into a coded form. Certificates are used to positively identify an individual or organization. Certificates can also be used to digitally "sign" documents. This proves that the source of the message is legitimately from the expected source.

■ RSA is an example of a public-key encryption algorithm. Messages to the private-key holder can be encrypted by using the public key, and the message can be decrypted only by using the private key. Contrast this method with single-key cryptography, where the same key is used for encryption and decryption. This method is not secure since the key must be transmitted without security.

■ Certificates are issued by a third party in order to avoid having anyone create falsified certificates. The authenticity of the issued certificates can be verified since each one is digitally signed using the third party's private key.

■ Custom authentication schemes can be constructed using ISAPI filters. The filter has access to the request information and can take this information and use it in a custom-developed authentication method.

What's Next

We've come to the end, so to speak. We haven't explored everything that the Active Server Platform has to offer, but you should have a firm understanding of the potential of the Active Server Platform. No doubt, you will want to learn more about this rapidly moving technology. Many excellent resources are available on the Internet that are dedicated to the Active Server Platform. You are encouraged to check them out. Good luck and, most of all, have fun!

■ Further Reading

- ■ http://www.activeserverpages.com—One of the largest sites, with many resources, it includes components and tutorials on ASP.
- ■ http://www.15seconds.com—An all-around good site, 15 Seconds has some of the more obscure information about the Active Server Platform.
- ■ http://www.kamath.com—The Active Server Corner has many cool things, too many to mention, but there is a very slick COM object that can generate HTML calendars!
- ■ http://www.aspzone.com—Run by John R. Lewis, the ASP Zone is a smaller site, but it contains the most useful code examples for COM components that can be found anywhere on the Web.

Installation and Configuration of IIS/PWS and Supporting Software

The first step toward utilizing the examples in this book is to install all the necessary support software. This appendix covers the installation procedures for IIS/PWS and also familiarizes you with some basic configuration techniques. You will want to make sure that you have adequate hard-drive space to install the software you require and that your computer's processor is fast enough and has enough RAM to run the software acceptably.

Windows NT 4.0 Option Pack

The Windows NT 4.0 Option Pack contains all the necessary software required to deploy Web sites using Active Server Pages. The Option Pack contains software for Windows NT Server/Workstation as well as Windows 9x (in spite of the confusing name). At the core of the software suite is Internet Information Server (IIS). The equivalent software for Windows 9x is Personal Web Server (PWS). The Option Pack also contains Microsoft Transaction Server, Microsoft Message Queuing, Microsoft Index Server, and other development resources.

Where to Get the Option Pack

Some of the sources from which the Windows NT 4.0 Option Pack can be obtained are as follows:

Microsoft Development Network (MSDN) Subscription—If you subscribe to this, the Option Pack 4.0 CD is a regular installment.

Web Download—http://www.microsoft.com/msdownload. There are versions for Windows 9x and Windows NT 4.0.

Included on the book's CD-ROM as part of the Visual InterDev 6.0 trial.

Installation Instructions

Installation of the Windows NT 4.0 Option Pack is fairly straightforward. The on-screen instructions will guide you through the process. You have the option of selectively installing many different components of the Option Pack. The examples and exercises in this book will use the Web Publishing Service, Microsoft Transaction Server, and Microsoft Message Queuing.

Note: If you are planning on using Microsoft Message Queuing (MSMQ), you'll need to have Microsoft SQL Server installed. MSMQ uses SQL Server to store queue data.

Setup

1. Launch the Setup.exe program of the Option Pack. The Welcome screen appears. (See Figure A-1.)
2. The Setup Program asks whether we are adding/removing Option Pack components or uninstalling the Option Pack entirely. Click the Add/Remove button to install components. (See Figure A-2.)
3. Select the components you wish to install. At the very least, you need to install Internet Information Server. Checking the box next to a component will install it and all its related subcomponents. You can choose which subcomponents to install by clicking the Show Subcomponents button. This will bring up another list that lists the subcomponents for the main component. (See Figure A-3.)

Message Queuing Install

If you elect to install MSMQ, the Setup Program will display some dialog boxes asking for additional parameters.

1. The first screen of the MSMQ Setup asks you what type of MSMQ installation you want to perform. If you do not have MSMQ installed on any server on your network, select the Primary Enterprise Controller (PEC) option. (See Figure A-4.)
2. You may be asked for the SQL Server data/log devices for queue data and the Connected Network Setup. If so, specify a size for the devices

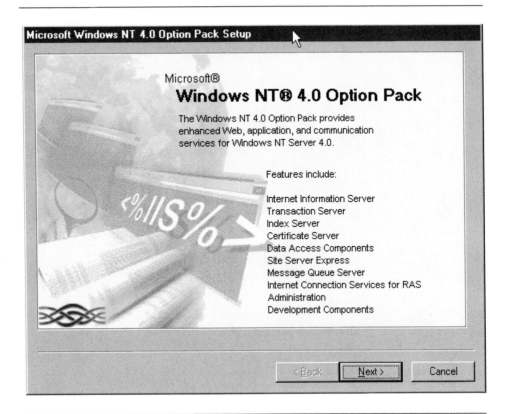

Figure A-1.   The Welcome screen.

that is appropriate for the storage available to you on the disk. At least one connected network must be specified as well. If you are developing your project on a single server, you can select your own computer for a connected network. (See Figures A-5 and A-6.)

Transaction Server Install

1. The Transaction Server Setup will ask you where you want to install the Transaction Server program files. Select a directory or use the default. (See Figure A-5.)

2 Transaction Server has a remote administration option. In order to use the remote administration option, you must select an account to use for remote administration. If you don't need to remotely administer Transaction Server, simply use the default Local option.

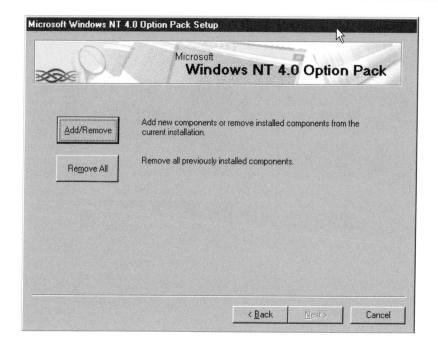

Figure A-2.   Selecting the Add/Remove option.

IIS/PWS Configuration

There are a few configuration steps we need to take to start programming Active Server Pages. The Internet Information Server Manager is implemented as a Microsoft Management Console (MMC) snap-in in IIS 4.0 (see Figure A-6) and as a separate configuration program (Personal Web Manager) on Windows 9x (see Figure A-7). Both of these have their own program group that is accessible from the Windows Start menu.

Setting Up the Home Directory

IIS 4.0

1. Right-click on the Default Web Site icon and select Properties.
2. The Default Web Site Properties screen appears. (See Figure A-8.) The following important options are available to us:

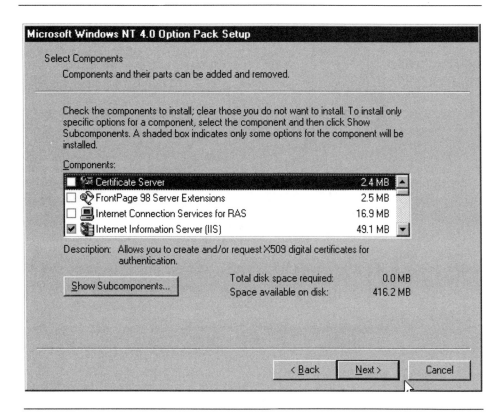

Figure A-3. Selecting the components to install.

■ The top group of radio buttons designates where the content of the Home Web directory comes from. The default option (and the one we'll use) is for the content to come from this computer.

■ Since we are specifying that the content will come from this computer, the Local Path box is the physical path where the content is located. You can change this if you wish by typing in a new directory or selecting one by clicking Browse.

■ The Access Control section controls what types of permissions are set for the Home directory. Our examples will require that the Read box is checked.

■ The Application Settings section allows us to specify a name for the ASP application and set up Scripts and Execute permissions. To run Active Server Pages, the Scripts option may be selected. You can

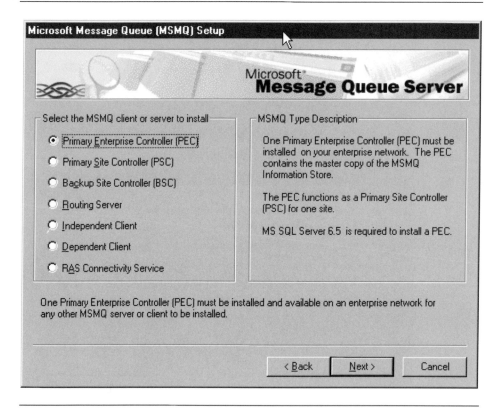

Figure A-4. Selecting the PEC option.

also select Execute, which will enable both CGI-based applications and Active Server Pages.

■ The Configuration button allows us to set advanced options for the Web application (virtual directory). If you wish to interactively debug (debugging is covered in Appendix B) your ASP application, the server-side debugging option must be enabled (from the Debugging tab).

3. Click OK to set the new properties.

Personal Web Manager

Before performing any of the following steps, it's a good idea to make sure the Personal Web Server is started. Start the Personal Web Server by clicking

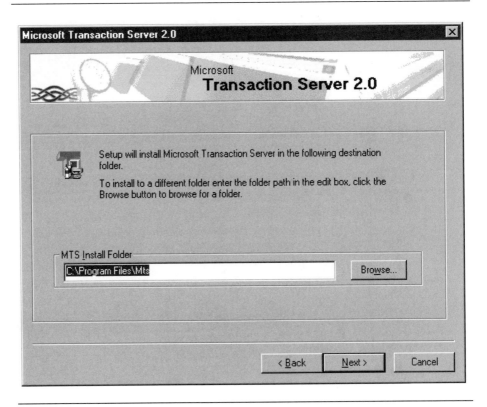

Figure A-5. Selecting where to install MTS files.

the Start button. The button toggles to a Stop button when the service is started.

1. To configure the main (Web root) directory, click on the Advanced icon in the left-hand side of the window. (See Figure A-9.)

2. In the Virtual Directories list, highlight the Home directory. If you want to enable a default document (a file that is automatically served when a Web directory is selected in a URL without a document), check the Enable Default Document checkbox and specify a filename. Checking the Allow Directory Browsing checkbox will cause the Web server to return a list of all the filenames in a Web directory in the browser window if a Web directory is specified in a request URL. Checking the Save Web Site Activity Log will log all Web requests to a

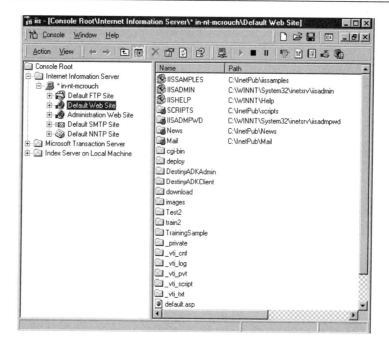

Figure A-6. The IIS 4.0 Manager.

file. Click Edit Properties to configure permissions for the Home directory.

3. The Edit Directory dialog allows you to set access for the directory. "Scripts" allows Active Server Pages to run in the directory. "Read" allows general read-access to the directory and is used when the directory contains only static files (HTML, graphic files, etc.). "Execute" allows CGI scripts and other Windows executables to run in the directory. The defaults (Read and Scripts) are fine for the examples in this text. (See Figure A-10.) Click OK.

Configuring Virtual Directories

IIS 4.0

IIS 4.0 provides a "wizard" interface for configuring virtual directories. The steps to the wizard are almost self-explanatory. You add a virtual directory to the Default Web Site as follows:

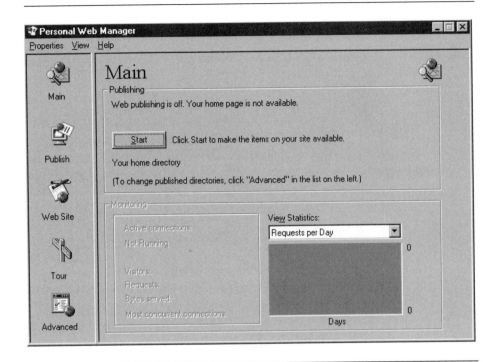

Figure A-7. The Personal Web Manager.

1. Right-click on the Default Web Site and choose New→Virtual Directory. (See Figure A-11.)

2. The first screen of the New Virtual Directory Wizard appears. Type in an alias name for the directory (this is the name that will be used to refer to the directory in URLs). Click Next to continue. (See Figure A-12.)

3. Enter the name of the physical directory that contains the content for the new virtual directory. Click Browse to select the directory. Click Next to continue. (See Figure A-13.)

4. The next screen allows you to select access permissions for the virtual directory. Remember that Scripts and Read must be checked to run Active Server Pages. Click Finish to create the virtual directory. (See Figure A-14.)

Personal Web Server

1. From the main screen, click on the Advanced icon.

2. Click the Add button in the Virtual Directories box.

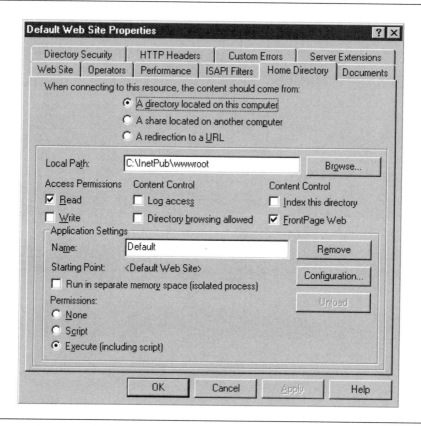

Figure A-8.   The Default Web Site Properties screen.

3. In the Add Directory dialog, select a folder on a volume by clicking Browse. Type an alias for the directory in the Alias box (this is the name used in a URL to refer to the directory). (See Figure A-15.)

4. Set any access permissions that are appropriate for the directory. Click OK.

Installing the Megabyte's Pizzeria Samples

1. Locate the Mega folder on the CD-ROM. This folder contains the Megabyte's Pizzeria files. Copy the files to a directory on your hard disk, keeping the directory structure of the Mega folder intact.

2. Create a virtual directory pointing to the Mega folder. Give this virtual directory Read and Scripts access.

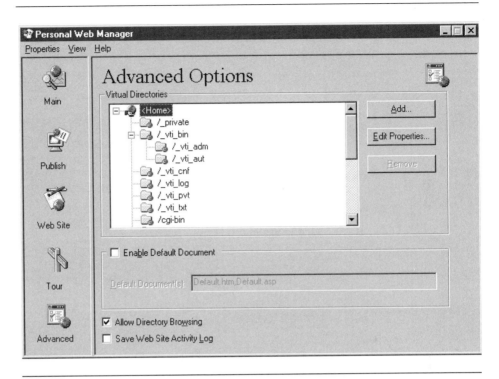

Figure A-9. Configuring the main (Web root) directory.

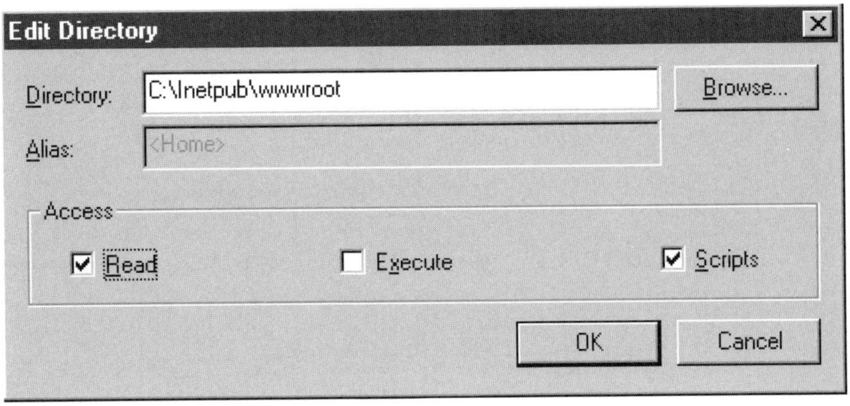

Figure A-10. The Edit Directory dialog.

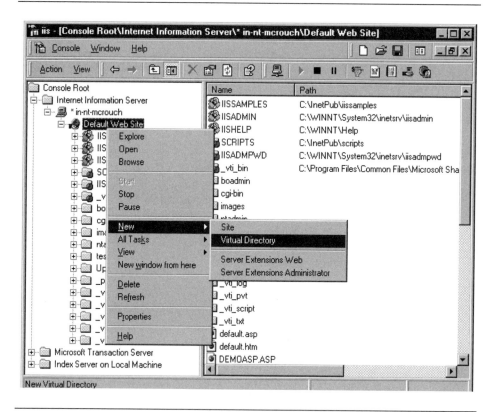

Figure A-11.   The Default Web Site icon.

3. To install the other examples and exercises in this book, create another virtual directory. Place the `.asp` files from the `Examples` directory on the CD into this virtual directory. Be sure to set Scripts permissions for the virtual directory before running the samples.

Note: SQL Server users should be aware that the Megabyte's Pizzeria connection strings may need to be modified to work with their database installation. In some cases, a username and password will need to be supplied in the connection string. The current connection strings in the default installation are set to work with Microsoft Access, which requires no username and password. See Chapter 8 for more details.

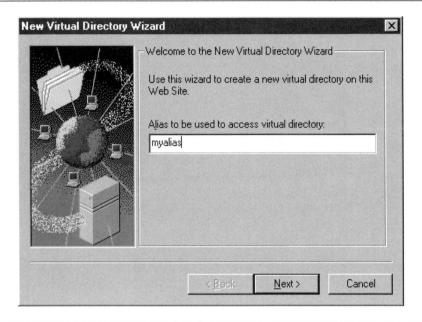

Figure A-12. The New Virtual Directory Wizard screen.

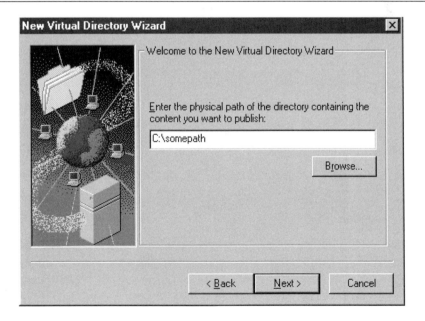

Figure A-13. Entering the directory name.

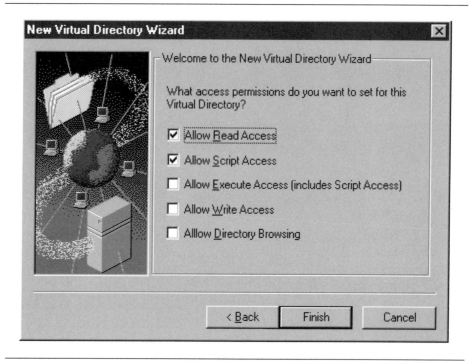

Figure A-14. Selecting access permissions.

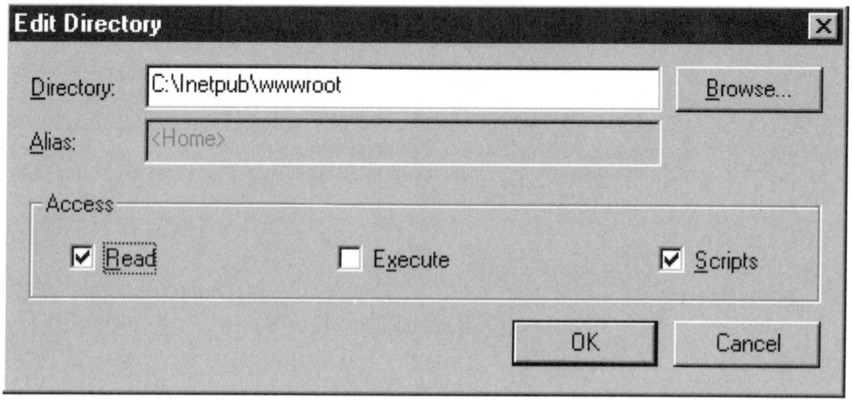

Figure A-15. The Add Directory dialog.

Debugging ASP Applications

As easy as it is to program using ASP and VBScript, you are going to mess up along the way. It's just a fact of programming life. So, we need to thoroughly debug our applications. In the early days of ASP, no debugger program existed. Debugging in those days required a lot of guesswork and good old "trace code" in the form of `Response.Write` commands. It was frustrating at best, and turnaround time was lengthy. With the introduction of the Microsoft Script Debugger and the Visual InterDev 6.0 software package came a facility to interactively debug your ASP scripts. These packages are very versatile and provide a rich set of features to make your debugging experience more productive. Setting up for debugging is a simple process.

The Microsoft Development Environment Debugger

The Visual J++ and Visual InterDev packages are grouped together in an IDE dubbed the *Microsoft Development Environment*. If the debugger is invoked, the Development Environment is launched with the script loaded into the main window. At that point, we are ready to debug our application. The Script Debugger is also available separately in the Windows NT 4.0 Option Pack if you don't own Visual InterDev 6.0. You'll need to install it before debugging ASP applications. Simply check the Script Debugger option during the Option Pack installation.

Note: Debugging ASP applications is supported only by IIS 4.0. Personal Web Server does not include support for the Script Debugger.

Invoking the Debugger

If you are already familiar with any of the Visual Studio tools, the debugging controls should look very familiar to you. Debugging ASP applications works in much the same way as conventional applications.

To invoke the debugger inside a VBScript block, simply insert the keyword `Stop` in your application. When the script interpreter encounters the `Stop` statement, execution halts. A dialog box will appear asking whether you want to debug the application. It will state that a runtime error had occurred, but, in reality, the script interpreter simply encountered the `Stop` statement. If you click Yes, the system will launch the Script Debugger. You may also encounter another dialog box asking whether you wish to open a project for debugging. This applies to applications created with Visual InterDev, so we will click No for this dialog. Here's a snippet of VBScript that shows use of the `Stop` keyword:

```
srt = ""
myarray = Array( "Testing", "One", "Two", "Three" )

' Invoke the debugger
Stop

For Each arg In myarray
      str = str & UCase( arg )
Next
```

This particular example will allow us to step through the `For Each` loop and watch the value of `str` change with each iteration.

Setting Breakpoints

A breakpoint is a signal to stop execution when the script interpreter encounters one. It is an alternative to using the `Stop` keyword in your code. This will enable you to look more closely at what is happening at that point in the code. You can toggle a breakpoint by clicking in the vertical gray bar on the left side of the code window, as shown in Figure B-1.

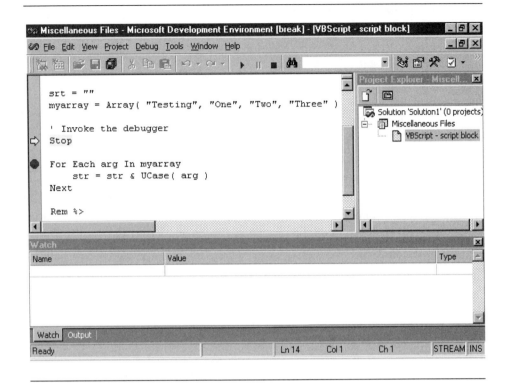

Figure B-1. Debugger window with breakpoint set.

The Debugging Controls

Here are some of the common controls that we will use when debugging ASP pages:

- *Continue*—Continue causes execution of the script to run until the next breakpoint is encountered or until the end of the script is reached.
- *End*—End causes the debugging session to terminate.
- *Step Into*—Step Into causes the Script Debugger to advance to the code inside a procedure. It is useful if your program is failing on a function call. You can run the Script Debugger and then step to the exact statement inside the rogue function that is causing the failure.

- *Step Over*—Step Over causes the Script Debugger to not enter the code inside a function. It is useful if you already know that a particular function works and don't want to bother stepping through all of its statements.

- *Step Out*—Step Out brings the Script Debugger out of the current procedure and back into the code block that called it. The pointer is positioned on the line of code immediately following the procedure call.

- *Insert/Remove Breakpoint*—Insert/Remove Breakpoint activates or deactivates a breakpoint on the current line.

- *Disable Breakpoint*—Disable Breakpoint just inactivates the breakpoint. Once inactivated, the debugger will not stop on that line. You may enable the breakpoint again at a later time.

- *Clear All Breakpoints*—Clear All Breakpoints removes all breakpoints set for the file.

- *Breakpoints*—Breakpoints brings up a window with a synopsis of all the breakpoints. You can also set a breakpoint when certain conditions in the code are encountered, such as when a counter reaches zero. To add a breakpoint, click on the Add button.

Setting Up to Debug ASP Components under IIS

The Visual C++ IDE offers a feature to debug the ASP components. You'll need to perform some initial configurations to get up and running.

Note: It is important that the COM object that you are trying to debug was compiled for Win32 Debug. This ensures that debug symbols were generated so that the IDE can step through the code. You can set this option in the Visual C++ by selecting Project→Settings from the menu. Select the Link tab, and make sure that the box that reads "Generate debug info" is checked.

Follow these steps:

1. Launch Visual C++.
2. Select Build->Start Debug->Attach to Process from the menu bar. The Attach To Process dialog box appears. Select the box that reads "Show System Processes." (See Figure B-2.)
3. Highlight the `inetinfo` process and click OK.
4. We need to tell Visual C++ what DLL we wish to debug. To do this, select Project->Settings from the menu bar. Click on the Debug tab,

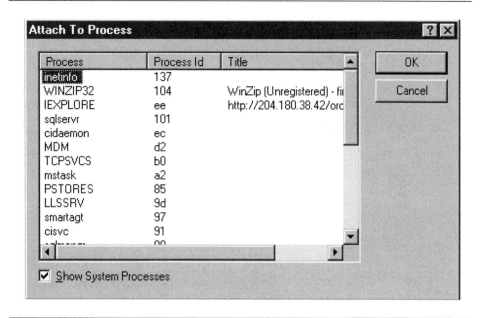

Figure B-2. The Attach To Process dialog box.

and select "Additional DLLs" from the category drop-down list. Browse for the component you wish to debug and add it to the list as shown in Figure B-3.

5. From the File menu, select the source file you wish to debug and open it.

6. Set breakpoints in the code where you want to begin debugging.

7. You are now ready to debug. Request the ASP page that executes your component. When your component is called, the Visual C++ debugger should begin and stop at your first breakpoint.

Note: You can continue to debug in this manner for as long as the debug session is alive in Visual C++. A few words of warning when debugging components in this manner: When you select "Stop Debugging" from the menu, this action will terminate the IIS process. When this happens, IIS will no longer respond to requests (in fact, the Services Control Panel will show the World Wide Web Publishing Service as not started). If you wish to run another debugging session, you must manually start the service again from the Services Control Panel.

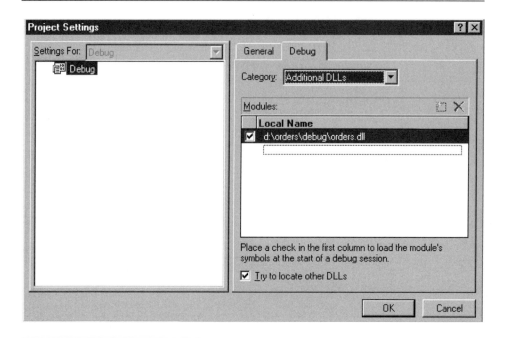

Figure B-3.   Specification of Additional DLLs.

In addition, if you want to make any changes to the COM object's code, you'll, of course, need to recompile the component. During the recompilation process, Visual C++ will delete the old DLL. More often than not, you'll see an error from the Visual C++ linker that it cannot delete the DLL. The reason is that the IIS process still has the DLL open. To remedy this, shut down any IIS-related services (World Wide Web Publishing Service, FTP Publishing Service, NNTP, and STMP) and the IIS Admin service using the Services Control Panel. Try rebuilding the COM object again. It should build successfully (assuming that no compile-level errors have been introduced). Then, restart the World Wide Web Publishing Service.

Setting Up to Debug ASP Components under MTS

Debugging components under MTS requires a different type of configuration than debugging for the IIS process. When we debug COM objects running under MTS, we need to specify an executable for the debug session.

Follow these steps:

1. Open the MTS Explorer and shut down any server processes that are currently running. To do this, right-click on the computer running MTS and select "Shutdown Server Process."

2. Make sure that your project is open for the component you wish to debug. Select Project->Settings from the menu bar. Click on the Debug tab. You should see options for the path to the executable for the debug session. The executable that controls server processes is `mtx.exe`. In a typical installation, this file is located in the `\winnt\system32` directory. This varies, so, if you cannot locate the file, perform a search for it using Windows "Find Files or Folders." Browse for the file and select it.

3. We need to specify some program arguments. The program argument to enter in this box is in the format:

```
/p: "packagename"
```

where *packagename* is the name of the package that contains your component.

4. Set any breakpoints that are necessary in the component's source code.

5. To begin debugging, select Build->Start Debug->Go from the menu bar.

6. The Visual C++ IDE will wait for the `mtx.exe` application to be launched. All we need to do now is request the ASP page that calls the component, and the debugger should start.

The ASP Intrinsic Objects

Server Object

- CreateObject(*progID*)—Creates an instance of a server COM component.
- HTMLEncode(*str*)—Applies and returns HTML encoding to a string.
- MapPath(*relativePath*)—Converts and returns relative or virtual path to the actual path on the file system.
- URLEncode(*str*)—Returns URL string as a properly encoded URL.
- URLPathEncode(*str*)—Returns URL path string as a properly encoded URL.
- ScriptTimeout—Is the time in seconds a script is allowed to run.

Request Object

- BinaryRead—Reads data returned by the client in a POST request.
- ClientCertificate—Is the collection of client certificate fields.
- Cookies—Is the collection of cookies sent by the user's browser.
- Form—Is the collection of HTML form element name–value pairs.
- QueryString—Is the collection of parsed items from the query string.
- ServerVariables—Is the collection of environment variables.
- TotalBytes—Is the total number of bytes in the client request.

Response Object

- AddHeader *header, headerValue*—Adds an HTTP header.
- AppendToLog *str*—Adds str to the Web server log for the request.
- BinaryWrite *data*—Writes raw data to the client (no character conversion).
- Clear—Erases any buffered output.
- End—Flushes buffered output and terminates current script execution.
- Flush—Immediately sends any buffered output to the client.
- PICS *str*—Adds PICS header (for content ratings).
- Redirect (*url*)—Redirects the browser to url.
- Write *str*—Writes character-converted content to the client.
- Buffer—Is the true/false value to turn buffering on (true) or off (false).
- CacheControl—Corresponds to the Cache-control HTTP header.
- CharSet—Is the HTTP header representing the character set to use.
- ContentType—Is the HTTP content type (MIME type).
- Cookies—Is the collection of cookies to send to the client.
- Expires—Is the time when content should be expired, expressed in minutes from now.
- ExpiresAbsolute—Is the date/time when content should be expired.
- IsClientConnected—Is the true/false value indicating if client is still connected to the server.
- Status—Means read-only, the HTTP Status header.

Application Object

- Lock—Prevents scripts other than the current one from modifying the Application object.
- Unlock—Allows other scripts access to the Application object.
- Contents—Returns a collection of contents associated with the application.
- StaticObjects—Returns a collection of static objects associated with the application.

Session Object

- **Abandon**—Destroys the **Session** object and its contents.
- **Contents**—Is the collection of items associated with the session (not static).
- **CodePage**—Is the code page used when writing text to the browser.
- **LCID**—Is the locale ID used for the text written to the browser.
- **SessionID**—Is the session ID for the current user.
- **StaticObjects**—Is the collection of static objects for the session.
- **Timeout**—Is the number of minutes for a session to last before timing out.

ObjectContext Object

- **SetAbort**—Aborts the current transaction that the ASP page is participating in.
- **SetComplete**—Indicates that the operations in the ASP page succeeded and that the transaction can continue.

ADO Reference

Table D-1. Connection Object

Method/ Property Name	Description	Parameters
Attributes	Property. Characteristics of the **Connection** object.	
BeginTrans	Method. Starts a transaction. Returns the transaction level.	
Close	Method. Closes the current ADO connection.	
CommandTimeout	Property. Seconds to wait for an ADO command to complete. Default: 30 seconds.	
CommitTrans	Method. Saves any changes made to the database inside a transaction.	
ConnectionString	Property. Information used to establish a connection to a data source.	
ConnectionTimeout	Property. Seconds to wait for an ADO connection to succeed.	

(continued)

Table D-1. (continued)

Method/ Property Name	Description	Parameters
CursorLocation	Property. The location of the cursor engine.	
DefaultDatabase	Property. The default database to connect to when the connection is established.	
Errors	Property. The error objects associated with the connection.	
Execute	Method. Executes the query, SQL statement, stored procedure, or provider text. Returns a **Recordset** object.	CommandText (in, string), RecordsAffected (out, long), Options (in, long)
IsolationLevel	Property. The transaction isolation level.	
Mode	Property. Indicates the available permissions for modifying data.	
Open	Method. Opens the connection to the data source.	ConnectionSTring (in, string), UserID, (in, string), Password (in, string), Options (in, long)
OpenSchema	Method. Opens a connection to a data source for the purposes of obtaining information about the data source (as given by the data provider). Returns a **Recordset** object. **SchemaEnum** can be: adSchemaProviderSpecific adSchemaAsserts	QueryType (in, SchemaEnum), Criteria (in, Variant), SchemaID (in, Variant)

(continued)

Table D-1. (continued)

Method/ Property Name	Description	Parameters
	adSchemaCatalogs adSchemaCharacterSets adSchemaCollations adSchemaColumns adSchemaCheckraints adSchemaraintColumnUsage adSchemaraintTableUsage adSchemaKeyColumnUsage adSchemaReferentialConstraints adSchemaTableraints adSchemaColumnsDomainUsage adSchemaIndexes adSchemaColumnPrivileges adSchemaTablePrivileges adSchemaUsagePrivileges adSchemaProcedures adSchemaSchemata adSchemaSQLLanguages adSchemaStatistics adSchemaTables adSchemaTranslations adSchemaProviderTypes adSchemaViews adSchemaViewColumnUsage adSchemaViewTableUsage adSchemaProcedureParameters adSchemaForeignKeys adSchemaPrimaryKeys adSchemaProcedureColumns adSchemaDBInfoKeywords adSchemaDBInfoLiterals adSchemaCubes adSchemaDimensions adSchemaHierarchies adSchemaLevels adSchemaMeasures adSchemaProperties adSchemaMembers	

(continued)

Table D-1.   (continued)

Method/ Property Name	Description	Parameters
Provider	Property. The data provider that the **Connection** object uses.	
RollbackTrans	Method. Undoes changes made to a database inside a transaction.	
State	Property. Indicates whether the connection is opened or closed.	
Version	Property. The version number of the ADO software.	

Table D-2.   Recordset Object

Method/Property	Description	Parameters
AbsolutePage	Property. Specifies the page of the current record.	
AbsolutePosition	Property. Specifies the ordinal position of the cursor in a recordset.	
ActiveConnection	Property. A reference to the **Connection** object that the recordset is using.	
AddNew	Method. Creates a new record in the recordset with the field names in **FieldList** and the corresponding values in **Values**. Both must have the same number of elements.	FieldList (in, optional, Array), Values (in, optional, Array)
BOF	Property. Flag indicating if the recordset is positioned before the first record.	

(continued)

Table D-2. (continued)

Method/Property	Description	Parameters
Bookmark	Property. Contains an ADO bookmark to the current record in the recordset.	
CacheSize	Property. The number of records in a recordset that are to be kept in local memory.	
CancelBatch	Method. Cancels a batch update.	AffectRecords (in, optional, AffectEnum);
CancelUpdate	Method. Performs an "undo" on any changes to a recordset prior to calling the Update() method.	
Close	Method. Closes the current recordset.	
CursorLocation	Property. Sets the location of the recordset cursor. Can be: adUseServer, adUseClient	
CursorType	Property. The type of cursor that the recordset is using.	
Delete	Method. Deletes the current record. The parameter can be: adAffectAllChapters (all ADO chapters), adAffectCurrent (default, the current record), adAffectGroup (records affected by the current filter only).	AffectRecords (in, optional, AffectEnum);
EditMode	Property. The editing status of the current record. Can be: adEditNone, adEditInProgress, adEditAdd, adEditDelete	
EOF	Property. Flag to indicate if the cursor is positioned past the last record in the recordset.	

(continued)

Table D-2. (continued)

Method/Property	Description	Parameters
Fields	Property. Collection of `Field` objects for the current recordset.	
Filter	Property. The filter of the recordset. Can be a filter string or one of these constants: `adFilterNone`, `adFilterPendingRecords`, `adFilterAffectedRecords`, `adFilterFetchedRecords`, `adFilterPredicate`, `adFilterConflictingRecords`	
Find	Method. Searches for a particular record in the recordset according to `Criteria`. `SearchDirection` can be: `adSearchForward`, `adSearchBackward` `Start` can be: `adBookmarkCurrent`, `adBookmarkFirst`, `adBookmarkLast`	`Criteria (in, sring)`, `SkipRecords (in, optional, long`, `SearchDirection (in, optional, SearchDirectionEnum)`, `Start (in, optional, BookmarkEnum`
GetRows	Method. Retrieves the records in the recordset into a two-dimensional array. `Rows` indicates how many row to retrieve. `Start` is the bookmark (`adBookmarkCurrent`, `adBookmarkFirst`, `adBookmarkLast`) to start retrieving records. `Fields` is an array of field names in the recordset to retrieve.	`Rows (in, optional, long)`, `Start (in, optional, BookmarkEnum)`, `Fields (in, optional, Array)`
LockType	Property. Indicates how to lock records when updating.	
MarshalOptions	Property. Indicates which records of the recordset are marshaled back to the server. Can be: `adMarshalAll`, `adMarshalModifiedOnly`	

(continued)

Table D-2   (continued)

Method/Property	Description	Parameters
MaxRecords	Property. The maximum number of records to return in the recordset.	
Move	Method. Move forward or backward for **NumRecords**. Positive values move forward; negative values move backward. Operation begins at the **Start** bookmark (**adBookmarkCurrent**, **adBookmarkFirst**, **adBookmarkLast**).	NumRecords (in, long), Start (in, optional, BookmarkEnum);
MoveFirst	Method. Move to the first record in the recordset.	
MoveLast	Method. Move to the last record in the recordset.	
MoveNext	Method. Move to the next record in the recordset.	
MovePrevious	Method. Move to the previous record in the recordset.	
NextRecordset	Method. Returns the next available recordset from a **Recordset** object that was returned by an ADO command that consisted of several recordset-returning queries.	
Open	Method. Opens a recordset. **CursorTypeEnum** can be: adOpenForwardOnly, adOpenKeyset, adOpenDynamic, adOpenStatic LockTypeEnum can be: adLockReadOnly, adLockPessimistic, adLockOptimistic, adLockBatchOptimistic Options can be:	Source (in, optional, Command Object/SQL Statement/Table Name/ stored procedure/ filename), Activeconnection (in, optional, ADO Connection/ Connection String),CursorType (in, optional,

(continued)

Table D-2. (continued)

Method/Property	Description	Parameters
	adCmdText (*SQL statement*), adCmdTable, adCmdStoredProcedure, adCmdUnknown, adCmdFile, adCmdTableDirect, adAsyncFetch, adAsyncFetchNonBlocking	cursorTypeEnum), LockType (in, optional, LockTypeEnum), Options (in, optional, long)
PageCount	Property. Indicates how many pages the records in the recordset occupy.	
PageSize	Property. Indicates how many records make up a page.	
RecordCount	Property. The number of records currently in the **Recordset** object.	
Requery	Method. Refresh the records in the recordset by running the query in **Source** again. Options are: adAsyncFetch, adAsynvFetchNonBlocking	Options (in, optional, long)
Save	Method. Saves the recordset to a file. PersistFormatEnum can be: adPersistADTG, adPersistXML, adPersistHTML	Filename (in, string), PersistFormat (in, Optional, PersistFormatEnum)
Sort	Property. An SQL ORDER BY clause to use for sorting the current recordset.	
Source	Property. The ADO command or SQL statement used as the source of the data in the recordset.	
State	Property. Indicates if the recordset is closed, open, or executing an operation. Can be: adStateClosed, adStateOpen, adStateConnecting, adStateExecuting, adStateFetching	

(continued)

Table D-2. (continued)

Method/Property	Description	Parameters
Status	Property. Result of recordset operations. Can be: adRecOK adRecNew adRecModified adRecDeleted adRecUnmodified adRecInvalid adRecMultipleChanges adRecPendingChanges adRecCanceled adRecCantRelease adRecConcurrencyViolation adRecIntegrityViolation adRecMaxChangesExceeded adRecObjectOpen adRecOutOfMemory adRecPermissionDenied adRecSchemaViolation adRecDBDeleted	
Supports	Method. True/false test for recordset functionality. CursorOptionalEnum can be: adHoldRecords adMovePrevious adAddNew adDelete adUpdate adBookmark adApproxPosition adUpdateBatch adResync adNotify adFind	

(continued)

Table D-2. (continued)

Method/Property	Description	Parameters
Update	Method. Updates the current record in the recordset. `Fields` is an array of field names to update, and `Values` are the corresponding values for those fields.	`Fields (in, optional, Array), Values (in, optional, Array)`
UpdateBatch	Method. Flushes all pending updates to disk.	`AffectRecords (in, optional, AffectEnum)`

Table D-3. Field Object

Method/Property	Description	Parameters
ActualSize	Property. The actual length of a field value.	
AppendChunk	Method. Appends data to a binary or large text field.	`Data (in, Variant)`
Attributes	Property. The attributes of the `Field` object. Can be: `adFldMayDefer` `adFldUpdatable` `adFldUnknownUpdatable` `adFldFixed` `adFldIsNullable` `adFldMayBeNull` `adFldLong` `adFldRowID` `adFldRowVersion` `adFldCacheDeferred` `adFldKeyColumn`	
DefinedSize	Property. The maximum width of the field.	

(continued)

Table D-3. (continued)

Method/Property	Description	Parameters
GetChunk	Method. Returns all or part of a binary or large text field.	Length (in, long)
Name	Property. The name of the field.	
NumericScale	Property. How many digits are stored to the right of the decimal point for numeric values.	
OriginalValue	Property. The value of a field before any changes have been made.	
Precision	Property. The maximum number of digits to use in numeric fields.	
Type	Property. The field's type. Can be: adEmpty adTinyInt adSmallInt adInteger adBigInt adUnsignedTinyInt adUnsignedSmallInt adUnsignedInt adUnsignedBigInt adSingle adDouble adCurrency adDecimal adNumeric adBoolean adError adUserDefined adVariant adIDispatch adIUnknown adGUID adDate adDBDate	

(continued)

Table D-3.   (continued)

Method/Property	Description	Parameters
	adDBTime adDBTimeStamp adBSTR adChar adVarChar adLongVarChar adWChar adVarWChar adLongVarWChar adBinary adVarBinary adLongVarBinary adChapter adFileTime adDBFileTime adPropVariant adVarNumeric	
UnderlyingValue	Property. The value of the field in the current database.	
Value	Property. The value of the field.	

Table D-4.   Command Object

Method/Property	Description	Parameters
ActiveConnection	Property. Contains the active ADO Connection object or connection string for the command.	
CommandText	Property. The text of the command.	
CommandTimeout	Property. The time, in seconds, that the command is allowed to take to execute.	

(continued)

Table D-4. (continued)

Method/Property	Description	Parameters
CommandType	Property. The type of the command. Can be: adCmdUnkown adCmdText adCmdTable adCmdStoredProc adCmdFile adCmdTableDirect	in] CommandType Enum plCmdType);
CreateParameter	Method. Creates a new Parameter object. Direction can be: adParamUnkown adParamInput adParamOutput adParamInputOutput adParamReturnValue	Name (in, String), Type (in, DataTypeEnum), Direction (in, ParameterDirectionEnum), Size (in, long), Value (in, Variant)
Execute	Method. Executes the command. Options can be: adCmdUnknown adCmdText adCmdTable adCmdStoredProc adCmdFile adCmdTableDirect	RecordsAffected (out, long), Parameters (in, Array), Options (in, long)
Name	Property. The name assigned to the Command object.	
Parameters	Property. Collection of parameters for the command.	
Prepared	Property. True/false value indicating whether or not the command is saved in a compiled version.	
Properties	Property. Collection of Property objects for the command.	

(continued)

Table D-4. (continued)

Method/Property	Description	Parameters
State	Property. The current state of the command. Can be: adStateClosed adStateOpen adStateConnecting adStateExecuting adStateFetching	

Table D-5. Parameter Object

Method/Property	Description	Parameters
AppendChunk	Method. Appends a large binary or text string to the **Parameter** object.	Val (in, Variant)
Attributes	Property. Attributes for the parameter. These can be OR'ed together. Can be: adParamSigned, adParamNullable, adParamLong	
Direction	Property. Indicates how the parameter is used by a command. Can be: adParamUnkown adParamInput adParamOutput adParamInputOutput adParamReturnValue	
Name	Property. The same of the **Parameter** object.	
NumericScale	Property. The scale of numeric values for the parameter.	

(continued)

Table D-5.   (continued)

Method/Property	Description	Parameters
Precision	Property. The number of digits to the right of the decimal for numeric values.	
Size	Property. Maximum size (bytes or characters) for the `Parameters` object.	

Type	Property. The data type of the parameter. Can be:
	`adEmpty`
	`adTinyInt`
	`adSmallInt`
	`adInteger`
	`adBigInt`
	`adUnsignedTinyInt`
	`adUnsignedSmallInt`
	`adUnsignedInt`
	`adUnsignedBigInt`
	`adSingle`
	`adDouble`
	`adCurrency`
	`adDecimal`
	`adNumeric`
	`adBoolean`
	`adError`
	`adUserDefined`
	`adVariant`
	`adIDispatch`
	`adUnknown`
	`adGUID`
	`adDate`
	`adDBDate`
	`adDBTime`
	`adDBTimeStamp`
	`adBSTR`
	`adChar`
	`adVarChar`
	`adLongVarChar`
	`adWChar`	

(continued)

Table D-5. (continued)

Method/Property	Description	Parameters
	adVarWChar adLongVarWChar adBinary adVarBinary adLongVarBinary adChapter adFileTime adDBFileTime adPropVariant adVarNumeric	
Value	Property. The value assigned to the **Parameter** object.	

Index

Addison-Wesley Computer and Engineering Publishing Group

How to Interact with Us

1. Visit our Web site

http://www.awl.com/cseng

When you think you've read enough, there's always more content for you at Addison-Wesley's web site. Our web site contains a directory of complete product information including:

- Chapters
- Exclusive author interviews
- Links to authors' pages
- Tables of contents
- Source code

You can also discover what tradeshows and conferences Addison-Wesley will be attending, read what others are saying about our titles, and find out where and when you can meet our authors and have them sign your book.

2. Subscribe to Our Email Mailing Lists

Subscribe to our electronic mailing lists and be the first to know when new books are publishing. Here's how it works: Sign up for our electronic mailing at **http://www.awl.com/cseng/mailinglists.html**. Just select the subject areas that interest you and you will receive notification via email when we publish a book in that area.

3. Contact Us via Email

cepubprof@awl.com
Ask general questions about our books.
Sign up for our electronic mailing lists.
Submit corrections for our web site.

bexpress@awl.com
Request an Addison-Wesley catalog.
Get answers to questions regarding your order or our products.

innovations@awl.com
Request a current Innovations Newsletter.

webmaster@awl.com
Send comments about our web site.

mary.obrien@awl.com
Submit a book proposal.
Send errata for an Addison-Wesley book.

cepubpublicity@awl.com
Request a review copy for a member of the media interested in reviewing new Addison-Wesley titles.

We encourage you to patronize the many fine retailers who stock Addison-Wesley titles. Visit our online directory to find stores near you or visit our online store: **http://store.awl.com/** or call **800-824-7799**.

Addison Wesley Longman
Computer and Engineering Publishing Group
One Jacob Way, Reading, Massachusetts 01867 USA
TEL 781-944-3700 • FAX 781-942-3076

CD-ROM Warranty

Addison Wesley Longman, Inc. warrants the enclosed disc to be free of defects in materials and faulty workmanship under normal use for a period of ninety days after purchase. If a defect is discovered in the disc during this warranty period, a replacement disc can be obtained at no charge by sending the defective disc, postage prepaid, with proof of purchase to:

Editorial Department
Computer and Engineering Publishing Group
Addison-Wesley
One Jacob Way
Reading, Massachusetts 01867-3999

After the ninety-day period, a replacement disc will be sent upon receipt of the defective disc and a check or money order for $10.00, payable to Addison Wesley Longman, Inc. Addison Wesley Longman, Inc. makes no warranty or representation, either expressed or implied, with respect to this software, its quality, performance, merchantability, or fitness for a particular purpose. In no event will Addison Wesley Longman, Inc., its distributors, or dealers be liable for direct, indirect, special, incidental, or consequential damages arising out of the use or inability to use the software. The exclusion of implied warranties is not permitted in some states. Therefore, the above exclusion may not apply to you. This warranty provides you with specific legal rights. There may be other rights that you may have that vary from state to state. The contents of this CD-ROM are intended for personal use only.

More information and updates are available at:

http://www.awl.com/cseng/titles/0-201-60460-4